Professional Examination

INTERMEDIATE LEVEL

Paper 11

Organisational Management

EXAMINATION KIT

CIMA

◆ FOULKS *lynch*

British Library Cataloguing-in-Publication Data

A catalogue record for this book is available from the British Library.

Published by Foulks Lynch Ltd
Number 4
The Griffin Centre
Staines Road
Feltham
Middlesex
TW14 0HS

ISBN 0 7483 5882 X

© Foulks Lynch Ltd, 2003

Printed and bound in Great Britain by Ashford Colour Press Ltd. Gosport, Hants

Acknowledgements

We are grateful to the Chartered Institute of Management Accountants, the Association of Chartered Certified Accountants and the Institute of Chartered Accountants in England and Wales for permission to reproduce past examination questions. The answers have been prepared by Foulks Lynch Ltd.

CONTENTS

Section

INTRODUCTION

This new edition of the CIMA Examination Kit for 2003 has been reorganised. Packed with exam-standard questions, this book will help you to successfully prepare for your examination.

The questions are organised by syllabus topics with separate sections for 'multiple choice questions' and 'practice questions'. The multiple choice questions are similar to the Section A questions you will come across in your examination and the practice questions include a wide selection of Sections B and C style questions.

This book includes an extensive selection of questions from past CIMA exams, including the latest papers. In addition, there is a mock examination with full answers.

SYLLABUS, LEARNING OUTCOMES AND EXAMINATION FORMAT

Format of the examination

		Number of marks
Section A:	Ten compulsory objective test questions	20
Section B:	Two compulsory question (20 marks each)	40
Section C:	Choice of two questions from four (20 marks each)	40
		100
Total time allowed: 3 hours		

Syllabus overview

This syllabus introduces students to the concepts, tools and issues of management in organisations of all types. The emphasis is on the role of the Chartered Management Accountant as supervisor and manager of staff in an open social system, and the relationships necessary with other specialists within the organisation. As well as their specialist role, Chartered Management Accountants are participants in the management process at the supervisory and managerial levels. This syllabus aims to provide students with an awareness of the skills required to operate effectively as a manager in the finance department of an organisation.

Aims

This syllabus aims to test the student's ability to:

- evaluate and recommend improvements to the management of organisations in an international context

- evaluate and recommend alternative structures for organisations

- apply human resource management techniques in the management of a finance department

- advise on the management of working relationships

- advise on the management of change.

Learning outcomes and syllabus content

11(i) ORGANISATIONAL MANAGEMENT – 25%

Learning outcomes

On completion of their studies students should be able to:

- explain the concept of strategy and its possible effect on the structure and management of business organisations;

- identify the stakeholders of an organisation and explain their influence on its management and structure;

- recommend appropriate organisational goals;

- analyse and categorise the culture of an organisation, and recommend changes to improve organisational effectiveness;

- explain the importance of organisational and professional ethics;

- recommend ways in which ethical behaviour can be encouraged in organisations;

- discuss ways in which the conflict between centralised control and individual creativity can be managed;

- explain the usefulness of both classical and contemporary theories of management in practical situations;

- explain trends in the general management and structure of organisations;

- evaluate the management of an organisation and recommend improvements.

Syllabus content

- The determinants and components of strategy.

- Organisational objectives (by which we mean stakeholder analysis and organisational mission, goals and targets).

- The reasons for conflict between the objectives of an organisation, or between the objectives of the organisation and its stakeholders, and the ways in which this conflict might be managed (for example, compromise or identification of a dominant coalition).

- The process of strategy formulation (by which we mean the steps required and the order in which those steps might be undertaken).

- The various approaches that might be adopted to determine an appropriate strategy for the organisation (by which we mean rational, adaptive and interpretative approaches).

- The determinants of culture, the different models available for categorising cultures (for example, Deal and Kennedy, Harrison, McKinsey 7-S, Peters and Waterman, Peters).

- The importance of culture in organisations (for example, the 'organisational iceberg').

- The expectations of stakeholders with regard to ethical behaviour, and the role of government (for example, Cadbury Report, ombudsman appointment) and professional bodies (for example, CIMA) in determining ethical standards.

- The different models of organisational management available to achieve goal congruence while maintaining individual motivation (for example, the creation of strategic business units and the encouragement of entrepreneurial behaviour).

- The views expressed by both classical and contemporary writers on business management and the practical value and limitations of the approaches they propose (for example, scientific management, administrative, human relations, systems and contingency approaches when compared with contemporary writers such as Peters or Handy).

- Trends in business management and structure as evidenced in the business press and other mass media (for example, demerger, strategic alliances, virtual organisations, service centres).

11(ii) THE FUNCTIONAL AREA OF ORGANISATIONS – 15%

Learning outcomes

On completion of their studies students should be able to:

- explain the relative merits of a range of different organisation structures;

- explain the relationships necessary between the functional areas in order for an organisation to achieve its objectives;

- analyse a range of organisations, identifying their component parts, the relationships between those parts and any problems with those relationships;

- recommend and evaluate changes to the structure of organisations;

- explain the general characteristics and operation of the main functional areas of an organisation;

- explain the relationship between the work of the management accountant and the functional areas of an organisation;

- explain the workings of the marketing function of an organisation and the major tools and techniques used by marketing specialists;

- analyse the information needs of managers in each of the main functional areas of an organisation.

Syllabus content

- The different structures which might be adopted by a business organisation and how the various components of those structures interrelate (by which we mean entrepreneurial, functional, divisional, matrix, network, complex).

- The general operation of the main functional areas of business (by which we mean operations, marketing, human resource management, finance, research and development, information systems management).

- The organisation and activities of the marketing function (by which we mean marketing research, market segmentation, marketing strategy formulation).

- The concept of the marketing mix and the major tools therein (by which we mean branding, product mix, pricing, advertising, sales promotion, public relations, packaging, distribution).

- The information required by managers in the various functional areas of a business organisation and the role of the Chartered Management Accountant in identifying and satisfying those information needs.

11(iii) HUMAN RESOURCE MANAGEMENT – 30%

Learning outcomes

On completion of their studies students should be able to:

- explain the process of human resource planning and its relationship to other types of business plan;

- produce and explain a human resource plan for an organisation;

- produce a plan for the recruitment, selection and induction of finance department staff;

- produce a plan for the induction of new staff into the finance department of an organisation;

- explain the importance of human resource development planning;

- evaluate the tools which can be used to influence the behaviour of staff within a business, particularly within the finance department;

- explain the process of succession and career planning;

- produce a training and development plan for the staff of a finance department and analyse the major problems associated with the design and implementation of such a plan;

- produce and explain the planning and delivery of a training course on a finance-related topic;

- evaluate a typical appraisal process;

- analyse the issues involved in managing the dismissal, retirement and redundancy of individual staff.

Syllabus content

- The relationship of the human resource plan to other types of business plan.

- The determinants and content of a human resource plan (by which we mean organisational growth rate, skills, training, development, strategy, technologies, natural wastage).

- The problems which may be encountered in the implementation of a human resource plan and the ways in which such problems can be avoided or solved.

- The human issues relating to recruitment, dismissal and redundancy, and how to manage them.

- The process of recruitment and selection of staff, using different recruitment channels (by which we mean advertisement, agencies, consultants, executive search).

- The content and format of job descriptions, candidate specifications and job advertisements.

- The techniques that can be used in the selection of the most suitable applicant for a job (by which we mean interviews, assessment centres, intelligence tests, aptitude tests, psychometric tests).

- The importance of negotiation during the offer and acceptance of a job.

- The process of induction and the importance thereof.

- A range of models of human behaviour and motivation and their application in a business context (for example, Taylor, Schein, McGregor, Maslow, Herzberg, Handy, Lawrence and Lorsch).

- The design of reward systems.

- The distinction between development and training and the tools available to develop and train staff (by which we mean education, training methods, management development programmes, promotion, succession and career planning, job redesign).

- The stages in the planning and conduct of a training course, the features and benefits of the various tools and visual aids used and the importance of feedback during and after a training course.

- The importance of appraisals, their conduct and the problems often associated with them.

- The relationship between performance appraisal and the reward system.

11(iv) MANAGEMENT OF RELATIONSHIPS – 15%

Learning outcomes

On completion of their studies students should be able to:

- explain the concepts of authority, power, responsibility and delegation;

- analyse the relationships between managers and subordinates;

- analyse situations where problems have been caused by the adoption of an ineffective or inappropriate management style, and recommend remedial action;

- explain the formation of groups and the ways in which groups and their members behave;

- identify the different roles adopted by members of a group, and explain the relevance of this to the management of the group;

- explain the problems of maintaining discipline and evaluate the tools available to help a manager to achieve it;

- explain how the legal environment influences the relationships between the organisation and its employees, and between the employees of an organisation;

- explain the responsibilities of the organisation, its managers and staff in relation to health and safety, and advise how a manager can promote the health and safety of subordinates;

- explain the various ways in which fair treatment of employees can be achieved, and the role of government in ensuring this;

- analyse the causes of intergroup and interpersonal conflict in an organisation and recommend ways in which such conflict might be managed.

Syllabus content

- The concepts of power, authority, responsibility and delegation and their application to organisational relationships.

- The characteristics of leaders and managers.

- Management-style theories (for example, Likert, Tannenbaum and Schmidt, Blake and Mouton).

- The advantages and disadvantages of different styles of management.

- Contingency approaches to management style (for example, Adair, Fiedler).

- Theories of group development, behaviour and roles (for example, Tuckman, Belbin).

- Disciplinary procedures and their operation, including the form and process of formal disciplinary action and dismissal.

- The nature and effect of legal issues affecting work and employment, including the application of appropriate employment law (by which we mean law relating to health, safety, discrimination, fair treatment, childcare, contracts of employment and working time).

- The sources of conflict in organisations and the ways in which conflict can be managed to ensure that working relationships are productive and effective.

Note: Only the application of general legal principles will be required in this exam, and the English legal system will be used in suggested answers purely as an example. Students will be free to use relevant law from their own country.

11(v) MANAGEMENT OF CHANGE – 15%

Learning outcomes

On completion of their studies students should be able to:

- evaluate the determinants of change in organisations and the different levels at which change must be managed;

- explain the process of organisational development and the problems associated with it;

- recommend ways in which planned change can be implemented at the organisational and departmental levels;

- evaluate how the organisation and its managers might deal with major critical periods in the development of the organisation;

- identify opportunities to improve the management of change, and communicate recommendations to appropriate managers.

Syllabus content

- The impact on the organisation of external and internal change triggers (for example, environmental factors, mergers and acquisitions, re-organisation and rationalisation).

- The stages in the change process.

- Approaches to the management of organisational development and major cultural and structural change (for example, Kanter, Lewin and Peters).

- The importance of managing critical periods of change (e.g. start-up, rapid expansion, reorganisation, merger, redundancy programmes, close-down), and the ways in which these periods can be managed effectively.

ANALYSIS OF PAST PAPERS

Pilot paper 2000

Section A

1   Human resource planning process

2   Description of organisational culture using a classification e.g. Harrison et al. Recommendations for the best organisational culture to fit the situation.

3   Causes of conflict. Overcoming conflict.

Section B

4   Relationship between management accounting and management. Changing role of the management accountant

5   Differences between deliberate and emergent strategy. Chandler: links between strategy and structure.

6   Financial incentives to improve motivation. Non-monetary methods of improving motivation.

7   Difficulties in implementing organisational change. Change management.

May 2001

Section A

1   Identification of stakeholders and description of their interests. Influence and power of stakeholders.

2   Motivation theory - merits and limitations. Advantages and limitations of share incentive schemes.

3   Application of a theory of management style. Inappropriate management style and possible remedial action.

Section B

4   Advantages of market segmentation. Variables useful as a basis for segmentation.

5   Effects on the role of the Management Accountant of developments in IT, management accounting techniques, corporate governance, increasing concern with the environment and globalisation.

6   Organisational development. The skills and qualities of specialists in that field.

7   Objectives of a performance appraisal system. Effectiveness of appraisals.

November 2001

Section A

1   Application of concepts of corporate culture and national culture.

2   The nature of different organisational structures and their relative advantages and disadvantages.

3   Benefits of the career ladder. Alternative career structures as a means of motivating staff.

Section B

4   Team working in organisations.

5   Models of organisational management: the learning organisation. Processes for selection.

6   Professional codes of conduct for management accountants. Professional bodies regulation of members' adherence to ethical behaviour.

7   Analysis of a scenario about organisational change. Identification of the sources of change and ways of tackling the change process.

May 2002

Section A

1   Problems leading to the failure of a start-up business. Models of organisational growth.

2   Differences between corporate, business and functional level strategy. Theoretical perspective on strategy formation.

3   General attitudes to training and development. Factors required in the production of an HRD plan.

Section B

4   The purchasing function and its role in the effective performance of organisations. The management of innovation.

5   Guidelines and rationale for disciplinary procedures.

6   The virtual organisation and factors that led to its development. Joint ventures and the advantages they bring to parent companies.

7   Induction plans and how they contribute to staff retention and the required performance of new recruits.

November 2002

Section A

1   Relationship between human resource planning and planning at the corporate and business levels. Applying planning techniques to a particular case.

2   The bureaucratic model e.g. Weber. Application of this model to the case of a growing organisation.

3   The marketing orientation, the ways in which the marketing concept can be implemented in practice and the way the marketing mix can be used to improve the competitive stance of an organisation.

Section B

4   The empowerment process, the problems involved in its implementation and how the process can be facilitated.

5   The concepts of power and authority and the application of these concepts of a specific case.

6   The factors that influence the determination of organisational goals and the justification of these goals from both a shareholder perspective and a stakeholder perspective.

7   Recommended 'best practices' for implementing planned change.

REVISION GUIDANCE

Planning your revision

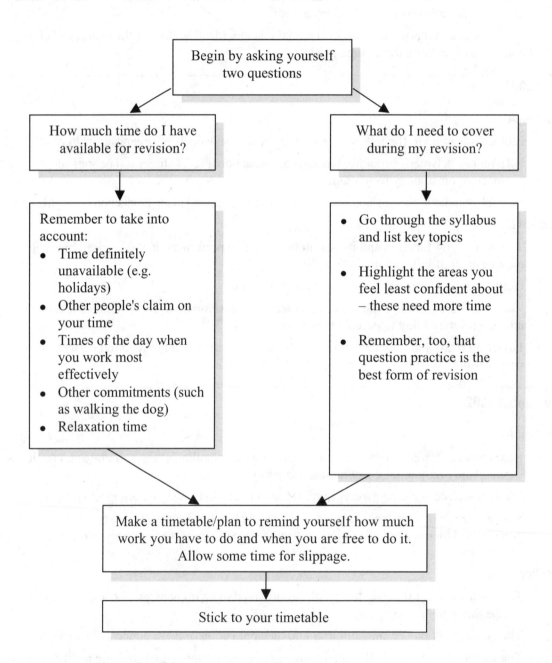

Begin by asking yourself two questions

How much time do I have available for revision?

What do I need to cover during my revision?

Remember to take into account:
- Time definitely unavailable (e.g. holidays)
- Other people's claim on your time
- Times of the day when you work most effectively
- Other commitments (such as walking the dog)
- Relaxation time

- Go through the syllabus and list key topics
- Highlight the areas you feel least confident about – these need more time
- Remember, too, that question practice is the best form of revision

Make a timetable/plan to remind yourself how much work you have to do and when you are free to do it. Allow some time for slippage.

Stick to your timetable

Revision techniques

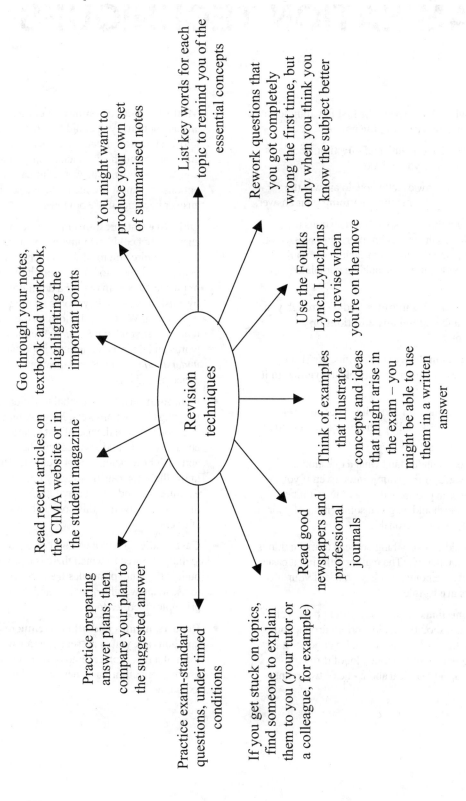

- Go through your notes, textbook and workbook, highlighting the important points
- You might want to produce your own set of summarised notes
- List key words for each topic to remind you of the essential concepts
- Rework questions that you got completely wrong the first time, but only when you think you know the subject better
- Use the Foulks Lynch Lynchpins to revise when you're on the move
- Think of examples that illustrate concepts and ideas that might arise in the exam – you might be able to use them in a written answer
- Read good newspapers and professional journals
- Read recent articles on the CIMA website or in the student magazine
- Practice preparing answer plans, then compare your plan to the suggested answer
- Practice exam-standard questions, under timed conditions
- If you get stuck on topics, find someone to explain them to you (your tutor or a colleague, for example)

Revision techniques

EXAMINATION TECHNIQUES

- You might want to spend the first few minutes of the examination **reading the paper**.

- Where you have a **choice of question**, decide which questions you will do.

- Unless you know exactly how to answer the question, spend some time **planning** your answer.

- **Divide the time** you spend on questions in proportion to the marks on offer. One suggestion is to allocate 1½ minutes to each mark available, so a 10 mark question should be completed in 15 minutes.

- Spend the last **five minutes** reading through your answers and **making any additions or corrections**.

- If you **get completely stuck** with a question, leave space in your answer book and **return to it later.**

- Stick to the question and **tailor your answer** to what you are asked. Pay particular attention to the verbs in the question.

- If you do not understand what a question is asking, **state your assumptions**. Even if you do not answer in precisely the way the examiner hoped, you should be given some credit, if your assumptions are reasonable.

- You should do everything you can to make things easy for the marker. The marker will find it easier to identify the points you have made if your **answers are legible**.

- **Essay questions**: Your essay should have a clear structure. It should contain a brief introduction, a main section and a conclusion. Be concise. It is better to write a little about a lot of different points than a great deal about one or two points.

- **Multiple-choice questions**: Don't treat these as an easy option – you could lose marks by rushing into your answer. Read the questions carefully and work through any calculations required. If you don't know the answer, eliminate those options you know are incorrect and see if the answer becomes more obvious.

- **Objective test questions** might ask for numerical answers, but could also involve paragraphs of text which require you to fill in a number of missing blanks, or for you to write a definition of a word or phrase. Others may give a definition followed by a list of possible key words relating to that description. Whatever the format, these questions require that you have *learnt* definitions, *know* key words and their meanings and importance, and *understand* the names and meanings of rules, concepts and theories.

- **Computations**: It is essential to include all your workings in your answers. Many computational questions require the use of a standard format: company profit and loss account, balance sheet and cash flow statement for example. Be sure you know these formats thoroughly before the examination and use the layouts that you see in the answers given in this book and in model answers.

- **Case studies**: To write a good case study, first identify the area in which there is a problem, outline the main principles/theories you are going to use to answer the question, and then apply the principles/theories to the case.

- **Reports, memos and other documents**: Some questions ask you to present your answer in the form of a report or a memo or other document. So use the correct format - there could be easy marks to gain here.

INDEX TO QUESTIONS AND ANSWERS

Section 1

MULTIPLE CHOICE QUESTIONS

ORGANISATIONAL MANAGEMENT

1   What can be described as 'a course of action, including a specification of the resources required, to achieve a desired outcome for the organisation'?

    A   Objective

    B   Strategy

    C   Procedure

    D   Policy

2   An advertising agency employs about 30 designers, copywriters, artists and account executives to develop advertising campaigns for business clients. When a new campaign is planned, a project team is established under the leadership of an account executive. This contains individuals with the necessary mix of skills to do the work.

The culture within the agency is that each team member is encouraged to contribute to the team effort to devise a successful campaign. Even the most junior and inexperienced individuals contribute ideas and suggestions for collective problem-solving within the project team.

Using the categories of organisation culture identified by Harrison, which type of organisational culture best describes the culture of the advertising agency?

    A   Task

    B   Role

    C   Power

    D   Existential

3   What is meant by the organisation element 'Skills' in the context of the McKinsey 7S model?

    A   Management culture

    B   The development of managers, both present and future

    C   Roles and responsibilities within the organisation

    D   The dominant attributes and capabilities of the organisation

4   In the McKinsey 7S model, there are seven interdependent organisational elements A weakness in any one of these elements creates a risk of organisation failure. The seven elements are grouped into three hard elements and four soft elements. Which of the following is a hard element?

   A   Staff

   B   Strategy

   D   Superordinate goals

   E   Skills

5   Mintzberg identified four forms of organisation. These are an entrepreneurial start-up, a machine bureaucracy, a professional organisation and an 'adhocracy'. To help explain these forms, he defined five basic organisational sub-units: a strategic apex, a middle line, a technostructure, support staff and an operating core.

   To which organisational sub-unit would the senior operations manager belong?

   A   Strategic apex

   B   Middle line

   C   Technostructure

   D   Operating core

6   Mintzberg identified four forms of organisation. These are an entrepreneurial start-up, a machine bureaucracy, a professional organisation and an 'adhocracy'. To help explain these forms, he defined five basic organisational sub-units to which its employees belong: a strategic apex, a middle line, a technostructure, support staff and an operating core.

   Which organisation structure is characterised by an operating core that seeks to minimise the influence of a middle line and a technocracy?

   A   Machine bureaucracy

   B   Entrepreneur start up

   C   Professional organisation

   D   Adhocracy

7   Peters and Waterman identified eight attributes of excellence in organisations. One of these attributes is:

   A   bias for action

   B   productivity through automation

   C   diversification

   D   profitability.

8   An employee who exposes the ethical misconduct of others in an organisation is known as a(n):

      A   ombudsman

      B   whisteblower

      C   stakeholder

      D   monitor.

9   'Simplicity' is one of eight attributes of excellence in organisations identified by Peters and Waterman. Simplicity can be described as:

      A   having few rules and procedures, but strong values.

      B   sticking to the core business.

      C   having few administrative layers and few senior staff

      D   organising into small semi-autonomous units.

10   Herbert Simon put forward a model of decision-making in organisations. A manager might reach a better decision by spending more time and money to reach it. Simon argued that in practice, decisions are reached through a trade-off between the quality of the decision and the time and cost of reaching it.

      This model of decision-making is known as:

      A   logical incrementalism

      B   bounded rationality

      C   muddling through

      D   rational planning.

11   Which of the following is not one of the management functions identified by Henri Fayol?

      A   Co-ordinating

      B   Controlling

      C   Motivating

      D   Organising

12   According to Mendelow, the significance of each stakeholder group in an organisation depends on two factors: the power of the stakeholder and the level of interest of the stakeholder in the organisation.

Level of interest

		Low	High
Power	Low	I	II
	High	III	IV

The management of an organisation should adapt their method of dealing with stakeholder groups according to their position in the above matrix, so as to avoid the risk of a damaging conflict.

What approach is recommended for dealing with stakeholders in quadrant III of the matrix above?

A   Develop strategies that are fully acceptable to the stakeholder

B   Keep the stakeholder satisfied

C   Keep the stakeholder informed

D   Minimum effort is necessary, because the stakeholder does not have sufficient influence to concern the organisation

13   French and Bell developed the concept of the organisational iceberg. Which of the following best describes this concept?

A   The informal (hidden) aspects of an organisation should concern managers more than with the overt, formal aspects.

B   Senior managers make just a few key strategic decisions, whereas a much larger number of smaller decisions are taken by middle-ranking and junior management.

C   The greatest rewards go a small number of managers at the top, and the majority of employees are not sufficiently rewarded.

D   An organisation drifts towards self-destruction when it is isolated from its environment.

14   Herzberg (Work and the Nature of Man) categorised work-related factors that cause satisfaction or dissatisfaction for employees as either hygiene factors or motivator factors.

Which of the following is a hygiene factor?

(i)   Job security

(ii)   Interpersonal relations

(iii)   Challenging work

A   (i) only

B   (i) and (ii) only

C   (i) and (iii) only

D   (ii) only

15   According to Deal and Kennedy (Corporate Cultures), the culture of an organisation is a function of two factors: the willingness of employees to take risks and the speed with which they receive feedback about how well or badly they have done.

What name did they give to a culture where the willingness to take risks is high and the speed of feedback is slow?

A   Bet your company culture

B   Hard macho culture

C   Process culture

D   Work hard/play hard culture

16   Which of the following features of an organisation and its management is not one of the eight attributes of excellence identified by Peters and Waterman (In Search of Excellence)?

   A   Listening regularly to customers.

   B   Achieving renewal through innovation.

   C   Giving autonomy to sub-units in the organisation and encouraging their management to think independently and competitively.

   D   Keeping in touch with the essential business of the organisation.

17   What is defined as 'the scope and amount of discretion given to a person to make decisions by virtue of the position he or she holds in the organisation'?

   A   Delegation

   B   Responsibility

   C   Power

   D   Authority

18   Power within an organisation comes from different sources. Which type of power within a company is associated with a trade union representative?

   A   Resource power

   B   Position power

   C   Personal power

   D   Negative power

19   Which of the following statements are correct?

   (i)   When the scalar chain of an organisation is long, the span of control will be wide.

   (ii)   There are fewer opportunities for promotion in a flat organisation than in a tall organisation.

   A   Statement (i) only is correct

   B   Statement (ii) only is correct

   C   Both statements are correct

   D   Neither statement is correct

THE FUNCTIONAL AREAS OF ORGANISATIONS

20   Which form of departmentation within an organisation offers the advantage of work specialisation?

   A   Product

   B   Functional

   C   Geographical

   D   Customer/market segment

21   A matrix management structure is inconsistent with the 'classical' management theory of:

    A   authority and responsibility

    B   unity of command

    C   delegation of authority

    D   line and staff authority.

22   A business school has a school of accounting, a school of human relations studies, a school of marketing and a law school. Each school has a head. Each degree course is the responsiblity of a member of the academic staff (the 'course director'), often a professor or a senior lecturer. The lecturers and tutors for each degree course are drawn from several schools.

    The organisation structure used in the business school is best described as a:

    A   departmental structure

    B   divisional structure

    C   project structure

    D   matrix structure.

23   What type of organisation might be described as one based on contact, communication and information-sharing between individuals or work units, normally with one individual or work unit acting in the role of co-ordinator?

    A   Matrix organisation

    B   Network organisation

    C   Entrepreneurial organisation

    D   Organic organisation

24   An identifiable group of customers with common needs, preferences or characteristics, who might be expected to respond in a similar way to marketing initiatives, is called a:

    A   focussed market

    B   market sector

    C   market segment

    D   target market.

25   A travel company has a web site giving details of the holidays it offers. Anyone visiting the web site can see what holidays are on offer, and make a booking. Which of the following elements of the marketing mix is the web site a part?

    (i)   Place

    (ii)   Promotion

    (iii)   Process

    A   (i) and (ii) only

    B   (i) and (iii) only

    C   (ii) and (iii) only

    D   (i) (ii) and (iii)

26   A supermarket has a limited period offer of three cartons of orange juice for the price of two. In which element of the marketing mix would this offer be categorised?

A   Price

B   Promotion

C   Place

D   Product

27   Which of the following are elements of the 'promotion' in the marketing mix for a brand of hair care products?

Item

(i)   Advertising

(ii)   Sales promotions

(iii)   Direct selling

(iv)   Public relations

A   (i) and (ii) only

B   (i) (ii) and (iii) only

C   (i) (ii) and (iv) only

D   All of them

28   Porter identified nine 'value activities' in an organisation, which he divided into two categories, primary activities and support activities. Which of the following value activities is a primary activity?

A   Procurement

B   Technology development

C   Human resource management

D   Service

HUMAN RESOURCE MANAGEMENT

29   There are four main objectives of human resource management (HRM):

(1)   to develop an effective human component for the organisation that will respond effectively to change

(2)   to obtain and develop the human resources required by the organisation and motivate them effectively

(3)   to create and maintain a co-operative climate of relationships within the organisation

(4)   to meet the organisation's social and legal responsibilities with regard to its employees.

Providing a pension scheme for employees to which the employer contributes is an aspect of which of these four objectives?

A   Objective 1

B   Objective 2

C   Objective 3

D   Objective 4

30   Which of the following activities is not usually a part of the human resources management function?

A   Manpower planning

B   Performance appraisal

C   Recruitment

D   Training schemes

31   Which theory of management is based on the premise that most people dislike work and responsibility, and will avoid both as much as possible?

A   Theory X

B   Theory Y

C   Theory Z

D   Hierarchy of needs

32   Handy takes a contingency approach to analysing what makes an effective group. He suggested that for any group, there are certain givens and certain intervening factors, which together determine the outcomes that the group achieves, such as group productivity or effectiveness.

Which of the following is not one of the intervening factors in his analysis?

A   Satisfaction of the group members

B   Motivation of the group members

C   Processes and procedures

D   Leadership style.

33   The HR department of AMZ has developed a human resources plan consisting of six elements: a recruitment plan, a training plan, a redevelopment plan, a productivity plan, a redundancy plan and a retention plan. The company has been concerned about the high rate of labour turnover amongst its specialist support staff, particularly it management accountants, and has developed plans for rectifying the situation. The plans for reducing labour turnover will be part of the:

A   redevelopment plan

B   recruitment plan

C   training plan

D   retention plan.

34   Which of the following provides the most suitable definition of job analysis?

    A   Assessing a job to decide whether it is worth maintaining in its current form

    B   Restructuring a job by changing the responsibilities and duties of the job holder

    C   Collecting information about a job and setting out its contents on the basis of the information gathered

    D   Specifying the requirements of a job and what the job holder is expected to do

35   Employers might use a range of tests to supplement interviews in the recruitment and selection process. One type of test seeks to measure the psychological dimensions of the job applicant and to give him or her a numerical test score on the basis of his or her answers. The score provides a measure of the individual's aptitude or personality, and the results can be compared with the results of the interview. What is this type of test?

    A   Proficiency test

    B   Intelligence test

    D   Psychometric test

    E   Psychological test

36   Which is the second lowest need in Maslow's hierarchy of needs?

    A   Physiological

    B   Esteem

    C   Safety

    D   Social

37   Herzberg's theory of individual motivation at work is based on the concept of hygiene factors and motivator factors. Which of the following aspects of work could be both a hygiene and a motivator factor?

    A   Job security

    B   Pay

    C   Gaining recognition

    D   Quality of supervision

38   Lawrence and Lorsch (Organisation and Environment: Managing Differentiation and Integration, 1967) studied the extent of differentiation or integration within organisations. Integration is a measure of the degree to which the units of an organisation are linked together and interdependent.

Do the following statements a correct explanation of some of their conclusions?

Statement 1:   In a dynamic and diverse environment, a low degree of differentiation is necessary to succeed.

Statement 2:   Conflict is reduced by differentiation.

A   Statement 1 only is correct

B   Statement 2 only is correct

C   Both statements are correct

D   Neither statement is correct

39   **Which of the following are aspects of human relations development (HRD)?**

(i)   Training

(ii)   Job re-design

(iii) Succession and career planning

A   (i) only

B   (i) and (ii) only

C   (i) and (iii) only

D   (i) (ii) and (iii)

40   **What is the term for an appraisal of an individual by his or her colleagues?**

A   Upward appraisal

B   Peer review

C   360 degree appraisal

D   Self appraisal

41   **According to Herzberg, which of the following approaches to job design is likely to result in a significant improvement in the motivation of the job holder?**

(i)   Job enrichment

(ii)   Job enlargement

(iii) Job rotation

A   (i) only

B   (i) and (ii) only

C   (i) and (iii) only

D   (i) (ii) and (iii)

MANAGEMENT OF RELATIONSHIPS

42   **Tannenbaum and Schmidt suggested that the appropriate leadership behaviour in any situation lies somewhere along a 'continuum of leader behaviour', ranging from boss-centred leadership at one extreme to subordinate-centred leadership at the other. (With boss-centred leadership, the boss makes the decisions and announces them, without any input from subordinates.).**

Put the following leadership styles in the order they occur on the continuum from boss-centred leadership towards subordinate-centred leadership.

Style

1   Manager defines limits and asks the group to make a decision within those limits

2   Manager puts a problem to the group, asks for suggestions and then makes a decision

3   Manager presents a tentative decision to the group but is prepared to change it

4   Manager allows subordinates to function freely within limits defined by the manager

5   Manager sells a decision to the group

A   Styles 5, 3, 2, 1, 4

B   Style 2, 3, 5, 4, 1

C   Style 3, 5, 2, 1, 4

D   Styles 5, 2, 3, 4, 1

43   **Fiedler's contingency theory of leadership includes the view that a task-oriented approach to leadership will be more successful than a relationship-oriented approach in some circumstances but will be less successful in others. The performance of a group depends on how certain factors interact. Most of these factors are variable, but one cannot change and is fixed.**

What is the fixed factor?

A   The personality of the leader

B   The formal authority of the leader

C   The task structure

D   Leader-member relations

44   **In Belbin's role theory, nine roles need to be fulfilled by team members in order to create a successful team. These nine roles are grouped into three categories.**

Which of the following is not one of those categories?

A   Cerebral

B   Action-oriented

C   Environment-oriented

D   People-oriented

45   **The four styles of management identified by Likert are:**

A   tells, sells, consults, joins

B   exploitative authoritative, benevolent authoritative, participative, laissez faire

C   task-oriented, people-oriented, result-oriented, middle-of-the-road

D   benevolent authoritative, participative, democratic, exploitative autocratic.

46 **Blake and Mouton's managerial grid assesses managers and management styles along two axes: concern for the task and concern for people.**

Each of these is graded on a scale of 1 to 9. What managerial style did they describe as 'team style'?

A   Very high concern for people but very low concern for the job

B   Very high concern for the job but very low concern for people

C   Very high concern for people and very high concern for the job

D   Very low concern for people and very low concern for the job

47 **Adair's action-centred leadership model suggests that the most appropriate approach to leadership of a group depends on three inter-related needs: the needs of the task, the needs of the individual group members and the needs of the group as a whole. The roles to which the leader gives relatively more or less time will depend on the priorities of these needs in the situation.**

The various roles of a leader are categorised as task roles, individual maintenance roles and group maintenance roles. Which of the following roles is a group maintenance role?

A   Information-seeking

B   Peace-keeping

C   Training

D   Counselling.

48 **Which of the following statements is correct?**

Statement 1: Authority is a form of power.

Statement 2: Responsibility can be delegated but authority cannot.

A   Statement 1 only is correct.

B   Statement 2 only is correct.

C   Both statements are correct.

D   Neither statement is correct.

49 **If a manager justifies an instruction to a subordinate by saying: 'because I am your superior', she is relying on which one of the following power bases?**

A   Referent

B   Reward

C   Legitimate

D   Expert.

50 **Tuckman identified four stages in group development. In which order do the stages occur?**

A   Forming, storming, performing, norming

B   Forming, norming, storming, performing

C   Storming, forming, performing, norming

D   Forming, storming, norming, performing.

51 The ACAS Code of Practice states that good disciplinary procedures should conform to certain standards. Which of the following is one of those standards?

A   There should be no right of appeal.

B   A worker should never be dismissed for a first breach of discipline.

C   The worker should have the right to ask for a public hearing.

D   The worker should have the right to state his or her case before a decision is reached.

52 In which sequence might the stages of a formal disciplinary hearing progress?

A   Formal oral warning, followed by written warning

B   Formal oral warning, followed by first written warning and final written warning

C   Informal oral warning, followed by formal oral warning, first written warning, then final written warning

D   Formal oral warning, followed by first, second and then final written warning

53 The finance director of GTR Limited, a UK company, is summarily dismissed without proper notice. His contract of employment gives an entitlement to one year's notice of termination of employment. Under UK law, the director could bring an action for:

A   unfair dismissal only

B   wrongful dismissal only

C   either wrongful dismissal or unfair dismissal

D   redundancy.

MANAGEMENT OF CHANGE

54 Training in the use of a new management information system is a means of overcoming resistance to change by:

A   facilitation and support

B   education and communication

C   participation and involvement

D   negotiation and agreement.

55 Greiner identified five stages in the life cycle of an organisation. These are, in order, growth through (1) creativity (2) direction (3) delegation (4) co-ordination and (5) collaboration. Each stage ends in a particular type of crisis. Which phase of Greiner's organisational growth model ends in a crisis of leadership?

A   Growth through creativity phase

B   Growth through direction phase

C   Growth through delegation phase

D   Growth through co-ordination phase.

56   In Greiner's model, in what sequence do the five stages in the life cycle of an organisation occur?

A   Collaboration, Creativity, Direction, Delegation, Co-ordination

B   Creativity, Direction, Delegation, Co-ordination, Collaboration

C   Creativity, Direction, Co-ordination, Collaboration, Delegation

D   Creativity, Co-ordination, Direction, Delegation, Collaboration

57   Burns and Stalker distinguished between mechanistic and organic organisations, and contrasted their ability to deal well with change. Which of the following statements is a correct representation of their views?

Statement 1:   Organisations with organic structures are more able than mechanistic organisations to deal with change.

Statement 2:   Organic structures are not necessarily good at exploiting creative ideas.

A   Statement 1 only is correct.

B   Statement 2 only is correct

C   Both statements are correct.

D   Neither statement is correct.

58   Rosabeth Moss Kanter (The Enduring Skills of Change Leaders) argued that organisational change has become a 'way of life' due to three forces. Which one of the following is not one of those three forces?

A   Globalisation

B   Information technology

C   Political change

D   Industry consolidation.

59   According to Kanter, organisations that are good at dealing with change share three key attributes, each associated with a particular role for its leaders.

Which of the following is one of those three key attributes?

A   The boldness to allocate resources to change

B   The openness to collaborate

C   The strength of mind to see through change

D   Financial strength.

60   Kurt Lewin put forward a 'force field theory' of organisational change. What are the forces he described?

A   Forces for decentralisation and forces for centralisation

B   Forces for change and restraining forces against change

C   Forces for growth and forces for break-up

D   Forces for improvement and a forces for deterioration.

61 Kanter identified seven 'classic skills' to be equally useful to CEOs, senior executives and middle managers for introducing change. Which of the following is not one of those skills?

A   Building coalitions

B   Acquiring technical skills

C   Learning to persevere

D   Tuning into the environment.

62 What is the Lewin/Schein three-stage approach to changing human behaviour?

A   Change individual attitudes, change group attitudes, change organisational culture

B   Coerce, manage resistance, adapt

C   Unfreeze existing behaviour, change attitudes and behaviour, refreeze new behaviour

D   Change top management attitudes, change management style, change employee behaviour.

63 Which of the following are three important factors for managers to consider when dealing with resistance to change within an organisation?

A   Cost of change, pace of change, scope of change

B   Timing of change, pace of change, manner of change

C   Costs of change, benefits of change, manner of change

D   Pace of change, manner of change, scope of change.

Section 2

PRACTICE QUESTIONS

ORGANISATIONAL MANAGEMENT

1 STRATEGY AND ENVIRONMENT

You are required:

(a)   to list **five** aspects of the environment which affect organisations;   **(5 marks)**

(b)   for **each** of these aspects, to describe the environmental trends likely to affect an international company during the next ten years.   **(15 marks)**

(Total: 20 marks)

2 STRATEGIC PLANNING

Describe the different components of strategic planning at its corporate, tactical and operational levels, and show the relationship between these components.   **(20 marks)**

3 CULTURE

Contrast the key features of 'role' and 'task' cultures.   **(20 marks)**

4 ETHICS AND SOCIAL RESPONSIBILITY

Social responsibility may be defined as the obligations that an organisation has towards society and the broad environment in which the organisation operates. Management, therefore, should concern itself with the way in which the organisation interacts with its environment.

Explain how and to what extent management should recognise social responsibility extending beyond the boundaries of the organisation.   **(20 marks)**

5 ETHICS AND THE PROFESSIONAL BODY

It has been suggested that one of the key issues surrounding the debate about the social responsibility of management concerns whether management is a profession.

(a)   Contrast the situation of a manager who is a member of CIMA with that of a manager who is not a member of a professional body.   **(12 marks)**

(b)   Discuss the case for setting social responsibility goals and policies in commercial organisations.   **(8 marks)**

(Total: 20 marks)

6   CONFLICT

(a)   Explain why the total effectiveness of a large and diversified organisation is likely to be adversely affected if any of its constituent departments or divisions pursue their own objectives.   **(5 marks)**

(b)   By what means may the various objectives, tasks and workflows within the organisation be properly co-ordinated and integrated, so that it may be effective as a whole?   **(15 marks)**

(Total: 20 marks)

7   CONTEMPORARY THEORIES

'The contingency approach to organisational design evolved as a direct reaction against the *one best way* panaceas of classical theory and the human relations school.' Outline the main features of the contingency approach and show how it can be distinguished from the other two theories mentioned in the quotation.   **(20 marks)**

8   CLASSICAL THEORIES

Compare the approaches taken by classical/traditional theorists with the human relations/human resources theorists in understanding the nature of organisations. **(20 marks)**

9   CONTINGENCY THEORY

Briefly state the main features of contingency theory and explain how it might help in designing an organisation.   **(20 marks)**

10   TRENDS IN GENERAL MANAGEMENT: FLEXIBLE WORKFORCE

Faced with a changing, uncertain and increasingly competitive environment, human resource managers are being required to develop a workforce which combines flexibility with quality performance.

Requirements:

(a)   Describe the features of a flexible workforce.   **(12 marks)**

(b)   Explain how you would go about achieving the twin objectives of labour flexibility and quality performance.   **(8 marks)**

(Total: 20 marks)

11   TRENDS IN GENERAL MANAGEMENT: REDUCING SIZE

(a)   Describe the major trends in reducing the size of an organisation   **(10 marks)**

(b)   Explain the reasons why such changes have become necessary.   **(10 marks)**

(Total: 20 marks)

12   CHANDLER

(a)   Explain why the actual strategy pursued by a company over a three- to five-year period may diverge from the deliberate strategy that the company initiated at the outset of that period.   **(8 marks)**

(b)   A D Chandler and others have argued that a multi-product organisation is best served by a divisional structure. Discuss the arguments for and against this claim. **(12 marks)**

(Total: 20 marks)

13   SFC

The Supreme Football Club (SFC), a profit-making company with directors and shareholders, has received a take-over bid from one of the satellite-broadcasting corporations. The club is currently assessing whether to accept the bid.

SFC is a multi-million dollar business. Its income consists of gate receipts, fees for TV rights, merchandising, sponsorship, conferencing and catering. The club is very successful; the team's performance on the pitch has made it a very popular club and this success has been reflected in growth turnover and profits in recent years. The advent of satellite TV has made football a worldwide spectator sport and the club has fans throughout the world.

The success of the club has not, however, prevented it from receiving some criticism. One of the issues causing continuing concern has been the constantly-changing replica shirts as worn by the club's football team. Parents of young fans have felt pressurised into spending large sums of money every year or so because the club has changed its shirt styles six times in as many years.

Another issue has been the increase in ticket prices over the past few years. These have risen far faster than inflation, and the fan club has made several representations to the board of SFC in protest at these increases.

The income from TV rights is much welcomed by the club, but matches have been rescheduled at short notice to suit satellite stations and their exclusive audiences. It is perhaps not surprising therefore that the bid to take over the club by the satellite-broadcasting corporation has been met with hostility by the fans and others who see the club they have supported and the game they love as being treated like any other profit-making organisation.

Required:

(a)   Who are the stakeholder groups of the SFC? Describe the particular interest of each stakeholder group in the club.   **(12 marks)**

(b)   Explain which stakeholder groups are likely to exert the most influence on the decision to accept / reject the takeover bid, indicating their power and influence.

(8 marks)

(Total: 20 marks)

14   FFC

A very successful multinational food company (FFC) from country S has just opened a small group of restaurants in country C, but a range of problems has affected the new venture. Customers have complained about the menus, the seating arrangements and the music that is played. Local residents have protested about the architecture of restaurant buildings, and the restaurant employees have complained about the style and practices of the managers from country S who run the business.

Required:

(a)   Using your knowledge of national and corporate cultures, explain why FFC is experiencing the problems noted in the scenario.   **(10 marks)**

(b)   Based on your analysis in answer to part (a), provide a set of recommendations to assist the board of FFC to resolve its problems.   **(10 marks)**

(Total: 20 marks)

15   PROFESSIONAL CODE AND ETHICS

Required:

(a)   Explain why it is necessary for chartered management accountants to adhere to a professional code of conduct.   **(10 marks)**

(b)   Recommend the steps that both professional accountancy bodies and organisations more generally can take to ensure that their members take seriously the ethical principles included in their organisations' codes of conduct.   **(10 marks)**

(Total: 20 marks)

16   THE E COMPANY

The E Company consists of automobile engine, marine engine and aerospace engine businesses. It has built its global reputation for engine design and quality on its engineering capability. Though the marine engine business has not been performing well for some time, the E Company has dominated the supply of engines for the luxury end of the automobile market for years. Unfortunately for the E Company, however, the market in luxury automobiles is changing. Exchange rate movements and increased production costs have made the E Company less competitive and its rivals are rapidly catching up in terms of engine quality and design. As a result, the latest annual report shows turnover down, margins reduced and the company barely breaking even.

You have just attended a strategy meeting at the E Company in which:

- Manager A argued that the automobile engine business strategy was wrong.

- Manager B claimed that the major problem had been the failure to properly implement functional strategies.

- Manager C said that more attention should be paid to the threats and opportunities of the external environment so that the E Company could position itself more realistically.

- Manager D claimed that the company should really be seeking to develop further its core engineering competence if it was going to regain its competitiveness in the market place.

After the meeting, a junior manager who had been in attendance asks you to explain what his senior colleagues had been talking about.

Required:

For the benefit of the junior manager, explain

(a)   The differences between corporate level strategy, business level strategy and functional level strategy in the E Company.   **(10 marks)**

(b)   The theoretical perspective on strategy formation adopted by manager C and manager D.   **(10 marks)**

(Total: 20 marks)

17   VIRTUAL ORGANISATION

(a)   Define the nature of a "virtual organisation", and account for the emergence of this organisational form.   **(10 marks)**

T is a newly-established mobile telephone company in N, an industrialising company. It has just formed a joint venture, J, with a large established European mobile telephone company, K. The purpose of the joint venture is to design, manufacture, market and distribute mobile phones in country N.

Required:

(b)   Describe the nature of a joint venture. Explain the potential advantages to Company T and Company K of setting up the joint venture J.   **(10 marks)**

(Total: 20 marks)

FUNCTIONAL AREAS OF ORGANISATIONS

18   RELATIVE MERITS OF DIFFERENT FUNCTIONAL ORGANISATIONS

You are required:

(a)   To draw a simple functional organisation structure, to explain three conditions under which it would be suitable and to give an example in each case;

(b)   To draw a simple chart illustrating territorial organisation structure, to explain three conditions under which it would be suitable and to give an example in each case.

(20 marks)

19   MERITS OF A RANGE OF ORGANISATIONAL STRUCTURES

Functional, product, market, territorial, project or matrix structures are all examples of organisational structure.

You are required to discuss *five* major factors which determine the choice of an appropriate structure.   **(20 marks)**

20   HR MANAGEMENT FUNCTION

The function of Human Resource Management is something of an oddity within organisations: Some writers have referred to the HR Manager as 'big hat – no cattle'.

Illustrate some of the issues and problems of HR within a functional organisational structure.
          (20 marks)

21   MANAGEMENT ACCOUNTANT'S RELATIONSHIP WITH FUNCTIONAL AREAS

(a)   Identify the political and psychological implications of managerial control in hierarchical organisations, and explain why a knowledge of these implications is of benefit to the chartered management accountant.   **(8 marks)**

(b)   In the event of resistance to managerial control, how can managers ensure their objectives are met?   **(12 marks)**

(Total: 20 marks)

22   MARKETING FUNCTION: THE PRODUCT LIFE CYCLE

You are required to explain the product life-cycle concept and why it is important to a company planning for the development of new products. Illustrate your answer using examples with which you are familiar.   **(20 marks)**

23   MARKETING FUNCTION: CONCEPTS

Marketing mix has been defined as 'the set of controllable variables and their levels that the firm use to influence the target market'. There are a great number of marketing mix variables, the most popular classification being the four Ps.

(a)   Outline the characteristics of each of the four Ps.   **(6 marks)**

(b)   Discuss how you would expect a manager to apply many, but not necessarily all, of the principles of the four P's to the marketing of a well-established tourist attraction eg, theme park, whose popularity is beginning to fall slightly.   **(14 marks)**

(Total: 20 marks)

24   FUNCTIONAL AREAS: VALUE CHAIN

The functional areas of a business link together to form a value chain. Describe the contrbution of ONE such area.   **(20 marks)**

25   MANAGEMENT ACCOUNTANT

You have been invited to give a talk to members at your local CIMA branch.

The chairperson of the branch is keen to encourage the involvement of students in branch meetings and has invited you to give a talk that will be of particular interest to students, but which will also be of some interest to the qualified, experienced membership.

In order to meet the different needs of both of these groups the chairperson has decided on two topics. The first of these - *the relationship of management accounting with other management activities* - will be aimed primarily at the student audience, while the second - *the changing role of the management accountant* - will be aimed at the membership as a whole.

Requirement:

Prepare a paper for a talk on the following two topics, including a series of headings supported by brief explanatory notes, that could be used as a basis for your overhead projector slides or whiteboard/blackboard headings.

(a)   Describe the general relationship between management accounting and the key activities of management.   **(12 marks)**

(b)   Describe how the role of the management accountant is changing and explain briefly the key forces driving the changes.   **(8 marks)**

(Total: 20 marks)

26   SEGMENTING

In the last few decades, companies have moved increasingly towards the targeting of particular customer segments rather than seeking to sell a single product range to all customers.

Required:

(a)   Explain the advantages that a company might hope to gain by targeting particular segments of the market.   **(10 marks)**

(b)   Describe three variables you think would be useful as a basis for segmenting the market for clothing sold by a large retail chain, and two variables for segmenting the market in paint sold to other businesses by a paint manufacturer.

Explain your reasons for the choice of all five variables.   **(10 marks)**

(Total: 20 marks)

27   COMPANY Y

Company Y began manufacturing a single product. As the company grew, it adopted a typical functional structure. More recently, as a result of both internal development and a series of acquisitions, it has become a multi-product company serving diverse markets.

Required:

(a) Explain the limitations of Company Y's functional structure, given its recent development into a multi-product company. **(6 marks)**

(b) In view of the growth of Company Y, identify the type of organisation structure that might be more appropriate, justifying your proposal. **(8 marks)**

(c) Discuss the potential limitations of the proposed new structure. **(6 marks)**

(Total: 20 marks)

28   C PHARMACEUTICAL COMPANY

It is now widely recognised that an efficient purchasing department can add significantly to the competitive advantage of an organisation.

Required:

(a) Describe the function of the purchasing department and explain how a well-managed purchasing department can contribute to effective organisational performance. **(10 marks)**

The C Pharmaceutical Company is in a state of crisis. The development of new drugs and treatments on which the very survival of the organisation depends has slowed dramatically in recent years. An investigation into the operation of the organisation's research and development (R&D) unit has revealed that the slow rate of innovation has much to do with the way the department has been managed.

The head of the unit, Dr Strong, regards it as his duty not to exceed the unit's budget allocation and has introduced strict controls to avoid this happening. Members of the R&D unit are set clear targets with time limits and expected to be working in the laboratory or office on a 9-to-5 basis every working day. This system of control is not to the liking of research staff and several of the most innovative members have left. The morale of the remaining staff is very low and further resignations are expected.

Required:

(b) Analyse why the problems in the R&D unit of the C Pharmaceutical Company might have developed. Recommend what actions could be taken to encourage creativity and innovation. **(10 marks)**

(Total: 20 marks)

HUMAN RESOURCE MANAGEMENT

29   HR PLANNING

(a) Describe the process of HR planning. **(10 marks)**

(b) What are the main problems and how can they be overcome? **(10 marks)**

(Total: 20 marks)

30   HOW TO DEAL WITH REDUNDANCY

Your organisation may cease trading altogether or might only have to close temporarily - depending on a financial restructuring proposal being considered by the banks and shareholders.

(a)   Outline the major issues facing the organisation in terms of planning for the future.

          (10 marks)

(b)   Describe the methods you could use to minimise the effect of redundancy on employees.   **(10 marks)**

          (Total: 20 marks)

31   RECRUITMENT: TWO-WAY SELECTION

(a)   Explain why it is beneficial to organisations as well as to applicants if selection is regarded as a two-way process.   **(10 marks)**

(b)   What factors need to be considered in drawing up a person specification for a newly-qualified management accountant to work in the accounting department of a company engaged in the manufacture and distribution of computer products?   **(10 marks)**

          (Total: 20 marks)

32   RECRUITMENT

(a)   Describe the process of recruitment.   **(10 marks)**

(b)   Discuss some of the major problems and issues for firms in selecting the right candidate.   **(10 marks)**

          (Total: 20 marks)

33   JOB DESCRIPTIONS AND PERSON SPECIFICATIONS

Getting the right person? How do job and person specifications become advertising 'copy'?

          (20 marks)

34   MANAGEMENT DEVELOPMENT

You are required:

(a)   to define 'management development';   **(4 marks)**

(b)   to describe the steps that an organisation should take to implement a formal management development system.   **(16 marks)**

          (Total: 20 marks)

35   INFLUENCING BEHAVIOUR: LABOUR PRODUCTIVITY

(a)   Describe the major factors which affect labour productivity.   **(12 marks)**

(b)   Explain, with reference to relevant literature, the relationship between labour productivity and the difficulty of achieving budget.   **(6 marks)**

          (Total: 18 marks)

36   INFLUENCING BEHAVIOUR: REWARD SYSTEMS

Describe and discuss the main features to be included in a reward system.   **(20 marks)**

37   TRAINING AND DEVELOPMENT STRATEGY

(a)   Discuss the role of training and development policies from a strategic viewpoint.

          (15 marks)

(b)   How does induction training become a strategic event?   **(5 marks)**

          (Total: 20 marks)

38   EXPLAIN THE PLANNING AND DELIVERY OF TRAINING COURSES

What are the main methods used in training to communicate ideas with delegates on courses? **(15 marks)**

39   EVALUATE A TYPICAL APPRAISAL

(a)   Discuss the process of appraising the performance of an employee. **(12 marks)**

(b)   How can this be related to a reward system? **(8 marks)**

(Total: 20 marks)

40   APPRAISAL AND REWARD

Discuss the link between Personal Appraisal and Reward, with specific reference to formal systems of evaluation and payment. **(20 marks)**

41   DISMISSAL, RETIREMENT, REDUNDANCY

Describe the various processes which lead to employees leaving an organisation, whether planned or unplanned. **(20 marks)**

42   REDUNDANCY

(a)   Explain what is meant by 'redundancy'. **(6 marks)**

(b)   Discuss how the process of redundancy can be managed to limit the effect on staff. **(14 marks)**

(Total: 20 marks)

43   X

Like many other companies, X has to respond to a variety of pressures for change. Increasing competition has forced company X to reduce costs by downsizing its personnel numbers and reducing the size of the head office. Further measures have included a greater concentration on its core business and processes. To date, these pressures have had a limited effect on the finance department, but the finance director is now under pressure to reduce the number of personnel employed in her department by 30 per cent over the next two years, and by a total of 50 per cent within a five-year period.

In the initial review of the task facing her, the finance director appreciates that she has to take into account a number of changes that are affecting the finance function. These include the ever-increasing application of IT, the increasing financial pressure to outsource transactions and other routine operations to large service centres, and the expectation by the chief executive that finance personnel will play a fuller part in the management of the business.

The department currently employs 24 people divided almost equally between three areas: financial accounting, management accounting and the treasury function.

The age/experience profile is a mix of older, experienced specialist staff, a young to middle-aged group of qualified accountants (many of whom also possess MBA degrees), and a group of trainees with limited experience who have yet to qualify.

Three of the older staff are within five years of the statutory retirement age; two more will move into this category within the time period set by senior management. One or two of the younger qualified staff have been looking for other jobs and one of the trainees has applied for maternity leave.

The finance director has arranged a meeting with the human resources director to discuss the development of a human-resource plan for future staffing, training and development of personnel in the finance department.

Requirements:

(a)   Describe the main stages of the human resource planning process and briefly explain how manpower planning fits into this process.   **(8 marks)**

(b)   Taking the role of the finance director, prepare a paper by way of preparation for your forthcoming meeting. Explain the key considerations that you will need to take into account in the development of a human resource plan for your department. **(12 marks)**

(Total: 20 marks)

44   MOTIVATION

The problem of keeping staff motivated is one with which managers in all departments have to cope.

Requirements:

Assume that you are the senior manager in the finance department of an organisation and that you have been asked to respond in writing to the following two requirements posed by a less-experienced colleague who has just taken up a similar post elsewhere in the same organisation.

(a)   Describe the use of financial incentive schemes as a means of improving employee motivation.   **(10 marks)**

(b)   Explain how non-monetary methods can be used to motivate employees.   **(10 marks)**

(Total: 20 marks)

45   B PLC

B plc, a large manufacturing company, is currently facing major problems in how to motivate its workforce.

For years, the company used share incentives to motivate its otherwise low-paid employees. This method worked very well during the period of the company's growth in the 1990s as the value of the shares offered to employees at a 20% discount increased in value year on year. Employees felt that their contribution was paying off for the company and for themselves and, as a result, tended to be highly motivated and loyal.

The start of the new century, however, has not been kind to the company. Increased competition has resulted in a decline in revenues and profits, and the share price of the company has been on a downward trend. This decline has significantly reduced the value of the individual portfolios which employees have amassed through the generous share incentive scheme. The company has noticed recently that the motivation and loyalty of employees have begun to decline.

The problems that B plc has experience in its use of the share incentive scheme are quite common but companies continue to make use of them.

Required:

(a)   Describe a theory of motivation on which such incentive schemes are based, and explain the merits and limitations of the theory you have described.   **(12 marks)**

(b) Explain the advantages and limitations of the share incentive schemes, and suggest ways in which financial rewards could be tied more closely to employee performance.

(8 marks)

(Total: 20 marks)

46 SMOG

The working practices of the Finance Department of the Smog retailing organisation are out of date. It operates as if developments in communications and information technology, developments in management accounting techniques, the increasing concern with the environment, demands for better corporate governance and the impact of globalisation had never happened.

But things are changing. A new chief executive has just been appointed and she intends to see that the Finance Department, like the rest of the organisation, will operate as efficiently as any of Smog's competitors. She has already seen to it that the department is re-equipped with the latest technology, and a new management information system (MIS) has been installed. Unfortunately, a lack of training has meant that as yet, the organisation has been unable to benefit fully from the investment in either the new technology or the new MIS.

Required:

(a) Explain briefly how each of the developments noted in the first paragraph of the scenario above has influenced the practice of management accounting in progressive organisations. **(10 marks)**

(b) Assume that you have been charged with the development of human resources in the Finance Department of Smog. Describe the various kinds of training and development programmes that would be required in order to make full use of the investment in the Finance Department and equip the staff to cope with the challenges of the modern era.

(10 marks)

(Total: 20 marks)

47 APPRAISAL

The performance appraisal process is now well established in large organisations.

Required:

(a) Describe briefly the most common objectives of a performance appraisal system.

(6 marks)

(b) Explain why appraisal systems are often less effective in practice than they might be, and advise what management can do to try to ensure their effectiveness. **(14 marks)**

(Total: 20 marks)

48 N PLC

When Josie began work at N plc, some years ago, opportunities for promotion appeared to be good. A vertical career ladder existed with a clear upward pathway from office junior through progressively more senior grades to the post of general manager.

In recent years, however, N plc has restructured by removing several layers of management and contracting out non-core activities. This has allowed N plc to react more quickly to changes in the market place, but for Josie and other managers in mid-career, it has been a traumatic period. Several colleagues have lost their jobs and others like Josie see little prospect of promotion in future.

Required:

(a) Discuss the benefits that the existence of a vertical career ladder provided for both Josie and N plc prior to the company's restructuring. **(10 marks)**

(b) Explain what N plc can do to maintain the commitment and motivation of its managers following the restructuring programme. **(10 marks)**

(Total: 20 marks)

49 S SOFTWARE COMPANY

Discussion of the human resource development plan in the S software company has revealed considerable disagreement between members of the management team. Janet, the managing director, and Jean, the human resource manager, have ambitious long-term plans for the training and development of staff. By contrast, Andy, the production manager, is concerned with how production will be staffed when this people "go on a company-paid training course at a luxury hotel". Colin, the marketing manager, is afraid that other firms will "recruit our newly-trained workers". Maurice, the management accountant, wonders whether the costs of training and development will ever show a return.

Required:

(a) Explain why Andy, Colin and Maurice have some concerns about training and development, and discuss the likely reasons for those concerns. **(8 marks)**

(b) Taking the role of Jean, describe to your management colleagues the key factors that you would have considered in drawing up the S software company's human resource development plan. Explain how the implementation of the plan could contribute to the overall performance of the company. **(12 marks)**

(Total: 20 marks)

50 R COMPANY

The finance department of R Company, a large hotel group, has experienced a range of human resource problems following the recruitment of a large number of professional members of staff. Several people have left within the first year and others have not performed as well as might have been expected.

The R Company's human resource management department has suggested that one possible reason might be the Company's lack of a systematic induction programme for new staff.

Required:

(a) Produce a plan detailing the key activities that need to be covered in a systematic induction programme for the R Company. **(10 marks)**

(b) Explain how an induction programme can help to overcome the problems experienced by the finance department of R Company as described in the scenario above. **(10 marks)**

(Total: 20 marks)

MANAGEMENT OF RELATIONSHIPS

51 SOURCES OF POWER

Gerald has been a qualified management accountant for some years and assistant management accountant in a division of a multinational organisation for the last two years. He has been particularly concerned with helping to introduce a new information system division. It is intended that this information system will be introduced throughout the organisation.

Gerald has now been appointed chief management accountant in another division of the same organisation, located in a different country. The organisation uses a common language in all the divisions so there is no language problem.

You are required to explain what sources of power Gerald possesses in his new job.

(20 marks)

52 AUTHORITY AND POWER

McGivering defines authority as the 'right to exercise power'.

Discuss how power can be exercised and the form it can take as authority.   **(20 marks)**

53 RESPONSIBILITY AND ACCOUNTABILITY

You are required to describe the concepts of accountability, authority and responsibility, and the relationships between them.   **(20 marks)**

54 DELEGATION

'The reasons for delegation are mainly practical, but there are a few that are idealistic'

(a)   What advantages, both practical and idealistic, may be gained from the delegation process in an organisation? Are there any potential disadvantages?   **(12 marks)**

(b)   What is needed in practice to ensure that delegated authority is matched with responsibility?   **(8 marks)**

(Total: 20 marks)

55 GROUPS AND EMPLOYEE COMMITMENT

(a)   Why has there been a renewed concern with the problem of securing employee commitment to organisational goals?   **(8 marks)**

(b)   In what ways can organisations secure the loyalty and commitment of their employees?   **(12 marks)**

(Total: 20 marks)

56 FAIR TREATMENT

(a)   Discuss what is meant by 'fair treatment' in employment matters.   **(10 marks)**

(b)   How can government assist in ensuring fair treatment by organisations?   **(10 marks)**

(Total: 20 marks)

57   MANAGING CONFLICT

(a)   Describe the effect of open conflict between departments on organisations. **(10 marks)**

(b)   How might such conflict be managed?   **(10 marks)**

(Total: 20 marks)

58   TR

TR is a transportation company involved in all aspects of the movement of people and goods around the country. Recently it has experienced considerable conflict between the Research and Development (R&D) department and the Operations department.

Research managers are responsible for developing operational innovations to improve efficiency, while operations managers are responsible for the scheduling and running of planes, trains, lorries and coaches. The conflict is manifested in constant complaints about 'the other department', and by a general sense of ill feeling and lack of co-operation between the staff of the two departments.

The operations managers are frustrated by the way in which the R&D department operates. They claim that research personnel take too long to carry out projects because, instead of seeking practical, cost-effective solutions to problems, they go in for 'the perfect solution' - which is often very costly and often late.

R&D managers are equally scathing about what they consider to be the unhelpful attitude of the operations personnel. They feel that Operations has been so uncooperative and resistant to adopting some of their innovations, such as the automated loading platform and the training simulator, that the point has now come for senior management intervention.

The personalities and attitudes of the heads of the two departments do not help the situation. Both are strong characters with authoritarian attitudes, and both are earnestly committed to achieving the aims of their respective departments. Communication, except for some routine interchanges and the usual abuse, has almost ceased between the departments.

Things have now come to a head and the chief executive has appointed a manager from within the organisation to investigate the problems affecting the relationship between R&D and Operations and to report back with findings and recommendations.

Requirements:

You are the manager from TR appointed to investigate and to write a report. Divide your report into two parts.

(a)   Describe how conflict is manifested in the TR case and explain the causes of this conflict.   **(10 marks)**

(b)   Explain how the conflict might best be resolved.   **(10 marks)**

(Total: 20 marks)

59   SOFT CORPORATION

Before taking up her position as Head of the Finance department of the SOFT Corporation, Joan Timmins had enjoyed a career in the Army where she had attained the rank of major. The military style of command had suited Joan's personality. She is by nature an assertive kind of individual, so giving orders is something that comes naturally to her.

The start of her new post as Head of Finance has not been easy. She has found that her previous style of management has not been well received by her new staff. Her enthusiasm for improving the way things are done in the department is not matched by that of her staff. In fact, if anything, an air of resentment seems to exist in the department. More generally, she is finding it difficult to adjust to the whole way of operating in the SOFT Corporation.

In her view, so much time seems to be spent in meeting and in consultation generally that she wonders how the organisation manages to compete in the market place as successfully as it does.

Required:

(a)   Using any appropriate theory of management style, explain why Joan Timmins is experiencing the difficulties described in her new post, and recommend the kind of management style which might be more appropriate.   **(12 marks)**

(b)   Discuss why Joan might have problems in adapting to the management style which you have recommended in your answer to (a) above, and suggest how these problems might be overcome.   **(8 marks)**

(Total: 20 marks)

60   T AEROSPACE COMPANY

The T Aerospace Company is in the early stages of planning the development of its latest commercial jet, the 007. The aircraft industry is a fiercely competitive one, dominated by a few large global players who operate at the forefront of technology. In this industry, competitors quickly copy any advance in technology or new management technique that might provide them with a competitive edge. Some of the T Aerospace Company's competitors have adopted team working as a means of speeding up their development and production processes.

The T Aerospace Company is thus considering the adoption of team working in its operations, but some of the traditionalists in the company are doubtful. They are concerned that the benefits of work specialisation will be lost. Some of the managers have had negative experiences with team working and so have strong reservations about the proposed changes.

Required:

(a)   Describe briefly the essential features of a team.   **(4 marks)**

(b)   Identify the benefits that the T Aerospace Company can expect to gain from the adoption of team working.   **(6 marks)**

(c)   Describe the difficulties that the company is likely to encounter in the management of its teams and recommend how it might overcome these.   **(10 marks)**

(Total: 20 marks)

61   NYO.COM

NYO.com was established in February 2000. Since then, the company, which provides online financial advice, has experienced rapid growth and the management has not really had the time to get all management systems and procedures into place.

The company has asked you to look at the way in which the company deals with its disciplinary problems and procedures. The chief executive officer has asked you to do two things.

Required:

(a)   Recommend guidelines for drawing up a disciplinary procedure.   **(12 marks)**

(b)   Explain why NYO.com should have a formal disciplinary procedure.   **(8 marks)**

(Total: 20 marks)

MANAGEMENT OF CHANGE

62   DETERMINANTS OF CHANGE

Describe the main features of the concept of 'change'. How far do these relate to issues of 'effectiveness'?   **(20 marks)**

63   ORGANISATIONAL DEVELOPMENT

(a)   Explain what organisation Development (OD) consists of.   **(10 marks)**

(b)   How can OD contribute to the success of an organisation?   **(10 marks)**

(Total: 20 marks)

64   IMPLEMENTATION

You are required to explain **four** strategies for managing change, giving the advantages and disadvantages of **each**.   **(20 marks)**

65   CRITICAL CHANGE FACTORS

You are required to describe the critical factors in successfully implementing change in a large organisation.   **(20 marks)**

66   OPPORTUNITIES TO COMMUNICATE

Many Japanese companies have long recognised the benefits of institutionalised learning based around quality improvement teams and associated issues.

Explain **five** competencies involoved in building learning organisations.   **(20 marks)**

67   DECLINE

(a)   Explain the three categories within which the causes of organisational decline can be grouped.   **(16 marks)**

(b)   Suggest ways in which managers can turn around decline.   **(4 marks)**

(Total: 20 marks)

68   INFORMAL ORGANISATION

(a)   Explain the nature of ' the informal organisation' **and** detail its disadvantages and advantages for a business.

(12 marks)

(b)   Explain the steps management can take to foster the benefits of 'informal organisation' whilst at the same time reducing its potential disadvantages.   **(8 marks)**

(Total: 20 marks)

69   Y

Y is one of the five main high street banks in the country. Since banking deregulation in the late 1980s, Y, like other banks, has been facing increasing competition, first from other existing financial institutions but more recently from new entrants who have started to offer deposit accounts and a number of other financial services.

In seeking to respond to these competitive threats, the bank's senior management has started to implement a number of changes. These involve a significant restructuring of the organisation with the removal of a number of layers of management, and a consequent reduction in staffing levels in most divisions. The closure of a number of high-street branches is also planned. The telephone-banking arm is being substantially enlarged, and a major investment in IT is being undertaken. The effect on staff will be considerable. A programme of voluntary redundancy and redeployment is planned and, given the demand for new skills, a considerable amount of training will need to be carried out. Despite clear evidence of the threat to the future of the bank, the plans set forth by management are meeting resistance from the workforce. The banking unions in particular seem determined to obstruct the changes wherever possible.

Requirements:

With reference to the above scenario:

(a) Explain why the implementation of organisational change often proves to be so difficult. **(8 marks)**

(b) Advise Y's management about the ways in which change can be facilitated.

(12 marks)

(Total: 20 marks)

70   DB COMPANY

The DB Company operates in an expanding market. It has been unable to take advantage of its opportunities because of what appear to be problems of co-ordination within the company.

A representative of the DB Company has approached a firm of management consultants for advice on these problems and they have recommended the services of a specialist in Organisational Development (OD). The chief executive office of the DB Company has never heard of Organisational Development and has asked for your advice.

Required:

(a) Explain the nature of Organisational Development and describe how it might be used to assist the DB Company with the problems indicated in the scenario. **(14 marks)**

(b) Describe the knowledge, skills and attitudes that the OD specialist would require, to take on the task of helping the DB Company with its problems. **(6 marks)**

(Total: 20 marks)

71   K COMPANY

K Company is experiencing rapid change. Increasing competition necessitates continual up-dating of its product offerings, its technology and its methods of working. Like other companies today, K Company has to be responsive to frequently changing customer requirements, the challenges posed by fast-moving competitors and the many other threats from a changing world.

One of the ways in which K Company might seek to cope with the challenges of the rapidly-changing environment is to become a "learning organisation".

Required:

(a) Advise K Company what would be involved in building a learning organisation.

(10 marks)

The changing environment has implications for K Company's selection process and, given the limitations of interviews and selection tests that constitute the traditional methods of selection, the company has decided to make use of an Assessment Centre to improve its chances of obtaining people who fit the needs of the company.

Required:

(b) Describe the key features of an Assessment Centre and explain why it is considered to be more effective than traditional methods of selection. **(10 marks)**

(Total: 20 marks)

72 F STEEL COMPANY

The recently-appointed Chief Executive Officer (CEO) of the F Steel Company is intent on making the organisation more competitive. He has made it clear that costs are too high and productivity too low. The trade union that represents the steel workers in the F Steel Company is well-organised and has promised the workers that it will defend their wage levels and working conditions.

The exchange rate of the local currency has been rising in value over the last year, and the company has to compete internationally with subsidised state steel companies. Though domestic demand for steel is weak, the market for steel in the Pacific Rim economies is still growing.

The company is suffering from a number of problems at the operational level. Deliveries have been late on a number of occasions and some customers have complained that the steel they have received does not match the agreed specification. Despite these problems, some of the F Steel Company's long-serving managers are complacent. They have seen the company come through many a business cycle and simply interpret the present situation as the trough of just another such cycle, which will pass. As a result, they see no need for any radical change.

Required:

(a) Analyse the forces for change and causes of resistance in the F Steel Company. Classify these according to whether they can be considered as deriving from internal or external sources. **(10 marks)**

(b) Recommend how the newly-appointed Chief Executive Officer in the F Steel Company might go about managing the process of change. **(10 marks)**

(Total: 20 marks)

73 BILL AND JOHN

Bill and John are two of several hundred employees who were made redundant by the X Steel Company. As part of the redundancy package, they received substantial lump-sum payments that they hope to use in setting up a business which will manufacture steel security gates. Both have the necessary craft and technical skills, and Bill has worked on a part-time basis in the recent past for a small company involved in this product market.

Despite possession of the essential skills, and some knowledge of the market for the product, Bill and John are a little nervous. They are aware of the high failure rate among start-up businesses in general and have no wish to take unnecessary risks.

Required:

(a) Explain why a high proportion of business start-ups, such as the one Bill and John hope to set up, fall within the first few years of operation. **(8 marks)**

Some years later, the SBJ business founded by Bill and John has prospered and is growing rapidly. From a start-up manufacturer of security gates, the Company has diversified into security consultancy and related insurance services. While pleased with their success to date, Bill and John are concerned about their ability to manage a diversified portfolio of businesses and an ever-growing number of staff.

Required:

(b)   Using any appropriate model of organisational growth, explain to Bill and John the problems they are likely to face at each stage of growth of the SBJ business. Recommend how they might overcome these problems.   **(12 marks)**

(Total: 20 marks)

Section 3

ANSWERS TO MULTIPLE CHOICE QUESTIONS

ORGANISATIONAL MANAGEMENT

1   B

Neither a policy nor an objective is a 'course of action' and neither specifies the quantity of resources required. The question describes a strategy, which is a course of action to achieve a high-level organisational objective. A strategy should be expressed in terms of a course of action, the intended objective and the quantity of resources required to achieve it. A procedure is a routine course of action, and cannot be described in terms of achieving a desired outcome for an organisation.

2   A

In a task culture, the process of management is seen as the completion of a continual series of projects or problem-solving problems. The focus is on completing each task that comes along. These organisations are flexible and change continually, with project teams/design teams being broken up when they have completed their task.

In contrast, the power culture or club culture is an entrepreneurial culture, where one person, perhaps the owner-founder, makes all the key decisions. A role culture describes a bureaucratic structure in which each employee has a defined position and responsibility for performance. An organisation with an existential culture exists to serve the interests of the individuals within it, such as the practice of a medical consultant. In a large organisation, different parts of the organisation might have differing cultures.

3   D

In the context of the 7S model, Skills are the core competences of the organisation. These are its dominant attributes that set it apart from competitor firms. In the 7S model, management culture is the element 'Style', the development of managers is the element 'Staff' and roles and responsibilities are the element 'Structure'.

According to the McKinsey model theory, the relative importance of each element varies over time.

4   B

The soft elements are Staff (people in the organisation), Superordinate goals (also known as Shared values – the shared belief of people in an organisation and why it exists), Skills (core competences) and Style (culture).

The three hard elements are Strategy (a set of actions), Structure (roles and responsibilities) and Systems.

5   B

The strategic apex in a company is the CEO and board of directors. The middle line consists of line management, including the head of operations, the head of sales and marketing, production managers and so on. The technostructure describes individuals who are not line management and who have specialist skills. It includes strategic planners, HR staff, company lawyers and so on. Support staff are employees who are not involved in direct operations and who provide support to the rest of the organisation – for example, include canteen staff, payroll staff, mailroom staff, and so on. The operating core consists of the employees who carry out the direct work of making a product, providing a service, and selling/delivering the products/services to customers.

6   C

In a professional organisation, such as a firm of accountants or solicitors, or a hospital, the operating core consists of highly-qualified individuals. These do not welcome the influence of managers in the middle line or specialised technocrats. Consequently, accountancy firms and legal firms do not have a large and influential middle line or technocracy. In a hospital, where the influence of line management is strong, doctors and administrators are often in conflict with each other.

7   A

A bias for action describes a tendency to do something rather than spend time talking about alternative options. Other attributes of excellence include 'stick to the knitting' (focus on core strengths and avoid conglomerate diversification), 'simplicity', 'hands-on, value driven', 'simultaneous loose-tight properties', 'autonomy and entrepreneurship' and 'productivity through people'.

8   B

In the UK, a 'whistleblower's charter' was introduced into law by the Public Interest Disclosure Act 1998. This gives protection to workers (against dismissal etc) when they disclose information that they reasonably believe to expose certain misconduct, such as financial malpractice and dangers to health and safety.

9   C

'Simplicity' has been described as 'simple form, lean staff'. Another attribute of excellence is 'simultaneous loose-tight properties', which means having few rules and procedures, but strong values to which employees in the organisation subscribe. Sticking to the core business of the organisation is the attribute of excellence described as 'stick to the knitting'. The attribute of excellence 'autonomy and entrepreneurship' means organising into small semi-autonomous units.

10   B

The resources of the decision-maker are limited, because managers do not have limitless time, information or processing ability. They use faster, simpler and quicker ways of reaching decisions. Simon called this 'bounded rationality'.

11   C

Fayol belongs to the 'classical' school of management theorists. He described the five functions of management as planning, organising, commanding, co-ordinating and controlling.

12   B

To avoid conflict with a stakeholder in a position of power but who has relatively low interest in the organisation is high but whose power is low, it will be necessary to keep the stakeholder satisfied. A powerful stakeholder who is dissatisfied might decide to take some action. (Keeping the stakeholder informed would be appropriate for stakeholders in quadrant II.)

13   A

The idea of the iceberg is that only a small proportion is visible above water, and most lies hidden beneath sea level. French and Bell argued that although organisation has a formal aspect, evident to everyone, this is just the 'tip of the iceberg'. Hidden beneath, there is a much more significant informal aspect, consisting of the feelings, attitudes and values of individuals. The informal aspect often creates a resistance to change. Managers seeking to introduce changes should not restrict their attention to the formal tip of the iceberg. What lies hidden will be far more important.

14   B

A hygiene factor stops an individual from disliking his job and his work. Hygiene factors include job security, interpersonal relations, salary, working conditions and the quality of supervision. Challenging work, on the other hand, can motivate an individual to want to perform better, and so is a motivator factor.

15   A

A 'bet your company' culture is characterised by the slogan: "Slow and steady wins the race". It is found in organisations with a willingness to take risks but slow feedback about performance.

In contrast, a process culture is characterised by low risk and slow feedback. It has cultural values focussing on attention to technical quality and detail and attention to procedures. Deal and Kennedy described the process culture as: "It's not what you do, it's the way that you do it."

16   B

The three attributes of excellence listed in the question are 'closeness to customers' (A) 'autonomy and entrepreneurship' (C) and 'hands-on, value driven' (D).

The other five attributes not mentioned in the question are 'productivity through people', 'a bias for action', 'stick to the knitting', 'simplicity' and 'simultaneous loose-tight properties'.

17   D

Authority gives a person the ability or discretion to make decisions. Authority comes from the position the person holds - i.e. 'position power' - (although some individuals acquire moral authority, or authority through their skills, expertise or experience). When authority is delegated to an individual, he or she is then responsible for exercising the powers properly and accountable for how it has been exercised.

18   A

Position power arises from the position of a person in the organisation structure. A trade union representative has position power within the trade union organisation, but not within the company. Although power might be used in a negative way, this is not an apt description of the power of a trade union representative. A trade union representative is in a position of resource power, because he or she controls/influences a key resource for the company, i.e. its unionised employees.

19   B

A long scalar chain is associated with a narrow span of control. For example, a manager might supervise 16 staff. Suppose another layer of management is introduced beneath him, so that he has four sub-managers, each supervising four of the original staff. The span of control will be reduced from 16 to 4 as a consequence of creating the taller organisation. Flat organisations offer fewer opportunities for promotion because there are fewer 'senior' jobs. However, flat organisations are more likely than tall organisations to empower their employees.

THE FUNCTIONAL AREAS OF ORGANISATIONS

20   B

Functional departmentation means that each department performs a specific function, such as production, marketing, accounts, human resources and so on. This form of departmentation is therefore built on work specialisation. The organisation might expect to benefit from economies of scale by concentrating all one particular area of activity into one department. However, there are also potential weaknesses with a functional department structure for the organisation.

21   B

Unity of command means that each individual takes orders from just one person, his superior in the organisation hierarchy. In a matrix management structure, individuals will take instructions from more than one person, for different aspects of their work.

22   D

Individual members of the academic staff do work for the course director of each course they teach, and must also report to their head of school. A project structure is not a good definition, because in a project structure, teams come together and then disband once the project is finished. The organisation of a degree programme at a university should be a more long-lasting arrangement than a project.

23   B

A network is a form of confederation, and a network organisation is a confederation of units linked by communication and information exchange. Often, one individual or work unit is identified as the network's leader, providing a key co-ordinating and communicating role. The units in a network structure could all belong to the same organisation, or could be a confederation of several different organisations or individuals. (Outside the world of business, an example of a network organisation is a golf society, where individuals meet occasionally to play golf. In many cases, such networks have one or two individuals acting as the main organiser and communicator.)

24   C

A market segment could be a group of either consumers or industrial customers. They are an identifiable group with common characteristics and needs, who would be expected to respond in a similar way to given marketing initiatives. A market segment might become a target market for an organisation, provided that it is accessible for the organisation and large enough to offer the prospect of reasonable profits.

25   D

The web site is a place where customers buy. It is also be used for advertising or promoting holidays. When customers book a holiday via the web site, it is also the first stage in the process of selling.

26   B

A 'three for the price of two' offer a short-term promotion. The basic price of a carton of orange juice is unchanged, so the offer is not an element of the price. (In contrast, offering a bulk purchase discount would be an element of price, provided a regular customer can always claim a discount.)

27   D

'Promotion' includes advertising, direct selling and PR as well as sales promotions. The hair products manufacturer has to sell its products to retailers, such as supermarkets and chemists.

Public relations work might also be a useful way of drawing the products to the public attention.

28 D

Porter's five primary value activities are inbound logistics, operations, outbound logistics, marketing and sales and service. The four support activities are the firm's infrastructure (general management, planning, finance etc), procurement, technology development and human resource management.

HUMAN RESOURCE MANAGEMENT

29 D

A contributory pension scheme is an element of pay for employees, which is an aspect of attracting and retaining staff, and motivating them. (There is no legal requirement to have a pension scheme to which the employer makes contributions.)

30 B

HRM managers will be involved in the planning of manpower requirements, in the recruitment and in arranging training for staff. Performance appraisal is a task for line managers.

31 A

McGregor distinguished two contrasting approaches to management, Theory X and Theory Y. Theory X is based on the idea that people dislike work, and management must therefore coerce, direct and control them. Theory Y is based on the idea that working comes as naturally to individuals as play or rest, and that individuals can be encouraged and can learn to seek responsibility and fulfil their potential. Management taking a Theory Y approach will be more democratic and encouraging in their approach to dealing with staff.

32 A

The 'givens' in any situation are the group membership, its environment, and the tasks it is given. These cannot be changed by management. The intervening factors are the way the work is done (processes and procedures), leadership style and group motivation, which can all be influenced by management decisions. The outcomes are group productivity and effectiveness, and also the satisfaction (or dissatisfaction) of the group members

33 D

A retention plan is a plan for reducing turnover of labour and holding on to staff, particularly staff with experience or skills that are difficult to replace. A key element of a retention plan is how to avoid wastage and reduce labour turnover

34 C

Answer A describes job evaluation, answer B describes job design and answer D describes job specification

35 C

Psychometric tests quantify the psychological dimensions of the individual, by assessing their characteristics. The individual is measured on a scale for each characteristic, to build up a score for his or her aptitude for doing a particular type of work or working in particular conditions or in a particular way. For example, psychometric tests can measure an individual's ability to manage pressure, work with others, use initiative, and so on.

36 C

The hierarchy, working up, is physiological needs (at the bottom), safety needs, social needs, esteem needs and self-actualisation needs (at the top).

37   B

Pay can be a source of dissatisfaction and needs to be sufficient to avoid this, i.e. pay is a hygiene factor. However, if pay is seen as a way of rewarding individuals for their achievements, it can be a motivator factor. Herzberg suggested that status could also be either a hygiene factor or a motivator factor. Job security and quality of supervision are hygiene factors and gaining recognition is a motivator factor.

38   D

Lawrence and Lorsch concluded that in a dynamic and diverse environment, a high degree of differentiation is necessary to succeed, but that conflict is increased by differentiation.

As differentiation increases, different parts of an organisation pursue different goals, develop differing views of the time-scale for achievement. Differentiation also brings changes in the way that individuals inter-relate with each other and the formality of their organisation structure. Lawrence and Lorsch suggested that integration is needed to hold the differentiated parts together. The degree of integration needed for an effective organisation must be consistent with the interdependence between the organisation's parts. The more differentiated the organisation, the more difficult it is to achieve integration.

39   D

Human relations development covers all aspects of personal and management development. This includes training (both formal training and on-the-job training) planning the succession for senior management positions, and career planning for individuals (particularly management recruits). Job re-design is also an aspect of HRD, because jobs can be re-designed to offer better or different learning experiences.

40   B

360 degree appraisal is appraisal from all sides, from the individual's boss, subordinates, peers and co-workers and possibly also customers, plus self-appraisal by the individual himself or herself. Upward appraisal is an appraisal by the individual's subordinates. Self-appraisal is an appraisal by the individual himself or herself.

41   A

Herzberg suggested that job enlargement, which involves giving the job holder a wider range of tasks, has little motivation value. Job rotation involves moving individuals periodically from one job to another, can reduce the monotony and boredom of working. Herzberg suggested that this might improve job satisfaction (and is a 'hygiene factor') but is unlikely to stimulate motivation.

MANAGEMENT OF RELATIONSHIPS

42   A

Tannenbaum and Schmidt suggested that the effectiveness of a leadership style depends on three factors: the nature of the work situation, the personal abilities and style of the leader, and the preferences and tolerance levels of the subordinates.

43   A

Fiedler suggested that performance of a group results from of the interaction of leadership style and 'situation favourableness'. Leadership style depends on the personality of the leader, which is fixed. A person cannot change his or her personality. Situation favourableness depends on three variable factors: the position power of the leader (formal authority) of the leader, the task structure (the extent to which the jobs of the group members are specified in detail) and leader-member relations (the degree to which the group members accept their leader).

44   A

Belbin's nine team roles are:

Action-oriented	Shaper	Challenging, dynamic, thrives on pressure
	Implementer	Disciplined, reliable, efficient
	Completer finisher	Painstaking and conscientious, completes work on time
People-oriented	Co-ordinator	Mature, confident, good chairman and good at delegating
	Teamworker	Co-operative, diplomatic: a listener
	Resource investigator	Extrovert, communicative, good at making contacts with others
Cerebral	Plant	Creative, imaginative: can solve difficult problems
	Monitor evaluator	Strategic, discerning: sees all options and has good judgement
	Specialist	Provider of specialist knowledge and skills.

45   D

Likert's four management styles were exploitative authoritative, benevolent authoritative, participative and democratic. (The tells, sells, consults and joins styles were suggested by the research unit at Ashridge Management College.)

46   C

Team style is graded (9,9) and represents a manager with both a very high concern for people and a very high concern for the job

47   B

Task roles include: initiating, information-seeking, opinion-seeking, diagnosing, evaluating and decision-making.

Individual maintenance roles include: goal-setting, feedback, counselling, training and recognition.

Group maintenance roles include: peace-keeping, clarifying, encouraging and standard-seeking.

48   A

Authority is a form of power. The authority that a person derives from his position in the management structure is sometimes called 'position power'. You can delegate authority but not responsibility. A manager remains responsible (and accountable to his/her own superiors) for the authority that is delegated to others.

49   C

'Legitimate' power is position power, derived from the person's position in the management structure.

50   D

In the forming stage, the team comes together. In the next stage (storming), the group re-assesses its targets and trust develops between the group members. This is followed by a period of settling down (norming), when the group establishes norms and procedures for carrying out their work. Finally, in the performing stage, the team executes its tasks successfully, having overcome the difficulties.

51   -D

The ACAS Code of Practice requires that: (1)there should be a right of appeal, normally to a more senior manager (2) worker should never be dismissed for a first breach of discipline, except in cases of gross misconduct and (3) procedures, witness statements and records should be kept confidential.

52   B

An informal warning is not a part of formal disciplinary proceedings. There are usually just three stages in formal disciplinary proceedings: formal oral warning, first written warning and then a final written warning. A record of formal warnings should be kept on the employee's file.

53   C

An action for wrongful dismissal is an action for breach of contract of employment. Here the contract provides for one year's notice of termination. The director can also bring a statutory claim for unfair dismissal under the Employment Rights Act. The Act gives employees a statutory right not to be unfairly dismissed. (With unfair dismissal, the case would be heard by an industrial tribunal). Redundancy is not an issue.

The director can bring an action for wither wrongful dismissal or unfair dismissal, but not both. He is likely to choose the course of action where the amount of compensation is likely to be greatest.

MANAGEMENT OF CHANGE

54   B

Training provides both education and communication of information.

55   A

The initial phase is the growth through creativity phase ('from garage to entrepreneur'). This ends with a crisis of leadership, when a need for leadership/management emerges. This leads on to the phase of growth through direction, when the organisation develops a functional structure and an accounting system.

56   B

The initial creativity phase leads on to a phase of growth through direction, when the organisation develops a functional structure. This ends in a 'crisis of autonomy', when employees start to demand a greater part in decision-making for the decisions that affect them. This leads on to a growth through delegation phase, in which there will be decentralisation of authority. Senior management then feels a loss of control, and a 'crisis of control' occurs. This leads on to the growth through co-ordination phase, when formal systems are developed for achieving greater co-ordination between different parts of the organisation. This leads to a 'crisis of red tape', when formal procedures get in the way of problem-solving and innovation. The fifth and final stage in the life cycle is the growth through collaboration phase.

57   C

Organic structures are better suited than mechanistic organisations for dealing with change, because a mechanistic organisation uses inefficient methods for dealing with the problems caused by change. However, organic structures are not necessarily good at exploiting creative ideas because they lack the discipline of mechanistic organisations and so are difficult to manage. Organisations can overcome the problem of managing change by having an organic structure in creative departments (such as R & D) and mechanistic structures for managing operations.

58   C

According to Kanter, the three forces that drive continual change in organisations are globalisation, information technology and industry consolidaton.

59   B

According to Kanter, one key attribute is the imagination to innovate. Management must encourage the development of new ideas. An organisation must also show the professionalism to reform and change itself. Thirdly, there must be an openness to collaborate with others outside the organisation. Management cannot bring about successful change simply by throwing money at the problem.

60   B

Lewin argued that at any time there are driving forces acting in favour of change and restraining forces acting to stop change. These forces come from individuals, organisations, ideas, the availability of resources, and environmental factors (PEST factors, etc).

When the driving forces for innovation are stronger than the restraining forces, conditions favour change. Occasionally, the driving forces for change are weaker than the forces pressing for a reversion to the old ways. In this situation, conditions favour 'relapse' and a return to the way things were.

61   B

The seven classic skills identified by Kanter are:

1   Tuning into the environment. 'Creating a network of listening posts', such as listening to customer complaints.

2   Challenging the prevailing organisational wisdom.

3   Communicating a compelling aspiration. You need a conviction to bring about change.

4   Building coalitions. Change leaders need co-operation and collaboration from the people with the resources, knowledge or political influence to make things happen.

5   Transforming ownership to a working team. Once a coalition is in place, a change leader can get others to implement the change.

6   Learning to persevere. Change will not go smoothly and there will be setbacks.

7   Make everyone a hero. Recognise, reward and celebrate the accomplishments of the team.

62   C

Lewin's approach to changing human behaviour is based on the idea of unfreezing attitudes, making a change and then re-freezing attitudes in their changed form. However, this approach has been criticised as being irrelevant to a continually-changing organisation, because re-freezing attitudes suggests the creation of a new status quo.

63   D

The three main 'change factors' to consider are how quickly the changes will be introduced, how extensive the changes will be and in what way the changes will take place. The timing of changes is an aspect of the pace of change. The costs of change will be considered when deciding whether change is desirable, but are not relevant to dealing with the problem of resistance to change.

Section 4

ANSWERS TO PRACTICE QUESTIONS

ORGANISATIONAL MANAGEMENT

1   STRATEGY AND ENVIRONMENT

Key answer tips

(a)   A simple list only is required for 5 marks.

(b)   A brief description of each of the five aspects carries only 3 marks, totalling 15 marks.

(a)   The five aspects of the environment are:

- Political

- Social

- Economic

- Technological

- Market.

(b)   In detail:

The political environment

The main political trends likely to affect an international company are:

Eastern Europe

The end of the eastern bloc and a unified Germany. The emerging countries of Eastern Europe present both marketing opportunities and competitive opportunities. There will be increased opportunities for possible joint ventures such as between Germany's Volkswagen and the Czech Skoda.

EC membership and directives

It is likely that EC membership will increase with Turkey and other countries wanting to be members. This will increase the market potential for existing members. The downside of EC membership is the impact of the Social Chapter from the Treaty of Maastricht. This will substantially increase the cost of employing labour. Already in Germany, full-time employees cost a further 85% of every mark paid in wages. This makes Germany a very unattractive country for investment.

South Africa

Now that South Africa is both a democracy and a member of the Commonwealth, it is no longer deemed politically incorrect to invest and trade with her. She is a rich country, with vast resources, and as she develops, the social demands of her newly enfranchised population will create a vast market for socially connected products such as building materials for roads, schools and houses.

Increased privatisation/deregulation

Airlines are finding that their governments no longer protect them. The deregulation of airlines in the United States has spread to international airlines that are finding it hard to compete. Profitability is now required and many were too over manned and inefficient to compete. Because of the competition in the telecommunications industry, BT are having to invest substantially in new technology to be able to keep up with developments that have been introduced since that market was deregulated.

The social environment

Environmental issues

There is a need for companies to respond to lobbying for environmental issues. It is no longer acceptable for European companies to use the North and Baltic Seas as dumping grounds. The nuclear industry is forced to consider the implications of transporting and reprocessing its waste. In complete contrast, Body Shop feel a responsibility to the Third World and obtain many of their raw materials from this source. They are also very concerned and responsive to the testing of products on animals.

Age pyramid

In the west, people are living longer. This creates a burden on pension provisions, especially those provided for by the state. Thus a new market is developing to encourage more people to take out private schemes or to extend their existing provision. This age pyramid is also putting new demands upon the provision of health care and accommodation. Again this has created a demand for a whole new industry. This population has a high level of disposable income and is a potential market for holidays and entertainment as well as care.

Working women

Equal opportunities have proved a double-edged sword. These provisions in the Employment legislation have increased the size of the labour market but most economies have not grown to totally absorb it. What has happened because of the high cost of employment is that women are being taken on because they prefer part time work and as a result are cheaper because they are exempt employment costs. The pattern of employment has also changed. The growth of a service based economy has created more jobs for women at the expense of traditionally male dominated employment sectors of extraction and manufacturing.

The economic environment

The price of oil and gas

The threat of wild fluctuations in the price of oil and gas is always going to concern industries that are dependent on it. When the price of petrol is low, many industries eg, car manufacture, experience periods of growth. As the prices of fuel edge up, these types of companies must look for alternative sources of energy or, in the car manufacturing industry, alternative solutions to engines that are inefficient.

Recession

In the UK, as in many other countries, we can look back at periods of recession followed by growth or vice versa. In the early 1990s the Tiger economies were enjoying a growth period while the UK, the United States and the Japanese economies were in recession. This position has been reversed over the last few years but there are still fears in the UK that our goods and services are too expensive and the strong pound is affecting our trading. Recession reduces the size of potential markets and forces companies to cut margins to remain competitive or even to survive.

Foreign exchange

Multi-nationals remain vulnerable to currency fluctuations. At present, the £ sterling, US dollar and the Euro have remained fairly steady, but the threat of interest rate rises to prevent falls or to prop up a currency is always present.

The technological environment

Improved information technology has made firms even more footloose. As a result, where labour is still an important cost, firms have taken advantage of the technology to optimise their locations where labour is cheap or wherever it is less likely to be parochial. In the UK the financial service industry favours towns like Swindon with its pool of labour while many new organisations use their Web site as their 'shop front'.

There is also a growing awareness of design. As a result, IT enables designs to be done by project experts. Using computer links, GM and Ford obtain design expertise for various parts of their automobiles enabling them to respond quicker and better to competition and customer demand especially by shortening development lead times.

Employment is affected by computerisation. In the main, manufacturing labour costs are now down to less than 10% of the product cost, if not below 5%. However, this does mean that overhead costs and fixed costs have increased quite substantially as a result of the new production technology.

The market

The past decade has seen the growth of many new markets. Telecommunications and new technology has made the ability to shop from home, using a TV or PC, a reality for many families. Owning a mobile telephone is no longer the exclusive domain of wealthy business people. The camera market has been extended by the introduction of digital cameras and DVDs are a recent addition to the home entertainment market.

Competition

The threat of competition can come from many areas. Over the past ten years the West has faced competition from the former communist countries of Eastern Europe, from China with its vast cheap labour force and from the Pacific Rim countries (Taiwan, Malaysia, Singapore, Indonesia and the Philippines).

This has increased the competition on western economies as well as attracting new markets. These emerging countries will provide bigger markets because, as their populations increase in both size and prosperity so does their propensity to consume.

2   STRATEGIC PLANNING

Key answer tips

Firstly, divide your answer into the three management levels.

Secondly, show the relationship between them as a separate section.

Strategic planning can be divided into three levels. These are corporate, tactical and operational. Corporate strategy consists of strategic planning at a corporate level and is not confined to one particular area, all areas being taken into account, and this includes marketing, personnel, production and operational activities, financial implications, etc.

1   Strategic planning at the corporate level decides on the objectives of the organisation, on changes in these objectives, and on the resources used to obtain these objectives.

Policies are then devised to govern the acquisition, use and disposition of these resources.

An essential starting point in corporate planning is a systematic appraisal of the strengths and weaknesses of a company. According to R A Chambers, this serves four main purposes:

(a)   To identify potential assets and unexploited opportunities

(b)   To determine changes in policy and organisation if long term objectives are to be achieved

(c)   To increase immediate profitability by better resource management

(d)   To prepare a defensive strategy for the minimisation of risk due to external factors.

The appraisal should cover four main areas:

(a)   profitability

(b)   product range

(c)   functional strengths and weaknesses

(d)   organisation of human resources.

In order to assess the external environment, the appraisal should cover relevant aspects of the following factors affecting the company:

(a)   legal

(b)   political

(c)   economic

(d)   competitive

(e)   technological

(f)   social

(g)   educational

(h)   philosophical

(i)   geographical.

Only an appreciation of these factors can allow the company, knowing its own strengths and weaknesses, to decide upon the strategy to adopt in relation to the uncertain future.

Based upon the strategic analysis, an organisation will be able to define and shape its decisions, which will determine its basic strategic choices. Such decision concern:

Organisational mission

This is a fundamental statement of the organisation's purpose. It defines the position of the organisation within its environment. Having already assessed its own performance and the anticipated future environment within which it will have to operate, the organisation can then approach the all important question of what business it is in, and whether this is the business that it wants to be in. An organisation's mission statement must also address the issue of how matters are to be implemented, thus allowing organisational objectives to be set.

Objectives

These satisfy in quite broad terms the actual targets to which the corporate effort is to be directed. Objectives will be set for such things as annual sales or the market share and they will cover new product development and innovation. There will also be objectives which will cover such things as operations, human resources, corporate financial return, product, customer service, reliability of product, and objectives which will encompass environmental protection, the treatment of employees or suppliers and social responsibility towards the community.

Strategies

These can be defined as the means by which the objectives will be reached. The organisational strategy is an organisational plan of how it intends to achieve its objectives and goals.

There are three main types of strategy:

(a)   The corporate or generic strategy, which is the strategy that determines how the organisation proposes to proceed or develop its business. These strategies might focus on such things as cost leadership in a volume business, market segmentation, differentiation of product etc.

(b)   Functional strategies or departmental strategies would be developed for specific functions such as marketing, quality, customer service, training, personnel, accounting and financial management etc.

(c)   Implementation strategies may include such things as close consultation with customers or clients, organisation and management development, staff training and development, financial and budgetary management. An implementation strategy would apply to all three levels of strategic planning.

With all strategies it is important that some sort of assessment criteria is associated with them and this should be done as the strategy is formulated. This assessment criteria will allow managers to ascertain whether or not strategies have been implemented or achieved and whether they have been achieved within the time scale laid down.

2   Tactical planning is more concerned with the contributions of the various functions and departments towards achieving the corporate objectives and strategies. Tactical planning is also concerned with resource allocation between the various departments.

At the tactical level the organisation is also concerned about the evaluation of alternative courses of action. Decision processes such as these may involve the estimation of the probabilities of different outcomes. Such decisions will also include the forecasting of the market and competitor responses.

At the tactical level, the objectives, criteria and standards for performance evaluation will be laid down. This is in order that the effectiveness of strategic implication and operational efficiency can be properly monitored and measured.

The tactical level will also be responsible for laying down details of policies. These policies establish contingency decisions, which will state a response to re-occurring situations. Policies are necessary in order to guide and standardise the organisation's response to particular situations. This then has the effect of achieving a consistent response.

3   There are a number of elements to operational planning, which include:

(a)   Establishing programs which specify a series of actions, procedures or rules that may be necessary in order to achieve a particular objective. Programs are also used in order to allocate tasks and responsibilities to individuals and also to lay down time scales in which these tasks need to be completed;

(b)   Laying down procedures which detail the way in which reoccurring issues or problems should be tackled. A procedure can be defined as a series of rules;

(c)   Establishing rules specifying a particular course of action which is to be followed in certain situations. Rules are used when it has been decided that individual discretion should be kept to a minimum;

(d)   Establishing a budgetary plan which involves planning, in detailed quantitative terms, the projected results for future periods. The projected results can be compared against the actual results. Budgetary planning is an important part at the operational level of the strategic plan, as it compiles a coordinated framework of estimated sales, output and productivity etc. Budgetary planning is a detailed expression of the plans and proposals which were originated in much broader context at the corporate or tactical level.

It can be said, therefore, that operational planning is concerned with the detailed planning, quantification and implementation of, at a departmental or functional level, the specified strategies and courses of action necessary to achieve the overall plans and objectives of the organisation.

3   CULTURE

Key answer tips

Split into 2 sections, begin with one culture. Then introduce the other while referring to the first.

Role culture comes from a bureaucratic form of organisation. In turn, it is suggested that this emanated from stable product environments, allowing organisations to create complex internal systems geared to produce standardised but high-quality processes. Often the overall structure would be a tall, functionally-based hierarchy.

The culture, or **organisational ideology**, would be one of control by sets of different rules and procedures. Decision-making would not be valued so much as the process of upward referral and so the strategic apex of the business becomes used to making decisions on trivial issues like dress code instead of envisioning future opportunities and threats. Communication tends to be formalised by memo and email and so is one-way, and attempts are made to put even small requests onto specific, numbered, forms each requiring some kind of approval from a higher authority or functional expert. Individual creativity is stifled by processes – such as quality assurance – where standard forms have to be filled in and each idea sanctioned at various levels to be finally authorised (if successful) months later. Hence, recruitment and selection procedures produce similar, unambitious, careful and obedient applicants which results in a kind of 'cloning'. Later behaviour ensures that following rules and regulations becomes more important than the end result. Tasks are well-defined by job descriptions, competence statements, person-specifications and targets; power is given to those at higher levels rather than those with expertise; communication tends to be downwards from those levels, and loyalty and obedience is required from subordinates.

This contrasts with the emergence of a **'task' culture**. This can be said to have arisen from turbulent and/or complex product markets where customer fashions change so frequently that decisions have to be made and implemented very quickly. This is made possible by an overall divisionalised structure either based on products or geographical regions, so that the organisation is 'close to customer'. Production often moves from mass lines to cells, and just-in-time techniques ensure stocks are low and product changes can be very quickly made.

In this environment, the number of levels in the hierarchy needs to be fewer so that the length of time taken to authorise a decision on, say, finance, is reduced – and frequently local task forces or interdisciplinary teams are empowered to make decisions rather than an arbitrary level of hierarchy. Communication is not always downwards or upwards – but horizontal, frequently informal and verbal and not based on seniority but expertise. Creativity is enhanced as is individualism and personal expertise.

Recruitment and selection procedures are careful to find enthusiasts who 'fit in' to the 'thriving chaos' rather than those who fit a standard specification. Few jobs are highly specialised – one car firm had only two job descriptions for all of its shop floor employees. Recruits are likely to come from different age groups, backgrounds vary, other industries experience is valued, and so the staff tend to be more varied and cosmopolitan.

Flexibility is the key personal attribute, aided by extended skill-sets, in order for changes in production to be effected quickly, or for absences to be 'covered' seamlessly by cross-trained multi-functional employees. Power rests with those who are experts and have 'can do' attitudes – promotion is on merit for those who demonstrate competence, despite often a cynical go-it-alone attitude.

Thus the two cultures are at opposite sides of the spectrum of control.

4 ETHICS AND SOCIAL RESPONSIBILITY

Key answer tips

Split your answer into 2. The 'how' - policies etc. and then 'to what extent' – the issues.'

Social responsibility is a hard term to define, but many would say it means acting with regard to social welfare. No organisation would ever admit to be socially *irresponsible,* and many organisations claim to act responsibly on social issues.

For an organisation to act with social responsibility, it should align its goals with those of the wider society of which it is a part. Whether a society as such has easily defined goals is hard to assess: the purpose and direction of society, not to mention the means by which those goals are achieved, are generally political concerns rather than commercial ones. Is the wider society limited to the national economy or the world as a whole? The consequences of a global corporation acting with 'social responsibility' in one society may cause it to act without social responsibility in another. Moreover, a business almost certainly has its own objectives, which, in the long term, it claims will enhance social welfare, if only that the creation of wealth as a result of business activities is felt to be of benefit to society as a whole.

However, the managers of organisations that seek to be socially responsible rarely start off with a theoretical notion of social responsibility, which they then seek to implement. Rather, organisations that act 'responsibly' do so in response to pressures from their various stakeholders. Some of these pressures are outlined below.

Employees - are internal stakeholders. Their relationship with the organisation is twofold. Firstly, it is their labour, which keeps the organisation in operational existence. Secondly, as citizens, they are members of the wider society in which the organisation exists.

Employees value the certainty and regularity of wages, in other words they expect that the employing organisation will honour the contract of employment. To act with social responsibility also implies a concern and respect for workplace and work practices, which are healthy and safe, whether this relates to equipment, buildings, or hours worked. (It is believed that repetitive strain injury arises from too much uninterrupted time at the word processor.)

An organisation's social responsibility towards its workers can also include the provision of a coherent career and training structure so that people can better themselves. It is believed that the level of workforce skills affects an economy's productivity, and so training is both beneficial for the trainee and for the country as a whole.

Other practices, which are examples of social responsibility, include adaptation to other pressures on employee's lifestyles. Workplace crèches, for example, are of great assistance to working women, but employers are unlikely to introduce them without any consequent commercial benefit: if the cost of labour turnover, for example, is higher than the cost of running workplace crèches and if labour turnover is reduced significantly by a workplace crèche, then the crèche can be financially justified.

Management has a certain amount of discretion, but law circumscribes this. Health and safety for example is subject to regulation, as it was felt that commercial imperatives would not justify the expense, and that employers are not necessarily altruistic. Other benefits are won as the result of the relationship between management and organised labour.

The exercise of social responsibility towards the workforce is constrained by the law, by organised labour, and in some instances by the recognition that social responsibility can be of benefit in encouraging employee loyalty and skill.

Customers - are stakeholders in that they pay for the organisation's output of goods and services. Here the situation is more complex. In some consumer goods sectors, public attitudes - with some direction from government and lobby groups - have made the environmental impact of an organisation's activities open to public comment. This has led suppliers to reduce CFCs in aerosol cans, and to introduce ranges of goods that are supposed to be friendly to the environment.

Suppliers - in multinational corporations, the exercise of social responsibility is distributed over several countries, but again, management will only let it override commercial objectives if it either is part of the inbuilt culture of the firm, or if the voice of public opinion in the market is strong. An example is the use of rainforest hardwoods: some consumer organisations are suggesting boycotting these products. A supplier may also make restrictions on the end-use of products a condition of sale. For example, a supplier of high-technology items may require that these are not re-exported to the enemies of the nation where the supplier is based.

Professional bodies - control is exercised over certain members of management by their membership of professional bodies, which have standards of ethics and conduct

Elected authorities - society's elected political representatives are external stakeholders and can affect management in a number of ways:

- by legislation as has already been mentioned,

- by influencing the climate of public opinion, or

- by trying to persuade commercial organisations to follow a particular line or policy. An example is business sponsorship of the arts in the UK.

Shareholders - are connected stakeholders. The main interest of shareholders is profit, and they might have objections to money being spent on projects which are socially responsible, but which reduce the return on the investment. As many shareholders are large institutions like pension funds, then their own duties can be adversely affected by the use of organisational resources on activities that do not make a profit.

It is possible that some shareholders, and other commentators, would assert that the creation of wealth is the only desirable social objective of a business, and anything that intervenes in this objective is damaging in the long run.

Conclusion: Management issues

Social responsibility has costs and benefits for an organisation, and management have to weigh up the conflicting demands of different stakeholders. There is also the problem of managing social responsibility policies so that the most effective use is made of the resources allocated for the purpose. This means:

(a)   monitoring the expectations people have of the organisation, as an enterprise which trumpets its environmental friendliness will be expected to live up to its claims in all areas;

(b)   achieving the maximum good publicity from the project;

(c) selecting appropriate choice of socially responsible activities which can be divided between:

    (i) ensuring that the firm's core activities are conducted in a socially responsible way;

    (ii) subsidising, supporting or sponsoring those activities which are for public welfare (eg, charitable donations, Prince's Trust) etc;

(d) clearly distinguishing between what are the minimum acceptable standards in a particular situation, and what are additional to them.

5 ETHICS AND THE PROFESSIONAL BODY

Key answer tips

(a) Remember to contrast – 'on the one hand' and 'on the other hand' Be very brief – 5 marks only.

(b) 'The case for requires no negative comments.

(a) CIMA members are regulated by a professional body that is among the largest and longest established in the UK, as well as having a strong representation globally. The main implication of this for managerial staff is in the quality assurance that their qualification gives to employers.

- CIMA members must pass a rigorous suite of examinations testing knowledge of a very wide range of business disciplines, as well as the ability to apply this knowledge in practical situations.

- CIMA members are encouraged to adopt a formal scheme of continuing professional development (CPD). A respected program of professional competences has been drawn up which many members use as the basis for planning their CPD.

The situation is very different for the wider ranks of managerial staff. Although one often hears of the 'profession of management', and indeed the term 'profession' is even used to describe such occupations as teaching where little managerial work is required, the key defining criteria of a profession listed above are absent in these cases.

In general, managers are drawn from many different backgrounds, with little in common in terms of formal qualifications, training, defined standards or regulation. The impact is that quality is likely to be variable.

(b) Social structures are the result of a variety of interacting environments created by groups of people. Business planners must always take account of structure alterations, and in particular society has an attitude towards businesses requiring new responses which conflict with the views and practices of older and accepted concepts of management.

Pressure groups in society persuade management to adopt four kinds of social responsibility.

- **Responsibility towards employees** - industrial democracy, sex and racial equality, safety at work, security of employment.

- **Responsibility towards customers** - value for money, quality of product, consumer protection organisations, the state and legal aspects, advertising standards.

- **Responsibility towards shareholders** - the private investor, institutional investment, shareholder intervention.

- **Responsibility towards society and the community in general** - social and economic performance of the enterprise, the physical environment, young people, the elderly, public decency and morality, participation in community affairs.

Managers are appointed to run businesses on behalf of others, typically on behalf of the shareholders in a commercial enterprise. Most commentators accept that managers have a responsibility above all to achieve the objectives of those who appoint them. This of course raises the issue of possible conflict between such objectives and aspects of social responsibility listed above.

Part of the solution may be to convince managers of ways in which this apparent conflict can in fact be reconciled. For example, only a very blinkered view of corporate objectives could lead to managers skimping on health and safety precautions. Money saved here will be more than outweighed by statutory penalties, not to mention the difficulty of recruiting quality personnel to an environment with a reputation for being unsafe.

This argument is more tenuous when wider social responsibilities are considered, but despite this the increasing attention paid to such issues has led managers to extend the argument. Being a good **'corporate citizen'** may bring only intangible benefits - and there are no specific penalties for failing to be a good citizen - but a long-term advantage is now thought to accrue to such responsible organisations.

To encourage managers to think in this way some organisations have attempted to incorporate social responsibility objectives into the assessment of managerial performance. To this end the concept of a 'social audit' has begun to emerge. It is fair to say that these developments are in their infancy.

6   CONFLICT

Key answer tips

(a)   Be very brief – 5 marks only.

(b)   Concentrate on 'co-ordination and integration' and discuss the objectives, tasks and workflow. with examples under several headings: controlled decentralisation, co-ordination, culture etc.

(a)   In a large and diversified organisation it is often the case that separate departmental objectives are set. This can have an adverse effect on the organisation as a whole. If, for example, the production department sets its own production goal without recourse to the amount of sales, the result could be a build-up in that particular product. The production department would be using corporate resources such as men, machines and materials in order to achieve its productive goal. Also, if the level of production continued to be higher than the level of the sales, warehousing problems would need to be taken into account. It can be seen, therefore, that a level of co-ordination and interaction needs to exist between separate department objectives. However, in a large organisation this is sometimes difficult to achieve.

If strategies are uncoordinated, this may lead to a variety of different and possibly conflicting strategies.

The lack of at least some unity of direction can also result in the incurring of a series of uncoordinated commitments. Sub-optimal behaviour can give rise to conflicting events such as a combination of commitments to cash expenditures beyond the total cash flow resources of the organisation. Also sub-optimal behaviour can lead to internal politics and dissent. This can have a negative effect on both the organisation and on the employees within that organisation; it can affect motivation and commitment to the organisation.

(b)   Within a diversified organisation it can be difficult to co-ordinate and integrate departments. However, there are a number of methods by which the various objectives, strategies, tasks and workflows can be co-ordinated, and these are as follows:

(i)   **Controlled decentralisation**

Control can be achieved by centralising the activities that sanction divisional or departmental objectives and strategies. The setting of the operational and budgetary perimeter within which a unit can work is also a means of control. Organisations can also control cash flows, performance standards, and set targets for each individual department to attain. In addition, treating departmental and divisional managers as a unified group, holding regular team meetings, and including some element of centralised work within their task portfolio will help to achieve a sense of belonging to the organisation as a whole rather than to one particular department. Depending on the type of organisation that is involved and the functions of each department involved, another way of using control is to move managers from department to department.

(ii)   **Co-ordination**

By the establishment of co-ordinating roles and departments, departmental or divisional objectives and attitudes, benefits of the whole organisation can be achieved. Lawrence and Lorsch and Handy suggest that:

(1)   they must be influential in decision-making within the area they co-ordinate;

(2)   they must possess expertise in all areas;

(3)   they must have the full backing and support of senior management;

(4)   they must be committed to confront and resolve raw conflict and inter-departmental conflict.

(iii)   **Culture**

In order to unify departmental and divisional direction it may be necessary to establish an appropriate culture throughout the whole organisation. This culture could place emphasis upon such activities as customer service, quality, innovation, and entrepreneurship. Such criteria as these are vital to the achievement of commercial success. Further, it also encourages employees to adopt an external focus.

It is the role of the organisation's chief executive and senior management to establish, reinforce and develop positive shared values towards the external features such as customer service, quality and innovation. The corporate culture is responsible for attitudes and values within the organisation. In order to be effective in unifying enterprise efforts, leaders will have to:

(1)   take a highly visible and consistent and supportive role;

(2)   lead by example;

(3)   show enthusiasm and statesmanship;

(4)   remain in touch with as many employees as possible (this is known as MBWA – management by wandering around);

(5)   create a positive climate especially towards the wider objectives of the organisation as a whole;

(6)   encourage employees to take an external view of the organisation as a whole.

(iv)   **Administrative procedures**

By standardising the administrative procedures throughout the whole organisation the incidence of fragmented or go-it-alone type activities can be reduced. Administrative procedures should be based on clearly formulated operational plans, policies, programmes, and objectives.

(v)   **Communication**

Within any large diversified organisation there will always be conflict between some departments. It is important that senior management are capable and willing to resolve these conflicts in order that the organisation as a whole can operate in a co-ordinated manner. Communication can be improved by the setting up of committees, project teams, and informal groups. It is important that departmental managers meet and communicate on an informal level as well as the more formal level within an organisation. It is often the case that managers can feel isolated; on-going management training can help provide a platform for managers to meet on a more formal level and build up informal friendships.

(vi)   **Team work**

Project teams can be set up in order to assemble a wide range of experience or skill from different departments or divisions. This can be particularly useful when dealing with specialised problems which may affect the organisation as a whole.

Employees must be made aware that the organisation as a whole can only survive and achieve its objectives by each department working to the overall benefit of the organisation.

7   CONTEMPORARY THEORIES

Key answer tips

Remember only to outline the main features of contemporary theory. (10 marks)

Then contrast it with the HR school and the Classical school. (10 marks)

Following the emergence of **the open systems approach** and its recognition of environmental influences on the organisation, an essentially pragmatic view was developed which argued that no single theory could guarantee the organisation's effectiveness. Essentially, 'it all depends'.

This **'contingency approach'** aims to suggest the most appropriate organisational design and management style in a given set of circumstances. It rejects the universal 'one-best-way' approach, in favour of analysis of the internal factors and external environment of each organisation, and the design of organisation and management as a 'best fit' between the tasks, people and environment in the particular situation i.e. tailored to the particular specific needs of an organisation.'

The contingency approach grew from the results of a number of research studies, which showed the importance of different factors on the structure and performance of an organisation and indicated that there is in fact no inevitable correlation between the structures and cultures prescribed by previous theories and organisational effectiveness. Joan **Woodward**, for example, demonstrated that 'different technologies imposed different kinds of demands on individuals and organisations and that these demands have to be met through an appropriate form of organisation'. **Lawrence and Lorsch**, and **Burns and Stalker**, found that different types of environment, with a different pace of change and degree of uncertainty, suited different organisation structures and cultures: Burns and Stalker's 'mechanistic' and 'organic' systems, for example. Fiedler, Handy and others suggest that group effectiveness is contingent upon a number of variables - not only the leader and the group but also the 'situation', the task and environment of the group.

This absence of 'prescription' is the main factor that sets contingency theory apart from classical and human relations 'theories', which attempted to formulate a set of principles which, if applied, would lead to the efficient and effective functioning of organisation.

The other main difference is in 'orientation'. **Classical theory was essentially an organisational theory, while human relations was a management theory**. Each concentrated on a particular aspect of the work situation, seen as most important at the time: in a sense, human relations emerged as a 'corrective' approach, from a critical perception of classical theory - in the same way that contingency theory evolved from a critical perspective on both.

The classical approach to management was primarily concerned with the structure and activities of the formal organisation. Effective organisation was seen to be mainly dependent on factors such as the division of work, the establishment of a rational hierarchy of authority, span of control and unity of command.

The practical application of **Taylor's 'scientific management'** approach was the use of work study techniques to break work down into its smallest and simplest component parts, and the selection and training of workers to perform a single task in the most efficient way.

The classical school contributed techniques for studying the nature of work and solving problems of how it could be organised more efficiently.

Mayo was responsible for the major early social research project known as the Hawthorne Studies, from which emerged the approach emphasising the importance of human attitudes, values and relationships for the effectiveness of organisations. It concentrated mainly on relationships and the concept of social man, with an emphasis on how employees' social or 'belonging' needs could be satisfied at work. This was called the 'Human relations' movement.

These ideas were followed up by various social psychologists – **e.g Maslow, McGregor, Herzberg and Likert** - but with a change of emphasis. People were still considered to be the crucial factor in determining organisational effectiveness, but were recognised to have more than merely physical and social needs. Attention shifted towards 'higher psychological needs for growth and self- fulfilment. This was labelled the neo-Human Relations School.

Contingency theory was founded on research evidence showing that the principles advanced by the two previous schools did not necessarily correlate with organisational effectiveness. The need for organisation structures to be adaptive (Lawrence and Lorsch, Burns and Stalker) rather than universal, on classical principles, became clear. Mayo's human relations ideas failed to make an impact at the Hawthorne plant once applied. Contingency thinkers moved away from particular aspects and into consideration of the 'whole' organisational system and its environment.

Another difference between the schools was the viewpoint of those behind them. The classical theorists were mainly early practising managers - such as Henri Fayol and F W Taylor. They analysed their own experience in management to produce a set of what they saw as 'principles' applicable in a wide variety of situations. The human relations approach, however, was pioneered mainly by social scientists - rather than practising managers - and was based on research into human behaviour, with the intention of describing and thereafter predicting behaviour in organisations. Contingency theory, as befits its flexible nature, has been championed by a wide variety of researchers, writers and managers in a number of disciplines.

According to Tom **Lupton**: 'It is of great practical significance whether one kind of managerial style or procedure for arriving at decisions, or one kind of organisational structure, is suitable for all organisations, or whether the managers in each organisation have to find that expedient that will best meet the particular circumstances of size; technology, competitive situation and so on.' Awareness of the contingency approach will therefore be of value in the following ways:

- **Encouraging managers to identify and define the particular circumstances of the situation** they need to manage, and to devise appropriate ways of handling them. A belief in universal principles and prescriptive theories can hinder problem solving and decision-making by obscuring some of the available alternatives. It can also dull the ability to evaluate and choose between alternatives that are clearly open, by preventing the manager from developing relevant criteria for judgement.

- **Encouraging responsiveness and flexibility to changes** in environmental factors through organisational structure and culture. Task performance and individual/group satisfaction are more important design criteria than permanence and unity of design type. Within a single organisation, there may be bureaucratic units side by side with task-centred matrix units (for example in the research and development function), which can respond to particular pressures and environmental volatility.

8 CLASSICAL THEORIES

Key answer tips

Compare – look for similarities and differences. Describe one theory then link the second one to it.

The **'classical' approach** is the oldest of the management concepts and it concerns itself with the correct design of the formal organisation, prescribing various rules in order that this may be successfully accomplished and keeping the subordinate subservient to the organisational needs. The rules, or principles, are intended to relate to all types of organisation.

In return, the organisation provides job security, equity, good remuneration, opportunities for individual endeavour and advancement. This is the essence of the principles of management established by Henri **Fayol**, and of scientific management attributed to Taylor, both stating that the needs of the organisation are paramount and that individuals have to accept this without argument.

Fundamentally this approach is less concerned with human beings than with the formal organisational structure: the work to be done, rather than the people undertaking the work.

Fayol called the vertical arrangement of direct authority and responsibility a 'scalar chain'. The length of the chain is the number of levels of authority and responsibility, which constitute the hierarchy. The principle refers to the vertical division of authority and responsibility and the assignment of various duties along the scalar chain. The main emphasis is on the superior-subordinate relationships.

Managerial activities were divided into planning, organising, commercial considerations, co-ordination and control. The undertaking's operations were categorised as technical, commercial, financial, security, accounting and managerial. His concern was for good order, power and authority within the departmental bureaucratic structure.

Taylor introduced the idea of 'functional authority' (by which was meant greater efficiency through specialisation). Taylor looked for specialists; at the lower operator level he looked for the most efficient shovellers of coal and iron ore and provided the system whereby men could work most efficiently for their mutual benefit. It is this concept, which led to the criticism that the scientific approach leads to dehumanisation of work.

The **'human relations' approach** emerged from the work of Elton **Mayo** undertaken first at the Philadelphia Spinning Mill then the Hawthorn experiments on worker-fatigue and its influence upon productivity. These studies showed that the behaviour of people at work is influenced less by monetary incentive than was supposed.

The scientific approach therefore depends on structure, individual selection and training, task setting and control. Later writers carried out other studies and the collective approach was that people's needs have to be identified and that people do not happily subordinate personal interests to organisational needs. The need for money, as indicated by Maslow for instance, is not paramount. The individual must find satisfaction of interests through working, and, at the same time, the work has to be so organised that organisations objectives are achieved. Mary Parker **Follet** contributed the idea that conflicts should be examined positively to solve problems (the concept of 'constructive conflict').

Neither approach suggests a complete answer to organisational problems. Rather, other factors will influence their suitability. For example, Taylor worked in the environment of heavy industry, which was highly labour intensive with high skill specialisation needs. The contemporary world, even at shop floor level, does not require such specialisation. It thus becomes pertinent to ask if Taylor's methods only apply in a highly coercive labour intensive environment. Fayol's ideas however readily adapt to the contemporary working environment, be it factory, office, college or charity. Conversely Mayo, and subsequent writers such as Likert, Maslow and McGregor, presuppose that people have aspirations for advancement and job satisfaction. However, many operatives are content to be part of the machine, to work their shifts as Taylor-style zombies.

Other features, such as management style, culture, economic environment and the nature of the job all influence the type of work environment. Once this has been identified it then becomes necessary to recognise how appropriate the schools of thought are. One organisation may be very Taylor-oriented, while other organisations are human relations oriented. But even then, only certain aspects of the human relations school may appear relevant. For example, consider two plants with the same group producing similar products. One is highly Taylor-oriented, and has low absenteeism, but only because of domination of the local labour market. The situation is one of latent alienation and poor productivity. The other plant, slightly more human, has better output despite higher absenteeism.

Taylor may be more appropriate to a large labour intensive shop floor while in the administration, where there are fewer people, the human relations approach may be more successful. The essential principle is that the environment must be appreciated first and given that one school may produce better results than the other, the suitability of either approach for a given situation must be considered.

9　**CONTINGENCY THEORY**

Key answer tips

List the main features of contingency theory and explain how they may help, giving examples where possible.

Contingency theory, rather than looking for the one best way to design an organisation, examines the functioning of organisations in the light of the particular internal and external pressures affecting a specific organisation.

The main contingent factors are:

(a)　type of personnel

(b)　nature of activity

(c)　environment

(d)　technology

(e)　size of organisation.

All of these factors have specific effects on organisations – the successful ones will be those designed in accordance with their contingent factors.

Organisations which adopt forms of structure consistent with the expectations and perceived needs of their personnel will tend to attract a greater contribution from such employees towards high performance. Although there is a great variability among personnel it is valid to recognise that the employees of an organisation constitute a major contingency in the design and operation of an organisation.

Handy claims that it is necessary to evolve different structures for the four main classes of activity found within an organisation – steady state, policy making, innovation and breakdown. Consequently, there is a clear implication that a number of different structures could exist in parallel within one and the same organisation.

Technology as a contingent factor leads to the conclusion that firms involved in unit, small batch and process production should have a more open, flexible and organic structure. On the other hand, firms in large batch and mass production require more mechanistic systems of management.

Environment is significant in that the stable environment can be dealt with by a relatively rigid bureaucratic structure but this is not the case with a volatile, rapidly changing environment. This will require a flexible, sometimes temporary, organic structure which can respond quickly and relevantly to the changes in the environment.

Researchers involved with the Aston Studies concluded that size was the most important contextual variable and that larger size led to more specialisation, standardisation and formalisation but less centralisation. In simple terms a more mechanistic structure is appropriate for the larger organisation.

In conclusion, contingency theory offers a significant step forward in organisational design by indicating how an organisation can organise itself to meet specific requirements.

10   TRENDS IN GENERAL MANAGEMENT: FLEXIBLE WORKFORCE

Key answer tips

(a)   Your description should be fairly long and detailed for 12 marks.

(b)   Split your answer into 2 sections, labour flexibility and quality.

(a)   A flexible work force has the following features:

(i)   **Fewer levels of management** and a removal of traditional barriers means a reduced demarcation by trades unions and little resistance of people to doing other people's jobs.

(ii)   **Communication and training programmes** ensure each employee can do at least one other job besides their main one. Multi-skilling allows employees to provide cover short term, and remain employable if the business's needs change in the longer run.

(iii)   There are many time-**flexing schemes e.g,**

- flexi-time;

- a mix of part-time and full-time staff, perhaps with job sharing;

- teleworking - some companies find it more appropriate to have staff working from home;

- out-sourcing and sub-contracting to push overhead labour into someone else's business and make it flexible in your own;

- contract and temporary staff to cover swings in business demand and labour availability.

Some of these schemes allow employees to be paid for working when they are needed, not for mere attendance for a fixed period. This makes labour more properly variable to business activity levels and less of a fixed overhead burden.

(iv)　**Pay linked to productivity schemes** allows employees to share in the success of the business and to be rewarded for actions that further the organisation's goals.

(v)　**Managerial flexibility to hire and fire at will**. As organisations move closer to this extreme, the more flexible they can be in expanding, shrinking and sorting through their work force as required.

(vi)　**Flexibility in the mobility of employees** - benefits the organisation when staff are prepared to move between sites and even spend periods abroad.

(vii)　**Project-based working** - makes staff more aware of the changing needs of the business and breaks down the tendency of people to settle into comfortable routines.

(viii)　**Team-based working** - demarcation of functions is eliminated and replaced by a team approach. Multi-functional workers can move quickly within the plant to meet the changing requirements of the customers. Non-direct personnel, such as management accountants can adopt the same kind of team approach. This weakens obstructive rigid hierarchies and departmental barriers.

(b)　I would seek to achieve the twin objectives of high flexibility and high quality by setting a clear strategy and timetable for introducing new procedures and practices. I would begin by negotiating these proposals with work force representatives so that any scheme introduced would have their approval and backing and would not cause any unnecessary conflict.

The Total Quality Management approach requires all employees to be introduced to a disciplined way of working where the individual takes responsibility for his or her own work. This requires good monitoring and measuring systems to be in place. Each employee must have a good safety awareness, environmental awareness, customer orientation etc, and concepts such as 'Right First Time' are central to this culture.

The following features are associated with **quality led management**:

(i)　**Effective recruitment and selection policy** that is geared to continuous improvement. This means upgrading each replacement, always seeking the best and trying to keep the best. It also means trying to balance the work force, mixing experience with youth and actively seeking to employ people with varied backgrounds, strengths and personalities. This has the effect of enriching the organisation's human resource pool.

(ii)　**Improvements in the quality** of, and increasing the level of training and multi-skilling. There can be a trade-off between multi-skilling and high-level expertise in one discipline but the more skills that people acquire, the more they can be imbued with the Quality Culture.

(iii)　**Improvements in the working environment** and job enrichment by which employees are engaged in self-improvement and optimising their own contribution, not treated as mere robots. Emphasis is paid to personal development and fulfilment.

(iv)　**The use of work systems and payment by results schemes** that are planned for efficiency, with clear job specifications and an appraisal system that sets clear agreed standards and objectives, monitors results, and rewards people for achievement. This allows standards to be maintained and continually improved.

(v) **Good management support for employees** where the methods they use are consistent - no sudden lurches in procedures, or changes in redundancy policy.

(vi) **A reduction in work demarcation** between workers, managers and departments. This encourages team working and project working.

I would try to introduce the above policies and management practices. The scheme to achieve the twin objectives of labour flexibility with quality performance would include:

(i) Agreeing with the employees, or their representatives, a programme of total quality management. This would also entail both an assurance of the programme's benefits to employees and a continuing future commitment to it. If employees enter into the necessary agreed changes as a package, the company must not be seen to renege on its commitments.

(ii) Setting up the new policies on recruitment, balance, appraisals and job enrichment.

(iii) Introducing multi-skilled project and team work. This would require cultural-change coaching for everyone in the organisation.

(iv) Improving each employee's awareness of the advantages of flexibility in the work force alongside a culture that is geared to quality performance.

The scheme outlined above would combine labour flexibility and quality performance using the positive 'human relations' approach of engaging and motivating people to achieve the organisation's goals. Another way would be to use a scientific management approach, where the methods used would deconstruct and simplify the elements of a job to allow it to be done with just the required level of skill and in so automatic and regulated a fashion that quality is consistent. This type of approach is no longer fashionable in management theory as it depends less on securing personal commitment and implies a manual, lower-skilled, less well-paid work force.

11   TRENDS IN GENERAL MANAGEMENT: REDUCING SIZE

Key answer tips

(a) Remember 'major' trends and the focus on how reduction is effected. Do not simply list ways of reducing organisational size.

(b) Environmental change is best handled by STEP factors.

(a) The major reductions in size have come about through de-layering, downsizing and outsourcing. Though there is some over-lap between these concepts each has a significant set of factors associated into it.

De-layering, as idealised, is simply the removal of a number of layers of management by reducing the tallness of hierarchy so that decisions can be made more quickly. Usually this involves mass redundancies of those in the affected levels, though some firms have simplified their grading instead, moving to 'broad banding' and replacing levels by teamworking and empowerment strategies. Many organisations aim for only five levels from shop-floor to boardroom.

Downsizing has sometimes been called 'right-sizing' in attempting to reduce the overall scope of the organisation to fit its best markets. Unwanted divisions are 'spun-off' or 'de-merged' and the remaining 'core' businesses receive the capital investment which was spread over a larger number previously. ICI's spin-off 'Zeneca' is a classic example, where the smaller company newly invigorated soon by passed its former parent in performance terms.

Outsourcing can be seen as a cost-cutting method, removing fixed costs (often of employment) and increasing variable costs (seasonal contracts for example). However, if strategic, it is a way of delayering and downsizing in one stroke, leaving a small expert 'core' able to concentrate on strategy, while the more mundane work, (often distracting senior managers' time) is carried out in the 'periphery' by contractors who are experts in their own field – such as logistics, training or IT.

(b)   The main influences in the environment can be usefully divided into four main factors.

Politically, free trade has opened markets and allowed foreign competitors to enter home markets; labour law has sidelined the trade unions to create a more flexible labour market, and the encouragement of inward investment signals the legitimisation by Government of different ways of working – particularly in Japanese 'transplants'.

Economic changes follows, in terms of globalisation and increasing scale economics per unit of finance. Hence, Unilever divested ('spun off') its profitable speciality chemicals businesses in 1999/2000 in order to concentrate capital investments in fewer areas. Competition is increasing to a point where firms are starved of cash to promote and develop new products and so are attempting to conserve internal revenues they can control – such as fixed costs – even selling assets and renting them back to release capital.

Sociological changes across the world have resulted in a rejection of communism and newly – industrialised nations have adopted a capitalist work ethic. Such countries provide new competition and at the same time national pride restricts the activities of multinationals, many having been nationalised. More sophisticated tasks and fashions mean that products must have more features (Toyota reportedly has 80 different styles of steering-wheel options) and so production becomes more complex as marketing planning becomes more risky in the turbulent consumer markets.

Technological changes happens both internally within firms and externally in terms of the products. Product sophistication follows sociological demands for gadgets, labour-saving 'white goods' and the use of micro-chips in vending machines, telephones, car seat adjusters – and so on. 'Consumerison' is assisted by globalisation and lowering of prices for goods in real terms. Internally, this has its costs. Old industries are under threat, while existing manufacturing of complex products like cars has had to provide a wider mix of products and a wider range of prices. From high-volume/low variety the mix is becoming low-volume/high variety. Such change requires sophisticated computer controlled or robot-operated machines, large factories, and cross-country manufacture to achieve unit/cost.volume targets. All of this requires very sophisticated IT-driven logistics.

12   CHANDLER

(a)   Strategy formulation is a continuous process of refinement based on past trends, current conditions and estimates of the future, resulting in a clear expression of strategic direction, the implementation of which is also planned in terms of resource allocation and structure. The strategy then comes about or is realised in actuality. This process is shown in the diagram below as the planned intended strategy (also known as the deliberate strategy). However, the actual strategy pursued by a company over a three - to five-year period may diverge from the deliberate strategy for many reasons, as outlined below.

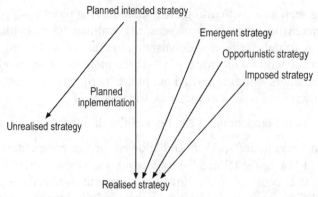

The obvious reason is that an intended strategy is not implemented because its underlying assumptions turn out to be invalid or because the pace of developments overtakes it. Factors affecting the strategy realisation will include changes in the organisation's external environment eg, changes in the market for the goods and services that the firm produces and in the nature of the competition facing the company, and also its internal environment.

Mintzberg argues that strategies can emerge, perhaps as a result of the processes of negotiation, bargaining and compromise, rather than being due to a deliberate planning process. This emergent strategy would be one that arises from an external stimulus not envisaged in the planned strategy. For example, a supplier pursuing modern ideas on supplier/customer relationships, might encourage a partnership approach to sourcing. It is easy to imagine that buyers in the customer organisation might see benefits in this, and could pursue the idea to the point where sourcing strategy took on an aspect not at all contemplated when planned strategic developments were laid down.

Sometimes changes from the intended strategy come about in opportunistic or entrepreneurial ways e.g, an enterprise can find a new process or resource that enables dramatic cost reductions.

Finally, strategy may be imposed. For example, recession and threat of a takeover may force a strategy of cost cutting and retrenchment. Technological developments may cause an organisation to develop new products to replace the ones that have become obsolescent.

(b) **Chandler** traced the growth and development of a sample of large US corporations from 1909 to 1959. His research showed that:

- diversification led to the need for a new administrative system that would ensure the efficient use of resources;

- the multi-divisional structure had evolved as an adaptive response to this need; and

- this created a type of managerial environment that placed a premium on economic performance and the skills of generalists.

The diversified corporations that Chandler was charting were about to become multinational corporations. As markets opened up, the evolution of a product-market strategy would impose changes on the organisation, leading to a transition from a functional to a multi-divisional structure, based on product-market relationships. This is how Chandler's idea that 'structure follows strategy' came about. He also argued that managers who are close to the operational base and its markets, deal with the day-to-day operations of a large organisation's various divisions more efficiently. Long-term strategy, on the other hand, he saw as best undertaken by those who can stand back and take an overview of the whole organisation.

Scott, following Chandler, developed a model of growth and development that viewed the corporation as moving through several stages as its product-market complexity increased. He saw firms as developing from one-person enterprises to functionally organised (sales, production and research) single business organisations. As the firm began to diversify and to develop multiple product lines, it would then adopt a multidivisional structure.

Subsequent studies by **Channon, Galbraith and Nathanson** confirm the general claim by Chandler that it is impossible for senior managers at the corporate centre to be sufficiently familiar with the different products and markets served by the different divisions of the corporation, and to make informed decisions. Divisionalisation enables each division to concentrate on the problems and opportunities of its particular business environment. The products/markets in which the organisation operates may be so different that it would be impractical to bring the tasks together in a single body. It is more sensible to split the organisation according to the different products/markets or operations and then to ensure the needs of each division are met by tailoring the operations within the division to the particular business needs.

Most writers seem to agree that organisation structure logically follows after strategy has been decided. However, there are some, including Mintzberg, who cast some doubt on this claim. They argue that, whilst the strategic activities need co-ordinating, the existing structure of the organisation is likely to provide a major barrier to change, as the vested interests of existing personnel are tied up in it. Their view is that the structure limits the strategic options and information flow and shapes strategic thinking. To the extent that such a situation prevailed it could then be argued that 'strategy follows structure'.

The view of modern contingency theorists is that there is a range of factors involved in the relationship between strategy and structure, and the structure that is actually selected is likely to be a compromise between pressures which pull in opposite directions. The assumption of any simple relationship is likely to be mistaken.

As with other areas of organisational management, it is not clear if there are any universal generalisations that can be made about the relationship between strategy and structure.

13   SFC

(a)   **Stakeholders** are people or groups with an interest in the success of an organisation. As described by Mintzberg's 'power in and around organisations' these can comprise internal groups (trade unions, managers etc) or external individuals (neighbours) or groups (suppliers, customers etc).

SFC has internal stakeholder groupings such as Directors, whose shareholding value and dividends depend on profit, and the manager, working staff and other support staff whose jobs depend on success directly or on the income generated. The players too, derive not only their salary, but also their worth on the transfer market by virtue of the Club's success.

SFC's external stakeholders include the shareholders, who have the same pecuniary interest as the directors but are more distant emotionally.

The fans are customers who pay at the gates and buy merchandise, but who have a more emotional link than perhaps some Directors and Officials as they are part of the local community and may have supported SFC all their lives.

The TV companies are also customers but incorporate SFC matches into their own internal value chain – in effect as wholesalers selling on the matches to a wider audience. They and other prospective buyers have an interest in buying SFC at the lowest price – a conflict of interest's vis-a-vis SFC's success.

The Governing Bodies of soccer and even the National Government are stakeholders because of their statutory obligations and also the Public Relations effect on the rest of the clubs and the wider society – such as violence of fans at matches or fire precautions.

(b)   The takeover of SFC can be influenced by external bodies if there is a wider public interest – and boycotts threatened by fans may worry institutional shareholders enough to affect the outcome. However, even if these forces are strong, if the pecuniary interests of the two parties (buyers and sellers) is stronger then the price will be the most influential aspect of whether the takeover goes ahead. Therefore the Directors are the most influential internal group – by virtue of their legal authority – and the Shareholders whose votes will count in the end are the most influential external group. However, only large tranches of shares held by institutions will be able to vote en bloc and so the effect may be muted. The price the buyer is prepared to pay is influenced in turn by its Directors, the balance sheet / profit and loss account, and ultimately its own institutional shareholders.

14   FFC

Key answer tips

This is a very straightforward question on national culture clash, where you should discuss the source of national culture, its interplay with corporate culture, and its susceptibility to change. Much of the answer below is common sense.

(a)   The FFC restaurants in Country C appear to be experiencing the effects of a clash of culture between the corporate culture of FFC, which has developed in Country S, with the national culture of Country C personified in the customers, the local residents and the local Country C employees employed by FFC.

There are a **large variety of ways in which national cultures can vary**, as a result of historical developments going back hundreds of years. National culture can be analysed according to the numerous factors that make a nation what it is – the background and mix of its people, its historic and current wealth, its artistic and religious heritage, its climate and geography, its experience of war and strife, whether there is only one language, etc. These can be summarised as factors of patterns of behaviour, beliefs, values and material artefacts, and it should therefore come as no surprise that the people of Country C have different approaches to food, seating arrangements, music, architecture and the way in which employees are managed.

FFC is an organisation that developed from Country S into a multinational company. While many of its characteristics in terms of corporate culture will be those of Country S, and these may be the real cause of the problems with the people of Country C, as an organisation it will have developed cultural characteristics of its own, which will not relate to a specific country. This means that it should be adaptable enough to cope with the problems in Country C – and indeed it has probably experienced such problems before. It may simply be that, having been very successful in many countries, the management of FFC have become complacent about the possibility of a culture clash. When setting up business to consumer operations in another country, any organisation should expect problems if they do not make the effort to research in advance the culture of the country concerned.

To overcome the problems being experienced the **management of FFC must be flexible and patient**, but must not lose sight of the rationale behind operating multinationally – namely, economies of scale and the benefits of operating a global brand. In addition, FFC should remember that, while most national cultures are strong but are not totally resistant to change and the influence of other countries, there are some countries which are maybe not suited to globalisation. This may be because of their historical culture or because of political instability at home which has made the resistance of globalisation a political cause in itself.

(b) Recommendations to the FFC Board for resolution of the problems of culture clash in Company C:

- Take care that the overall approach of FFC is measured and conciliatory. The problems being experienced are not huge and should not be allowed to escalate

- Meet the groups of people who have complained and listen very carefully to what they say

- Research and analyse similar problems experienced before in other host countries, and how FFC handled them

- Research and analyse the national culture of Country C with more care, especially with regard to eating out, music, and architecture

- Research and analyse the management styles adopted by indigenous Country C companies, and by other multinationals who have set up successfully in the country

- Check that the recruitment and selection procedures operated by FFC in Country C are appropriate

- Formulate a plan based on all this research that addresses the specific issues of menus, seating, music and architecture which will be effective yet not too costly

- Formulate a recruitment, selection and training plan that will ensure the staff of the restaurants are suitably motivated to accept the FFC culture, adapted if necessary, while dealing with the people of Country C in the way that is desirable. This may or may not require the use of Country S employees on secondment.

15   PROFESSIONAL CODE AND ETHICS

Key answer tips

Professional codes of conduct and ethical behaviour are very important issues and you should make sure that you could produce a good answer to a question like this in the exam.

(a) A **professional code of conduct** is a set of rules to which members of a professional body subscribe for the conduct of their professional affairs. The rules incorporate standards of behaviour and competence which members of the professional body are expected to meet, and there are usually sanctions if they are not met, administered by the professional body itself.

The UK Chartered Institute of Management Accountants (CIMA) has a code of conduct which, among other points, requires members to meet the following standards of behaviour and competence:

- To act with due care

- To be professionally and technically competent

- To behave with integrity and objectivity

- To maintain quality of service to clients

- To maintain client confidentiality

- To serve the public interest

Active compliance with the code of conduct promotes a very positive image for both the member and the professional body itself. Because clients have learnt to value the competence of members over unregulated non-members, chartered management accountants can expect to enjoy repeat business from their clients and new business from people who have received recommendations. They can charge good rates for this.

Failure to act in the manner set out can result in serious consequences for the client if misleading, inaccurate or just bad advice is acted on. The persons affected include companies and their stakeholders: senior management, shareholders, lenders, employees, customers, suppliers, government and regulators, and the public at large. Where these stakeholders identify the source of their problems as incompetence etc by a management accountant then the professional body to which that person belongs is also brought into disrepute.

Non-compliance with the code of conduct will also reduce repeat and recommended business, so gradually the volume and the rate charged for business will decline.

In extreme cases, non-compliance may indicate that the management accountant is not operating to high standards and may prompt further investigations by the professional body and even the tax and criminal authorities. While this may be unwarranted, it is not something that any professional person would want.

Whether there is simply non-compliance, or fraud itself, such acts on the part of chartered management accountants bring the reputations of the professional body and all its members into question. Stakeholders begin to question the existence of professional standards, and the value of paying good rates to people who then do not live up to them. In this way, the reputations and therefore the livelihoods of all professional people are damaged.

(b)   Ensuring that both professional accountancy bodies and organisations more generally take the ethical principles contained in their codes of conduct more seriously requires a 'carrot and a stick' approach – make it worth their while to comply, and make sure there are sanctions available if they do not.

First, it is also worth evaluating why people would choose *not* to take them seriously. Largely this is down to self-interest. Some people will make the following calculation: can I benefit financially from non-compliance, and are the chances of discovery and/or sanctions small? Conversely, some people will feel so pressurised by their employer or client *not* to comply that they feel they have no choice.

These are difficult issues to deal with, but if an organisation or professional body feels that, overall, it is worth the effort to attempt to override selfishness and bullying with institutionalised ethics, then progress can be made. The main aim should be to encourage an ethical atmosphere, but there should also be clear expectations and a framework for enforcement.

The following approaches can be used:

*   **Draft a mission statement** which clearly incorporates ethical principles

*   **Develop a formal corporate code of conduct**, encompassing the values which are implicit in the corporate culture

*   **Ensure that policies are written** covering issues such as employee welfare, community participation and stakeholder concerns

*   **Provide ethical training** to current employees and as part of the induction of new employees

*   **Incorporate ethics and employee welfare issues** etc into the specific objectives of managers and staff

*   **Set up an ethics or code of conduct committee** which can track compliance, and recommend action or amendment of the code

*   **Conduct social audits** into the organisation's activities and promote the results widely if they are good

- **Make ethical behaviour** and concern for stakeholders **part of the corporate culture** by means of promotions, charitable fund-raising etc

- Encourage 'whistle-blowing' or at least do not discourage whistle-blowing. This means that members or employees who perceive breaches of ethics in their workplace should let someone in authority know about it.

16   THE E COMPANY

Key answer tips

(a)   This is a straightforward question based on textbooks which most students will have had little problem with gaining most of the 10 marks.

(b)   This asks for two sub-parts, explaining the actions of the two managers in terms of the theory of schools of strategy. This would have posed difficulties for many candidates unfamiliar with the Examiner's CIMA article published in 'Financial Management'. Most texts do not delineate the three 'schools' of strategy in an easy to digest form, and many answers would tend to be very descriptive of the actions: difficult to gain ten marks here.

(a)   E company is large enough to have separate levels. The corporate level states the *raison d'etre*, the rationale for the business E is in. A frequently asked questions is what business are we in?, followed by 'do we want to be there?' and 'what better segments might we like to enter?'. E has a diversified but related portfolio of products and must allocate the right structures (both financial and organisational) and resources to them depending on the estimation of returns to capital.

Each of the diversified businesses then has its own business level of strategy, coping with **PEST** and **SWOT** factors and the more local **5 Forces** which affect it specifically. Here, it competes head-to-head with similar firms with similar issues and has to try to create better value as perceived by its customers. This can be by finding a unique selling point. Here, **Porter** refers to a cost-leadership or a differentiating (quality-enhancement) strategy. These can both have a broad or narrow (niche) focus.

Within a business strategy, numbers are collected for benchmarking purposes, and where possible these are applied to different functions. Whereas **Henry Ford's** original 'River Rouge' plant produced everything from cast items to tyres, engines and electrics. Most industries have developed 'supply chains' of specialists. These are on the basis of firms which can develop better quality and cheaper items than can be provided by the main 'client' firm. Each function can be subject to a 'best practice' audit and if it fails to satisfy strategic criteria, can be outsourced.

(b)   Manager C has in mind development whereas Manager D considers a narrower growth perspective.

For C the task is more difficult as he has to engage in environmental scanning using boundary-spanning activities like market research. Then this data has to be interpreted and analysed such as in a SWOT analysis or in the more complex BCG or GE matrices which demand more precise information. Given some pointers from these, C has to position the products into the correct area – such as Dog, Problem Child for difficult 'weak' products, or Stars and Cash cows for 'strong' ones.

This might require an organic structure capable of reaching to the various STEP factors which affect each of the products in their market position.

Manager D has a similar strategic perspective: **Drucker** described it as 'managing for results' which demands a concentration on core products, resourcing these fully, and intensifying activity to beat off competition. Scope and breadth are narrowed and R&D focused. This resource–based perspective is giving favour:

Unilever recently sold off its profitable speciality chemicals business because it could not in future find cheap capital to fund each one. D is riding the crest of a trend and so should find favours at Board level, especially if it leads to a cost-leadership strategy.

17 VIRTUAL ORGANISATION

Key answer tips

(a) Students choosing this question will be aware of the idea of the flexible firm and core competences and the step factors, so good marks should be scored on this straightforward explanation.

(b) This is in three sub–parts. The first is an explanation; the second ,the advantages to T; the third, the advantages to K. Fairly straightforward 10 marks.

(a) In its extreme form, a **'virtual' organisation** may consist of a simple entrepreneur with a bank account, mobile phone and internet connection. All that is needed is a market for products/services and customers can be supplied from the entrepreneur's contacts, each being billed by the entrepreneur separately.

At the other extreme is the vertically-integrated company which has an extensive value-chain which is staffed and whose capital assets are all owned by the company.

Inbetween lie and number of alternative **'quasi-firms'**. Manufacturers often buy-in components and may create a joint venture (i.e. with capital injection) or an alliance (cooperation and legal contracts only) to support a close working relationship. At the various stages along the value chain, activities can be outsourced to contractors, and marketing and other facilities shared with competitors.

The driver for change has been often described as 'the crisis of capital' but returns on investment, measures of efficiency, and the perceptions of investors (often institutional) have pushed firms to limit capital spending and lower their labour costs in order to heighten financial ratios.

Assisting these underlying features has been the growth of a **'flexibly specialised'** economy where small firms become far more important innovators. This is in turn aided by developments in manufacturing and operations (JIT, FMS, MRPI, MRPII, TQM) which increase flexibility production, lower costs and enable establishment in areas of high unemployment (as location is not dependant on the availability of raw materials). In those areas labour costs are also low.

Communication technology also allows for greater control and at the same time more efficient marketing and distribution through intranets, websites and extranets. As these are becoming progressively cheaper and more efficient (ISDN and Broadband) this is likely to increase 'teleworking' and lead to more 'virtuality'.

(b) **Joint ventures** are usually distinguished by the creation of a (usually temporary) third party legal entity in which the partners invest capital and other resources (under accommodation etc) often these are limited by shares and the partners take various holdings. Royal Dutch/Shell used to be 50-50 but is now 60% Royal Dutch 40% Shell, as the trading pattern changed.

Company T will have the advantage of the higher-level managerial expertise of K especially its working skills; it will also have access to K's production facilities at lower cost and contribute via increased volume to better scale economies for both firms. Presumably T knows the local culture of N and its newly-established position should allow it to operate individualistically, entrepreneurially and flexibly without having to spend time and resources on the activities is can buy-in from K.

Company K will have similar advantage of scale economy in manufacturing of T's volume becomes significant and its products do not require additional capital equipment to manufacture. Presumably K has no knowledge of country N and so has the 'back door' – a joint venture with T – it can gain not only some of T's technical skills but also its detailed knowledge of the culture and market of N. As it is likely to be more politically sophisticated and produce other products from T it may use the JV as a 'wooden horse' to penetrate other markets, be seen as a responsible inward–investor and thereby contribute to N's economic development and so gain access to more markets and perhaps cheap Government capital, manufacturing facilities or tax breaks.

FUNCTIONAL AREAS OF ORGANISATIONS

18   RELATIVE MERITS OF DIFFERENT FUNCTIONAL ORGANISATIONS

Key answer tips

(a)   Your answer should be in two parts: draw a functional structure and describe three conditions with three examples.

(b)   The same as for (a) using geographical (territorial) divisional structure.

(a)   A simple functional organisational chart could be:

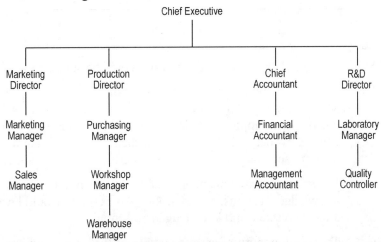

Such a functional organisation chart would be suitable in the following circumstances.

(i)   Where it is necessary to group skills and expertise together, so that a central concentrated effort will occur, not a widespread effort. In the chart above, Research and Development is grouped together and not spread over different production processes or markets. This enables exchange of research results, optimum use of equipment and availability of advice from specialists who are based in that area.

(ii)   Where customer requirements dictate that functions should be separately presented, for example, where customers wish to deal with a technical person and not a generalist. Most garages split servicing from spares from car sales. Customers discussing servicing requirements for their car wish to talk to a technical person not a general sales or clerical person.

(iii)   Where the nature of the business dictates that functions be separated. This can arise when an organisation is providing services to the outside world but also, internally within its parent organisation. This can be artificially proposed as in the example of 'Chinese Walls' blocking the flow of potentially illegal 'insider dealing' information between functions of a financial institution.

In general, functional organisational structures tend to occur at an early stage in a company's development. Logically, an expanding small company will seek to recruit a specialist and appoint that person to head an area of responsibility, where the proprietor or Managing Director feels an expert is needed.

(b)   A simple territorial organisation structure could be:

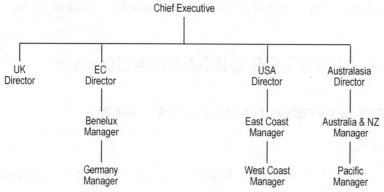

Each of these territory managers could have functional heads reporting to them. For example,

Such a territorial organisational structure would be suitable in the following situations.

(i)   Where it is important for an organisation to develop a 'profit by area' culture. Many trading organisations expand by moving into overseas areas, often by takeover. Examples include Tesco's move into France and Ratners takeover of Kay's Jewellery Chain in USA. In such situations it is important to keep the territory separate so that true profit performance is available.

(ii)   Where customers demand a local organisation to meet expectations of local knowledge, customs, expertise etc. An example would be an estate agent where a local presence and knowledge is essential.

(iii)   To exploit opportunities and conditions that are particularly local. For example, a country may have Government Assistance Schemes for companies registered in that country only. In addition many organisations find it is necessary to be organised by territory so that local managers can be delegated to take charge of the local unit and respond to local initiatives without needing to refer to head office. For example, a UK wine importer may own vineyards in France, Australia and Chile. There is little advantage in having a wine producing manager overall since each territory has its own product and its own harvesting problems.

In general, territorial organisation is often linked with functional or product organisation or two tiers in a company's structure.

19   MERITS OF A RANGE OF ORGANISATIONAL STRUCTURES

Key answer tips

Do not discuss the structures but the factors determining structure. Discuss five major factors only.

Among the factors to be considered when deciding on the structure appropriate to a particular organisation are:

Size

Clearly a business controlled by one entrepreneur has quite a different structure from a multi-million pound, multi-national giant. A decentralised (territorial) structure may be suitable in a large company, whereas a functional structure in such a company might lead to excessive bureaucracy.

Chosen strategy

A company pursuing a growth strategy will probably need a different organisational structure from one pursuing a non-growth, low risk strategy. It must be able to move quickly, so the organisational structure must allow quick decisions. This means that chains of command should not be too long, and this suggests perhaps a product or matrix structure.

A department specifically concerned with promoting change is needed. The research and development manager will have a high status in the company. The organisation must be forward-looking; it cannot afford to dwell on yesterday's mistakes.

Management style

An ideal organisational structure cannot be imposed on an organisation regardless of management style. For instance, a programme of decentralisation, however desirable in other circumstances, will be doomed to failure if the chief executive is an autocrat who is reluctant to relinquish control to any appreciable degree.

Diversity of products, markets and geographical locations

With very diverse operations there might even be negative synergy if top management try to interfere in areas they do not understand. This points to decentralisation. Similarly, the greater the geographical distance from the centre, the greater the necessity for decentralised control.

Technology

The research undertaken by Professor Joan Woodward established that variations in structure were related to three technological categories:

- small batch and unit production;

- large batch and mass production;

- process production.

A linear relationship was present between a company's technical complexity and certain features involving the formal organisation eg, the length of line of command, the control range of the chief executive and finally Woodward discovered the ratio of managers to total personnel was ever increasing, starting from small batch through to process production.

20   HR MANAGEMENT FUNCTION

Key answer tips

An open question asking for 'some'

-        'issues' (not problems)

-        'problems'

This is tricky to organise, unless theory is used.

Firstly, if we refer to **Mintzberg's** structuring diagram for organisations, we can see that HR lies in all probability in the Support Structure along with administrative tasks. Some aspects of HR are clearly administrative such as payroll. This distances HR both from the technostructure (where a 'technical' function like legal may be located, as well as R&D) and the Operating Core. HR, if it is located in the support structure, therefore acts as a service to the other functions. In some organisations it may not be represented in the Strategic Apex or may have a reduced role. A recent UK newspaper article (October 2000) described one of the director's exit from a major UK retailer as almost inevitable as 'she had a Personnel background'. Thus Personnel, in even large organisations, may be seen as a reactive, administrative function.

Some employers such as Mars however assign HR to line functions on shiftwork so that there is integration of goals and mutual learning and support – though these cases are exceptional.

HR has a problem of having usually a small staff of its own ('no cattle') but being required to generate policies affecting all of the organisation's staff – big hat! How far HR managers understand the needs of their line colleagues is a thorny problem; many advertisements for HR managers require 'a business orientation' but are not specific as to what this means. Even then, where HR is 'sensitive' to line issues these may pull in opposite directions. Production Day Supervision has very different needs from its Shift Supervision; R&D scientists have orientations to work far removed from those of Sales Staff.

Even if HR were sensitive, and had policies to match the needs of the staff, its reduced power-base as a supplier of services has often led to **outsourcing**. Service power bases need a dependency relationship if they are to become more influential. Establishing dependency requires a high level of knowledge and skill outside the ambit of line managers and also the ability of HR staff to create uncertainty in that area. Most line managers have interviewed, been interviewed, trained, and been trained so to establish credibility in these areas HR must present something novel – outside the line manager' experience – such as 'competences'.

'**Competences**' are emerging as ways of assessing individuals for recruitment, promotion training etc. and if they can be shown to be effective, line managers may jettison their current methods and take on such new HR initiatives. A clear area for HR influence is the law: Health and Safety, discipline and dismissal, grievances and so on which are complex, knowledge-rich and, critically, highly risky areas. It is here that HR is likely to survive being outsourced, so long as the relationship to the line is retained and a 'policing' role avoided.

21   MANAGEMENT ACCOUNTANT'S RELATIONSHIP WITH FUNCTIONAL AREAS

Key answer tips

(a)   Split the answer into political and psychological, then explain briefly as there are only 8 marks.

(b)   Open question on circumventing resistance – remember it asks 'how?' , so be positive.

(a)　(i)　**The political implications of managerial control** may be identified as follows:

Managerial control in hierarchical organisations can be implemented through policies, procedures, hierarchies of authority, specialists and defined roles that govern all control aspects in the organisation. Power is based on the position in the hierarchy and control is by decision-making, rules and regulations. For this to work effectively and for management to feel confident that they can achieve their goal, there must be clear, unambiguous management control within the hierarchical structure.

Managerial control can lead to smoother operations, but the existence of a power structure can foster a culture of jostling and positioning for personal advantage amongst managers. This aspect of managerial control can produce goal conflict amongst the managers seeking to exercise control.

If the managerial control is excessive, it can lead to alienation of subordinate staff and to a culture of 'them and us'. This can cause resistance and conflict, often involving unionisation. Effective control can only really take place in organisations where there is positive commitment from employees with a corporate culture of shared values, beliefs and traditions. Excessive control can lead to inefficiency.

Managerial control through policies and procedures will include budgets. These are of benefit to the chartered management accountant as they act like checkpoints to monitor the activities.

(ii)　The **psychological implications of managerial control** may be identified as follows:

People tend to function better when they know their place in the organisation and they are part of a stable structure with clear lines of control. It also helps if there is a common understanding and acceptance of the organisation's vision and mission.

Goal congruence is better where managers exercise clear control and where subordinates feel that their interests are being served. There is respect for the management and workers defer to and do not overtly challenge their decisions. However, some may feel that this is an anti-democratic way of operating an organisation. Strong managerial control involves a few making decisions on how the many will work, without the many having much say in the matter.

If a manager can understand how managerial control can affect the behaviour of employees, he or she can assess the undercurrents in the organisation, avoid friction, defuse tension and optimise organisational culture. As a person who has to select, interpret and present meaningful information about the business, the chartered management accountant benefits from an appreciation of such matters.

(b)　**Management has a duty to maximise business performance**, part of which depends on effective control of human resources. This means ensuring employees are keeping to procedures, working towards targets and keeping in line with job descriptions. Within a business, individuals and groups will each have slightly different goals and priorities from those set out by top management.

Some resistance within the organisation can be overcome by operating a stable system in which each employee's place and role are clearly set out in detail. The more formal the system, the less likely is casual, 'test-the-water' resistance. However, management control in hierarchical organisations cannot depend on the structure to achieve objectives. The structure is limited and cannot be successful if the organisation adopts the wrong strategy or does not possess the requisite skills.

Obviously, there are occasions when the divergence of views becomes extreme and subordinates will begin to resist the will of top management. To avoid this resistance, management should be sensitive to any divergences and should find ways of allowing dissenting views to be communicated and accommodated. Consultation and participation should be encouraged by specific mechanisms and by the general cultural framework. The communication channels within the hierarchical structure can bring conflict into the open and allow managers to listen to, and act upon, the views of subordinates. This may help to establish goal congruence.

When there is a **breakdown in control** bordering on high-profile opposition, management can take certain steps to overcome it. They can adopt a strict disciplinary regime with low tolerance of poor conduct. This type of regime requires strict supervision, where verbal and written warnings that lead to possible dismissal form the basis of the discipline. Organisations that experience severe resistance can manage to create a 'listening' atmosphere whilst actually manipulating events to get what they want. This means channelling and absorbing resistance, so that it remains manageable at all times and under management control.

Where there is an **undercurrent of resistance**, rather than high-profile opposition, management can use the carrot, rather than the stick approach. Company awards such as pay rises, perks and bonuses can be used to favour specific conduct and encourage commitment by employees to the objectives set by management. Promotion can be used to signal to employees the attributes and attitudes the business wants to build on. Training and personal development programmes can also help to shape the attitudes of the work force.

22   MARKETING FUNCTION: THE PRODUCT LIFE CYCLE

Key answer tips

Split your answer into 2 sections, explaining the life cycle concept and explaining why it is important.

Remember 'new products' and to include examples.

Many products pass through a number of stages in their history until they eventually decline in the face of outside competition or a change in consumer tastes. As illustrated below, it is important to consider carefully when to start developing new products in order to achieve a steady rate of growth in both turnover and profits for the whole company.

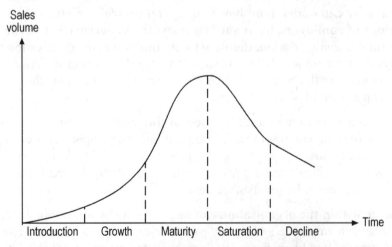

It should be noted that periods are only shown in the diagram as being of equal size for convenience. For example, product development may take three years but the product may be in decline for four years after market introduction. If this were the case, the product development of the second product would need to be started before market introduction of the first.

Some products have much longer life cycles than others - basic foodstuffs have much longer lives than more fashionable products such as clothes, although perhaps the days of the plain white loaf are numbered (unless sliced for sandwiches, toast etc). The time required to develop a product also varies tremendously - forty years so far have been spent developing the fast breeder nuclear reactor and it is still not commercially viable. Conversely, it now takes about four years to develop a new car although the Mini took fifteen years.

It should also be realised that within an industry different products will have reached different stages, which might not be typical of the industry as a whole. It is commonly believed that the electrical domestic appliance market has reached the maturity stage. However, although refrigerators are already in 90% of homes, microwave ovens have less than 15% ownership and it is consequently hardly surprising that the Japanese have decided to focus on this segment in order to enter the industry globally.

Marketing activities will change as a product passes through its life cycle. For example, strategic issues at the development stage of a grocery product would be concerned with such questions as 'What business are we in?' whilst marketing research would be concerned with new product testing. Marketing mix considerations would be at the planning stage although sales training would be taking place.

During the market introduction of the product the overall strategic decision would be whether to continue or to cancel. Marketing research would be directed at customer and consumer reactions which could lead to modifications to the product or to the pricing policy which could initially have been based on skimming or a penetration price. Promotion would be concentrating on the 'creation of demand' while the sales force would be dealing with unforeseen problems and gaining new distribution outlets.

In the growth stage the company can take risks with over-capacity and even with quality in order to establish a market position - profit margins will permit production inefficiencies. Strategic issues would include how to deal with private brands and marketing research would be focusing on brand share information. Price falls are likely and new variants would be introduced as a result of new product development. Promotion would be building up brand loyalty as the sales force battled for shelf space. Distribution would have to cope with the surge of demand as new outlets stocked up.

During maturity and saturation efficient use of plant and close attention to production costs become much more important. Strategy will be concerned with the introduction of new products and the relation of these to existing products. Marketing research will be looking for signs of market saturation and stagnation. Price will remain steady if no private brands exist; otherwise it will fall, particularly as large outlets pressure for special terms. 'Below the line' promotional expenditure will rise if private brands exist.

The decline stage will raise the question 'Do we wish to remain in business?' and how much will depend on the forecasts provided by marketing research. Prices would continue to fall and there would be greater promotional expenditure in an attempt to maintain sales.

It can therefore be seen that the product life cycle concept is not only a useful tool for analysing demand but is also valuable in managing the marketing mix during the introduction of a product and throughout its life cycle.

23   MARKETING FUNCTIONS: CONCEPTS

Key answer tips

(a)   Simply 'outline' each for 6 marks.

(b)   Concentrate on the theme park idea and develop your arguments to prevent decline by considering what changes can be made in areas of:

- Product

- Price

- Promotion

- Place

(a)   Any discussion on marketing mix will include consideration of the 'Four Ps'. These are product, price, promotion and place (or distribution). Their main characteristics are as follows.

Product - is anything that is offered to the market for use or consumption. Factors to be taken into account will include quality, any branding, variety, special features, style, packaging and fashion. Generally, people want to acquire the benefits of a product so they will also be looking for the characteristics of guarantees, after-sales service and general reliability.

Price - is important because it is the only element that produces revenue. Normally this will be characterised by reference to being fixed to both market conditions and also costs of production. Other characteristics will embrace discount policy for quantity or early payment, as a 'weapon' in the introduction of a new product or complementing another line, and also trade-in allowances.

Promotion - is the way in which the product is drawn to the attention of the market place. It covers advertising in all its forms (eg, press, commercial TV, outdoor hoardings, etc), personal selling, sales promotions and publicity through media coverage.

Place - the purpose of this is to get the product to the consumer, hence the alternative names of placement and distribution. Its characteristics are the channels of distribution and the physical distribution activities. It is also concerned with the location of sales outlets and the infrastructure of warehousing and transport facilities.

(b)   The scenario given is one where the skilful application of the four Ps has meant new life for an attraction with declining popularity. Working in the favour of the manager is the fact that with increased prosperity and leisure time for many people, there are opportunities to retrieve the situation and to exploit the attraction very profitably. Two obvious examples in the UK are Alton Towers and Madame Tussauds.

It is essential to recognise that one element on its own cannot be manipulated to give success. It is important that each element be considered as part of the overall approach and that the effect be co-ordinated to ensure improvement. However, for ease of presentation, it may be appropriate to consider each item individually.

Product - the manager must consider just what he is selling and what is so special about his product that encourages tourists to travel to visit the attraction, sometimes at very great expense eg, a walk in the main street of Stratford-upon-Avon on any summer's day will confirm the worldwide interest in this particular product. Here, of course, the products are all associated with William Shakespeare and this is very skilfully exploited by the theatre, the Shakespeare Trust properties and all the other attractions that constitute 'the product'.

With this example, the basic concept underpinning what the tourist expects is self-evident. For a museum or theme park, the manager must carefully research the product. Does the visitor want an educational visit, an 'experience', a 'white-knuckle' ride or passive entertainment? Possibly the visitor might want all of these. There are many examples where museums have changed their image, so that instead of passively viewing relics, people can actively experience some of the items on display.

Once the manager has determined his underpinning approach, he can consider what other complementary facilities should be provided. Obvious ones are good rest areas, souvenir stalls, convenient catering provisions and possibly even hire of cameras (as in Tussauds). If the quality is good, there is every likelihood that the additional revenue earned would greatly enhance the profitability of the attraction.

Price - coupled with any changes or developments in the image for the theme park or the museum must be reconsideration of the pricing policy. Typical problems that need to be addressed are as follows.

(i)   How does the price level proposed compare with competing attractions? Will it be seen as value for money?

(ii)   Should there be one overall admission price covering all activities, or would a separate admission charge with extra tickets for rides and other attractions be more appropriate?

(iii)   Will the price level proposed and the estimated attendance ensure that a profit is made?

(iv)   What family schemes, concessions for children and senior citizens, or coach parties, should be arranged?

(v)   A popular development is the provision of package deals for admission and overnight accommodation, eg, Legoland, Seaside Sun centres, etc. Would this be possible?

(vi)   Should there be different peak charges at weekend and bank holidays?

(vii)   Would the price level be acceptable both to home visitors as well as overseas tourists?

(viii) What price should be charged for franchises such as food and souvenir kiosks?

Promotion - here the concern must initially be with the development of the 'product' and the image it is to portray. Is it a family day out or an educational experience, or should the 'fun' aspect be stressed? Once decided, then the most appropriate means of promotion must be determined. Several outlets might be used. For example, press and commercial television advertising would be satisfactory to attract home visitors but are unlikely to be seen by overseas tourists. Hence, knowledge of what most people do on their first night of a holiday would be appropriate. After unpacking, many people congregate in the reception area of the hotel or campsite picking up leaflets for the local attractions - and this approach was found to be one of the most effective in promoting the new image of Tussauds. Where a small discount token is printed in the leaflet, than it is found that many people cannot resist this bargain.

Place - As the theme park or museum is in a fixed location, particularly in the short to medium term, then consideration of channels of distribution is inappropriate. There are other elements, which may be explored, such as exploitation of the location, and the provision of car parking and conveniences for public transport. Market segmentation is considered under this heading and here there can be opportunities to attract different consumers at different times. One example is the use of a holiday camp for different activities at varying times of the year: for example, holidays during the period April to September and conferences outside these dates. If the marketing manager reconsiders the approach under these headings and is bold in his approach, then popularity of the attraction will be high again. However, having once carried out this exercise, he must not 'rest on his laurels' as people are continually looking for new experiences and he must work all the time to maintain the position.

24 FUNCTIONAL AREAS: VALUE CHAIN

Key answer tips

A very open question. Depending on the area chosen, different frameworks are possible.

One of the most important areas especially in a manufacturing business is that of **Production or Operations**. This is a 'line' department and part of Mintzberg's 'operating core' and 'mid line'; it is a key element in Porter's value chain as a transformational process converting inputs into outputs. This function exists in primary (extraction), secondary (manufacturing) and tertiary (service) sectors of the economy. On a global scale, however, the concept of World Class Manufacturing makes operations management a highly important differentiator and an effective contributor to strategic advantage.

There are different aspects to production, but two elements – volume and quality – stand out. Cost, for example, though important, is subject to volume and quality factors in the first instance. Technology underlines all of these, in that artisan or craft production – Woodward's unit/small batch category – has mainly been transformed into mass production by the investment of capital into machinery: hence 'capitalism'. This form of production requires a high division of labour (or specialisation of function) to deliver high volume. Adam Smith in 1799 showed how a pin factory could be transformed from craft to mass production using the same work force and machinery by an efficient division of the task into eighteen separate operations. This increased the number of pins made from a few hundred to 48,000. Such massive returns on investment triggered the Industrial Revolution and later Taylor's 'scientific management'. Henry Ford added the idea of a moving assembly line and true volume production was then possible along an almost continuous process.

Taylor recommended a vertical separation between workers and management, the former paid on piecework rates, while the latter developed continuous improvements. Such a system existed in production facilities in the UK car industry until the mid – 1970s when measured Day work replaced piecework, but vertical divisions remain, even where teamwork is advocated, though empowerment has removed some barriers to workforce-based creativity.

Such moves were necessary as volume production was often of low quality, resulting in re-work and waste. The Japanese experience, using 'quality gurus' from USA, highlighted the outmoded production systems which relied on high stock levels, were often unbalanced resulting in work-in-progress excesses, and in which employees who made the product had no responsibility for quality, only for volume.

Production systems moved to decrease stocks by the **Kanban method**, to devolve quality to groups of workers (via Quality Circles) or to individuals (via Total Productive Maintence), and to involve those worker in decision-making through Autonomous Groupworking, and representation at senior management meetings. Continuous improvement ('Kaizen') became a method of quality control and enhancement, involving employees both directly and by wider decision-making task forces or scheduled cross-functional meetings ('ringi – Ko').

While taking both suppliers and customers for granted was even implicit in **Porter's value chain**, modern production departments devote resources to both the supply chain management and to customer focus groups which assist in designing the product itself. Current manufacturing firms aim to introduce new products more quickly than competitors, resulting in 'time-based competition' which gains competitive advantage. Wide product ranges require quick-change set ups of machines and labour, the latter becoming both flexibly employed (e.g. temporary or part-time contracts) and multi-skilled: a far cry from Henry Ford's River Rouge plant where he had to double the daily pay to attract workers, so vile were the conditions.

25   MANAGEMENT ACCOUNTANT

(a)   **Management role**

Management is not an activity that exists in its own right. It is really a description of a variety of activities carried out by those members of organisations whose role is that of a manager - having formal responsibility for the work of at least one other person in the organisation.

Management as a description of its activities

The activities of managers have generally been grouped in terms of:

- planning;
- organising
- motivating
- communicating
- controlling.

They do not depict the full account of what constitutes management but they are a convenient way of describing the key aspects of the work of managers in practice.

Activities of management accountants

We can discuss the relationship between management accounting and these key activities of managers by comparing the activities performed in general by management accountants. A recent survey suggests that these activities include the following:

- Interpretation and management of accounts and cash flows - this involves the analysis and allocation of costs.
- Managing and organising others in the finance function.
- Operations planning, budgeting and budgetary control.
- Investment appraisal - involving analysis of funds before they are committed to projects and advising on operational decisions, programmes and projects;
- The design, development and operation of financial and management information systems.

Type, size, level and structure of organisation

As with any other role in an organisation, there will be variations due to the type of industry and size of business that the management accountant is employed in, the level at which he or she operates and the structure of the company (divisional, functional or a matrix combination). The amount of time and effort devoted to each of these activities by a particular management accountant will vary according to these factors.

Relationship between management accounting and the key activities of management

- **Planning in the longer term** - the management accountant helps to formulate plans for the future by providing information that will help managers in the various functional areas to decide what products to sell, what markets to enter and at what prices and to evaluate proposals for capital expenditure.
- **Planning in the short term** - the management accountant makes a contribution in the budgeting process by providing data on past performance as a guide to future performance. By establishing budget procedures and timetables, the management accountant also co-ordinates the short-term plans from all the various functions or sections of the business, so that they are in harmony with

each other. This is achieved by assembling all the various plans into an overall plan (master budget) for the business as a whole.

- **Organising** - the management accountant will often be included in the management team to advise on the kind of organisational structure that will be most useful for the development of an internal reporting system.

- **Motivating** - management accountants play an important role in the motivation process using budget and performance reports. Because budgets represent targets, they can be used to motivate people to improve their performance, if they are used carefully. They are designed to do this by communicating performance information in relation to targets set. The management accountant may also advise on incentive schemes and their likely impact on labour costs

- **Communicating** - by advising on how to install an effective communication and reporting system, the management accountant assists in the organisation's communication process. When communicating budgetary information, an effective reporting system enables budget plans to be conveyed to functional managers, as well as providing feedback at various times to show whether or not the departments concerned are within budget. As a communicator, the management accountant has a role to play in educating functional managers in the ways that financial information can help them in the fulfilment of their duties as managers of the various functions, whether in marketing, R&D, production, distribution or after-sales service.

- **Controlling** - management accountants assist in the control process by providing performance reports that compare actual outcomes with planned outcomes for each of the business area functions or responsibility centres. Using the management-by-exception process, a manager's attention is drawn to particular activities that do not conform to agreed budget limits or to planning targets. This type of control activity frees managers from unnecessary concern with those operations that are sticking to agreed limits and plans.

(b)   Many of the roles in an enterprise are changing because of changes in the business environment, associated changes in organisations and developments in information technology. The role of the management accountant is at the forefront of these changes.

Key forces driving the changes

The key drivers of change in management accounting include:

- globalisation and internationalisation;

- changes in the business environment;

- organisational restructuring;

- communications; and

- information technology.

There are other trends, which must be considered eg,

- quality and continuous-improvement initiatives - including the spread of accounting knowledge amongst an increasing number of managers;

- outsourcing - of routine accounting transactions,

- new management accounting techniques eg, activity-based costing, benchmarking, business process re-engineering and the 'balanced scorecard';

- developments in the education and training of accountants. and the spread of accounting knowledge amongst an increasing number of managers.

How the role of the management accountant is changing

The major changes to the management accounting role arising from these drivers include:

Globalisation and internationalisation – where management accountants are employed in global organisations they need to be more involved with the provision of information on the activities on a world basis, reporting on matters that affect the organisation in other countries. Details of the basis of trading with foreign countries, such as fluctuations in exchange rates, political payments at home and abroad, labour policies on pay and pension schemes as well as policies on safety, health and green issues, must be accounted for.

Changes in the business environment – it is crucial that the organisation interacts effectively and efficiently with its external environment. To achieve this, chief executives need better advice in an increasingly turbulent and uncertain environment and they are encouraging management accountants to take a more proactive strategic role in business decision-making. Crafting strategy involves:

- managing stability
- detecting discontinuity
- knowing the business
- managing patterns
- reconciling change

The organisation's management information system must be flexible enough to enable the management accountant to use the financial models to describe the effect of emergent strategies. Developments in both the education and training of management accountants and the number of new management accounting techniques are providing the means to enable accountants to meet these demands.

Environmental concerns and the demands of corporate governance are also increasing the requirements for management accountants to provide new types of information for a wider range of stakeholders. There are always pressure groups representing the public's concern about something eg, GM products, the treatment of waste and the safety procedures and safety records of companies.

Information technology – the development of accounting software packages, allowing easier collection, storing, manipulation and accessing of financial data, has led to a reduction in the importance of some of the traditional contributions of management accountants eg, measuring and reporting costs and performance. This data is more accessible to managers, who are themselves now much better educated, both in accounting matters and in the use of IT, than they were in the past. However, the widespread use of management information systems allows accountants to conduct sensitivity analysis, improving their ability to carry out their analytical tasks more efficiently and to present relevant and timely information to managers.

Communications – developments in IT have also made location of the management accounting function less important than in the past. The use of electronic data transmission means that accounting transactions can be carried out at more remote and cheaper locations than major cities. Some large companies have taken advantage of these developments and outsourced their routine transactions, either in-house or to service centres.

26   SEGMENTING

(a)   Market segmentation is a scientific, rational process of trying to match the needs of specific groups of customers with the organisation's products and services.

The idea is that different groups in society have different needs, aspirations, statuses etc and that even a humble product like a bar of soap possesses different 'meanings' for the different groups.

The advantages for firms marketing efforts are many:

Firstly, the same product can be advertised in different media to target different customer groupings-trade journals for professionals, leisure magazines for general customers, local newspapers for local clients, websites for international buyers and so forth. This may be expensive (in time and money) but should increase sales to offset costs.

Secondly, product packaging and branding can be changed to represent different products for differing segments. Expensive wrapping using gold and black can change the 'meaning' or status of the soap bar to move it 'up-market'. This need not be expensive, especially if the only thing that changes is the name. Some car companies use the same body or engine but brand the car differently-the manufacturers' name and model name are changed.

Thirdly, the actual product can be altered or enhanced to suit the needs of different customer groups. This is an expensive option involving re-design and production re-tooling and should be part of ongoing development.

Thus, the advantages are in the efficiency and accuracy of the marketing plan and the increased returns to investment as against a 'one size fits all' undifferentiated strategy.

(b)   Three variables of the clothing market would be:

(i)   Gender - males and females have very different requirements and view clothes differently in terms of their perception of the 'meaning' these generate to others-male 'fashion' is virtually non-existent.

(ii)   Age - within the gender category, there are clear differences with regard to age-for example school uniforms or general school wear for secondary school age children; young people's leisurewear; older people's formal/business attire and leisurewear. Size also varies with age and so it is essential in clothing to differentiate by age.

(iii)   Lifestyle - under the age category, leisurewear is more common for those not in work. Between 20 and 60 both men and women who work require more formal outfits and a greater number of these than children or retired people.

In terms of the paint manufacturer, these are two variables that can be used to segment the market:

(i)   **End-user**: some businesses are virally wholesalers and supply the general public, so these would require more stylish tins with colour charts and advice leaflets. Other businesses are strictly 'trade' and would require a narrower range without the enhancements.

(ii)   **Size:** a big customer would require large batches with quantity discounts, a special salesperson allocated to them etc. A small high-street trader would require only occasional visits by a representative, but might need help merchandising/displaying the paints effectively. There would be hundreds of these and so a dedicated service would not be feasible – re-ordering would be made easier for the small trader for example.

27   COMPANY Y

Key answer tips

The circumstances described in the question would seem to indicate that the product division structure would be the most appropriate as the company has become diverse. This is the approach followed through in this answer, though if you had selected a matrix or a hybrid structure you would still have gained marks.

(a)   In most manufacturing companies with a functional structure, operations are typically divided into the following functions:

- Production

- Sales and marketing

- Finance

- Research and development

- Personnel

This structure ensures that specialists in each area are grouped together in functional departments and report to a functional manager. This tier of management then reports to the owner or the most senior manager. In a **single product manufacturer**, therefore, the structure works well. Decisions as to how the product should be marketed and sold are straightforward for instance, and depend simply upon the characteristics of the one product and the one market. The departments can be interdependent and the major decisions can be taken by the person in overall charge if there is disagreement.

However, when a company becomes involved in the **manufacture of multiple products** this simple structure can become unwieldy, with a lack of coordination and scheduling. Each functional department will continue to focus on its particular area of expertise without reference to the fact that choices may need to be made for the benefit of the organisation as a whole. This can lead to conflict. For example, the Sales and Marketing department may be aware that Product X needs to be manufactured in preference to Product Y, but because the manager of the Production department finds Product Y easier to manufacture there may be disagreement. Similarly, the marketing of Product X may require different types of employees than the ones currently employed, yet the Personnel department may be unaware of this, or may be unwilling to get involved.

An additional problem in multi-product organisations such as Company Y is that the costs to be attributed to each product in the portfolio may be difficult to identify except for the straightforward raw materials and production time costs, as the overheads in the support functions may be difficult to allocate.

(b)   Company Y has grown due to both internal growth and acquisition. It now has many products and diverse markets. The latter point in particular suggests that the functional structure will not be sustainable, as it is very possible that the acquisitions have different structures which may not be adaptable.

The most obvious structure to be adopted by Y is a product division structure. This would involve setting up a number of autonomous divisions, each of which has the full set of functional departments as listed in part (a), with managers who are totally focussed on the one product/market area, reporting to one manager and supported by specialist functions as required. Each division will stand or fall on its own financial success and will develop its own means of competitive advantage.

How far this process should be taken depends obviously on the nature of the products and markets. However if, for instance, Company Y includes both retail fashion and gas turbine production, the two divisions will encounter totally different products, markets, personnel, technology and financial considerations. There is thus little scope for either division dovetailing to any degree, so they should be completely stand-alone.

The **advantages of a product division** structure are as follows:

- The financial viability of each division is easy to evaluate

- Problem areas in each division can be identified quickly

- The response of each division to changes in its environment can be speedy because all its managers are focussed purely on that environment

- The strategy for the division can be decided without reference to the needs and activities of the other divisions

- Managers learn how to coordinate all the functions of the division to achieve the division's desired aim

- As divisional managers are held accountable for the profitability of their own division, the product division structure provides good training for future senior managers of the group as a whole

- The senior managers of the group have flexibility in terms of divestment and investment. Selling off a division is quite straightforward as it does not impact on the operations of the other divisions. Acquiring a new division does not require reorganisation of the existing ones.

The product division structure therefore seems to be the most appropriate form for Company Y, unless the products and markets that the company has become engaged in are all related to each other in some way. If this is the case, then a matrix structure might be considered whereby, for instance, the group support functions report to, say, the production functions of each division. Similarly, a hybrid structure may be appropriate

(c) The **product division structure may not be the most effective** for the following reasons:

- There will be a considerable duplication of effort and resources in that Company Y will have several support functions such as Finance and Personnel across the divisions. This means that many of the advantages of increased scale of operations are lost

- Production resources will not be used in the most efficient way. For example, idle machine time in Division A could be used by Division B if they were not separated by the structure adopted. Economies of scale in purchasing and logistics will also not be exploited

- The separation of the divisions could become a source of competitiveness between them which means that the managers may become focussed purely on the day to day results that they are producing, so as to 'beat' the other divisions

- The very precise way in which the divisions' results can be evaluated may also create this sort of short term thinking, in that managers become discouraged from investing for the future in favour of 'good' results in the short term.

28   C PHARMACEUTICAL COMPANY

Key answer tips

(a)   Straightforward justicfication of purchasing which most students would gain most of the 10 marks on.

(b)   More difficult reflection on how creativity is influenced by structure, reward systems, culture etc. So long as several elements are included, reasonable marks for this part should be attainable.

(a)   Purchasing has always been necessary and as such perhaps has been a 'Cinderella' department until quite recently. Porter's use of the **value-chain concept** and the emulation to some extent of the Japanese prime-and-contracting (core/periphery) strategy has put purchasing – or procurement – at the forefront of strategy in manufacturing. In tertiary sectors of the economy however it has far less importance as raw materials are not important in the value-chain. In the primary sector of extraction (as opposed to agriculture and fisheries) purchasing of essential commodities is more a political and strategic function. This is because the raw materials are simply vital for the survival of mineral, oil and chemicals, among many others. In food processing as well there is a global trade in agricultural 'futures' – buying future crops of coffee and rubber.

The major accounting basis for the importance of purchasing lies in the simple difference between gross sales and net income. A saving of £10K in purchasing is a real saving in case; a generation of £10K's worth of sales however is a gross measure and with margins of 10%-20% most firms would net only £1,000-£2,000 for each £10K of sales.

Where purchasing contributes in manufacturing is the ability to use the specialist markets of contractors to outsource heavily-loaded actives and so clear overhead. This demands high levels of skill in assessing tenders and structuring contracts with 'credible commitments' to ensure the compliance of supplies.

(b)   CPC seem to have an inappropriate, Taylorist, system which works reasonably well when the work is not self-paced – though it still has its problems of morale. In R&D however, the culture is more like a **'star'** system – a person culture – which relies on the self-paced work of technicians. These people are motivated by self-esteem needs more than safety and security under Maslow's hierarchy. They therefore need, as Burns and Stalker noted in their book *The Management of Innovation* (1961), a more organic than mechanistic structure.

The form of structure defines the form of control; organic ones concentrate on **Mintzberg's** 'standardisation of norms' rather than of inputs, outputs or direct supervision. Clearly CPC staff have slowed down the pace of their work – in terms at least of the pace of innovation as measured by the number of new drugs developed.

To re-evaluate those staff we need first to discuss Dr Strong, as not only is he/she incapable of operating in another area, it will send a positive signal to staff that senior management treat their morale as a very serious matter. Subsequently an OD approach could be used to develop the idea of staff for methods of organising the work of the R&D unit. This will avoid the NIH 'not invented here syndrome and **use Kotter and Schlesinger's** 'involvement and participation' strategy.

Probably what will emerge will be a matrix–like structure based on important projects – these being the basis of teams, AWG's (autonomous working groups). The career progression and status needs of the scientists will need close question on a team structure often tends to make individual contributions rather anonymous. A service-based increment system, or a democratic voting procedure might be used amongst these professionals to highlight individual contributions. Support for research papers could offer a similar solution.

HUMAN RESOURCE MANAGEMENT

29   HR PLANNING

Key answer tips

(a)   A simple answer, but ensure enough detail is given for the full 10 marks.

(b)   Split into: problems of HR planning and solutions.

(a)   **HR planning** is the new name for the process which used to be called manpower planning. It followed a set routine when organisations existed in fairly simple, stable environments. Nowadays the idea of planning has become more flexible and plans more integrated into strategy.

The HR plan should begin with an **analysis of the current state of the business** and so should be strategic. If there are changes planned, especially to strategic direction, then technical expertise and managerial or marketing skills may be needed which are new to the organisation, or as additional measures to an existing department. Thus, the first stage is an estimate of future needs in terms of skills and numbers, including retirements and labour turnover rates.

Given this, the organisation may look to current employees - under a training and development plan perhaps - to see if the needs can be staffed internally from promotions and/or training. Any movements here create knock-on effects where departments have to release staff to new ventures - these need to be assessed in terms of disruption to current activities.

An **assessment is then made of the external recruitment** market for the staff required: at the senior level especially the use of Agencies including 'headhunters' is a common way of speeding up this assessment.

Finally a **plan is drawn up** which indicates the key inflows and outflows, new positions being created and approved and job descriptions and person specifications written so as to facilitate recruitment advertising.

This is often not an exact science and most large organisations recruit a general intake of trainees each year to allow for 'natural wastage'. These include apprentices, university graduates, and technical and administration trainees.

Nowadays the use of government training schemes is a way of staffing-up in the short term, and provides a pool of labour familiar with the organisation which can be used to fill permanent vacancies.

(b)   The increasing complexity and instability of environmental forces has created the problem of forecasting for firms.

Many have moved away from quantitative techniques towards qualitative approaches such as building up scenarios of possible alternative futures.

Also, because of uncertain skill needs, firms are looking to use the flexible labour markets where available, and general sources of intelligent labour to create development systems. Here, the adaptability of existing staff through training and on-the-job development assignments can mitigate against future emergencies.

Building-up skills however creates marketable staff and so thought has to be given to motivating retention and loyalty on deferred - reward schemes such as pensions, service-related-pay, benefits and so on.

30 HOW TO DEAL WITH REDUNDANCY

Key answer tips

(a)   Remember 'major issues' – do not list everything – try the STEP factors.

(b)   More open question about methods. As there may be 1 or 2 marks for each method, a list may be adequate.

(a)   This situation is the worse of both worlds from a planning viewpoint as each alternative presents different options.

       If the organisation is closing temporarily, then it will need to keep records of the staff it loses so as to offer them work when trading volumes rise. Of course, those with poor records may not be offered re-employment but these staff need to be identified before the redundancy exercise commences. If a total closure is possible, then staff will not be re-employed and the important issue is to retain the goodwill in the community or nationally.

       The organisation must first decide what the loss of business actually involves. It may be that one main section is affected or that cost-cutting is the main reason and this may be achieved by overall reductions of, say, 20%. Alternatively, indirect labour could be cut by more than the direct workforce so as to keep customers satisfied.

       Given the numbers of staff and their locations have been ascertained, the issue of fair selection is paramount. Even if volunteers are called for, the organisation may not want to lose certain categories, especially if the reductions are short-term. Consultation with staff and/or with recognised trade unions may help identify and communicate the various criteria for selection. Often, LIFO (last-in-first-out) will operate but this is not essential. Next, the organisation may need to identify timings and select those who go first. It will also need to calculate redundancy or severance pay and notify Government agencies etc.

(b)   The process can be made easier in several ways. One of the easiest is to ensure the financial package is perceived as generous - negotiating with the Trade Unions will assist here. Other policies may include limiting the numbers- by banning recruitment, cutting overtime, encouraging early retirement, writing good references for potential leavers, terminating contracts of agency temps, part-time or ancillary workers, re-arranging work tasks and offering alternative employment. Frequently volunteers are called for and their package enhanced. Also, a good length of time prior to the actual dismissals is often used to enable staff to find alternative employment locally or nationally

31 RECRUITMENT: TWO-WAY SELECTION

Key answer tips

(a)   Split into 2 sections, benefits to organisations and benefits to applicants. Remember to highlight only 'benefits'.

(b)   Consider whether IT experience is also required - Consider the factors under Rodgers 7 point plan, or Munro-Fraser's 5 point plan.

(a)   **Selection** is the choosing from a number of candidates the one most suitable for a specified position. This means using methods to find out if candidates have the required knowledge, skills and aptitudes. The process continues with the selection interviews to make the actual choice and the introduction of the new recruit to the organisation to ensure that they start with enthusiasm and settle down quickly. This selection process can be very costly; not only are there the cash payments for recruitment agents, advertising and relocation, but there is also the opportunity cost of interviewing, effort and induction programmes. Unfortunately, many new appointments turn out to be failures, because one or other of the parties is dissatisfied. For the organisation, the cost of getting it wrong can be even more daunting than the joint costs of recruitment and the salary paid to the employee. At the same time, a recruitment error can be damaging to the employee concerned.

If the organisation views the **selection process as a two-way exercise**, it should help to reduce the number of recruitment errors and assist in the development of best practice in managing the recruitment and selection process. It is important that the potential recruit sees an honest picture of the job, the workplace and the organisation in general before being asked to join the organisation. The candidate should also be encouraged to be equally open in the interests of avoiding a painful mistake. An organisation that has a developed a user-friendly recruitment and selection approach will generally attract, and possibly also retain, better candidates and build a better reputation for its enlightened treatment of people.

(b)   The main problems involved with all types of specification are **detail and flexibility**. Some writers feel that over-specification is as bad as being too vague, in that too detailed a specification may be aimed at the ideal candidate who just does not exist; it may, therefore, prove to be too limiting in the recruitment and selection exercise. Probably the most appropriate policy is to apply a detailed specification with a certain degree of flexibility. Several classifications have been produced, the most famous of which is undoubtedly the Seven Point Plan devised by Alec Rodger in the 1950s. This is a checklist of points about what the job entails and the kind of person they should be looking for.

Category	Job	Individual
Physical make up	The job does not involve physical strain. It is not fatiguing, nor is it carried out under trying conditions	Reasonably good health but not a relevant issue for this type of job.
Attainments	A reasonably high standard of general education with some previous experience. CIMA member preferable.	Membership of CIMA or another accredited accountancy body would be desirable. A period of relevant experience in a similar post. Proven competence in a similar computer industry.
General intelligence	Reasonable degree of intelligence.	(Possibly) good to high intelligence which is implied by having required attainments.
Special aptitudes	An understanding of modern costing techniques, computer systems, and modern software packages - especially spreadsheets. Sufficiently motivated to work on their own, and to be accurate in the technical aspects. Competence and confidence in individual and team interaction and in explaining arguments. Ability to handle both routine work and the cope with the unexpected.	Experience in modern costing techniques, preferably using spreadsheets and computerised systems. Flexibility, tenacity and a team approach are also important as is an interest in the computer sector.
Interests	No special requirements in social, practical, intellectual or physical activities	
Disposition	Easily acceptable to other people, steady and reliable	Fulfils requirements
Circumstances	May need to travel, undertake further training.	Ambitious for personal and professional growth

32   RECRUITMENT

Key answer tips

(a)   Simple question – but note it is not about selection, only recruitment.

(b)   A more tricky question about selection – define 'selection' and analyse the problems.

(a)   The standard procedure is to first obtain an agreed vacancy: in some firms nowadays the first question after receiving a resignation is not 'where do we get a replacement from' but 'do we need to replace?' If there is a need, then the process should begin by reassessing the job and person description to see if it is current - and if not, altering the duties and/or the qualifications or skills in the person specification. This may be best done by the incumbent who has just resigned, with his or her supervisor.

From here, many firms create **internal job advertisements** first, which go up on notice-boards ahead of any external advertisement. Indeed in some cases, either from experience or from a formal development plan, there is no perceived need to advertise externally: internal candidates may even be identified straight away (such as the incumbent's deputy or assistant) and interviewed. In many cases there may be no competitive interview - just an appointment.

Where time is of the essence, media such as agencies and 'head-hunters' may be used, perhaps to fill the position on a temporary basis. Simultaneously, depending on the level of the job and the expert of the perceived labour market, local newspapers and magazines, TV and radio and the Government Employment Agencies can be used to advertise. National jobs markets require advertisements in trade publications, quality daily papers and Sunday newspapers.

Attracting a good field of candidates is often seen as essential and a 'long list' of people who match the criteria can then be whittled down to a 'short-list' either by a paper-sift looking for the best-qualified, or by preliminary interviews. Where there is a national recruitment for a major expansion (eg, in retail, hotel and catering, market research or sales) interviews can be held locally using hotels or conference centres.

Second or final interviews usually involve senior staff at a Head Office location and may be extended towards an assessment centre format where different skills of the applicant are tested and often an aptitude or personality test given.

(b)   At the stage of selection, the major problem is to find a way of ensuring the selected applicant will do a good job in the real world the firm operates in: this is called 'validity'. To make selection valid it should be as objective as possible, though this is reflected by how far the people the candidate has to work with actually **like** him or her. Thus 'fitting in' is subjective but should be considered an essential part of the process - introduction to colleagues and subordinates may pave the way for a more open relationship later.

Objectivity can be increased by involving several different interviewers (i.e. not one line manager), using the same job and person specification and a structured interview where more-or-less the same questions are asked. Interviewer bias should be circumvented by Panel Interviews and standardisation of questions. However, the use of an assessment centre approach brings in other skills - a group problem-solving exercise; a presentation; an in-tray exercise; a personality test. These are now marketed by major occupational psychologists and are becoming popular.

However, they are artificial. If a sales person has had several jobs with excellent results and does poorly on the selection process, does this mean that the process itself has not been pre-tested? This is the most common failing - the assumption that what you are testing really measures what it sets out to.

33 JOB DESCRIPTIONS AND PERSON SPECIFICATIONS

Key answer tips

Simple open question. Split into 2 sections, job description (what elements to advertise) and person specification (what attributes to advertise).

Lengthy description required under each (for 10 marks × 2).

Job descriptions (JD), though having some fairly simple and straightforward information about jobs often include quite profound and useful statements which can attract or repel applicants and so act as a filter in advertisements. Sometimes the job title itself is a key aspect - for instance **'Personnel Manager'** implies a rather old-fashioned organisation as HR Manager is more trendy.

'Personnel Services Manager' is apt to put off those aspiring graduates who do not want to be lumbered with a host of ancillary 'services' like security, canteen, cleaning contracts. Many JDs have a job purpose and can be usefully edited down to provide copy. Often, phrases like 'reporting to the MD you will be responsible for . . .' appear direct from the JD in the advert, followed by objectives, key tasks or duties. In some cases JDs include wage/salary ranges bonuses, overtime etc and describe the environment of the job including opportunities for development within the job, and/or its importance or stress level - such as at year-end or stock-taking. All of these contribute to succinct phrases in the final advert.

The personnel specification (PS) is developed from the JD, and nowadays the use of competence statements has added a more thorough and scientific dimension to the PS. Typically, in the past, the JD may have included desirable or essential qualities demanded of the applicant - probably for job evaluation purposes. Such attributes, like qualifications and experience, transfer easily to the PS, as do extensions of the phrases to do with temperament - creativity and stress - resistance for example. The PS can also be developed to include useful 'contra' indications' for the advert: such phrases as 'those currently earning less than £40K will probably not have the experience required' are occasionally seen and act as a filter. When listing attributes in a PS it is of course essential to avoid direct and indirect discrimination. Direct discrimination is fairly easy to spot, but some requirements like minimum height indirectly exclude more women than men. In the UK there are 'genuine occupational qualifications' in the legislation which do allow discrimination - such as recruiting an Asian waiter for an Indian restaurant - but these are not fixed and applicants can challenge them through Employment Tribunals.

Thus, the final advert may often be rather vague and most frequently paints a positive picture rather than a realistic one. For some reasons this is seen as necessary, even though it attracts the wrong type of applicant and leads to high expectations of what are quire often mundane and boring rules.

Even the location is glamorised, and can appear to sound like an Estate Agents blurbs. The best adverts are strictly factual, based on the JD and PS with salary range and benefits as attractors rather than phrases like 'a wonderful opportunity for a high-flier and located in the beautiful North West (near the Lake District)' which turns out to be a job introducing job evaluation into a factory in Carlisle.

34 MANAGEMENT DEVELOPMENT

Key answer tips

(a) A simple definition for only 4 marks is needed.

(b) Try to use major 'steps' rather than a list in the implementation of a management development system.

(a)   **'Management development'** has been defined as 'the progress a person makes in learning how to manage effectively' (Weitrich). However, as a system, management development is aimed at improving management effectiveness in all areas by a planned process of evaluation, training, experience and performance improvement.

Many reports in the past five years have shown that management in the UK lags behind our major competitors. It is calculated that Germany spends five times as much as the UK per head of management population.

(b)   The following steps could occur in a **typical management development programme**:

(i)   The organisation's strategic plan will identify corporate objectives for the next three or five years. This plan should be analysed in terms of manpower needs. A key part of this manpower plan will be the definition of management positions over the coming years. For example, consider a company planning to establish a manufacturing unit in Eastern Europe; the necessary management positions can be defined and a specification of skills and experience levels stipulated. The strategic plan together with the proposed organisation structure provides the basis for this schedule of management positions over the short and medium term and an outline for the longer term.

(ii)   Having defined the future needs, the next step could be to evaluate the existing management team. An analysis by skills, experience, age, promotability, past appraisals, career pattern etc, will provide categorisations which can be put alongside the future management schedule. It will be necessary to adjust the present management list for likely turnover for future years. Some turnover, such as retirements can be forecast accurately. Elsewhere, past statistics can be used to anticipate likely numbers leaving in main categories.

(iii)   Any specialist skills necessary should be highlighted for separate consideration. Where such skills/experience are rare, the organisation may seek to head hunt selected individuals rather than issue a general advertisement.

(iv)   By matching the adjusted basis of present management people against the expected management needs of the future, a gap will emerge. The organisation is now in a position to state the number of managers at particular levels of skill and experience that will need to be developed to fill these gaps. Some general principles will be established as guidelines eg, younger understudying older, minimum three people identified as development for any management position.

(v)   To close the gap, individual managers will need to be developed through training, selective experience, project work etc, whilst other positions will need to be filled through recruitment.

The training section will devise specific individual training programmes where necessary. These may overlap, or form part of, general training courses aimed at developing management effectiveness overall. Also selected periods of experience will be prescribed to develop and test potential of individuals. For example, any individual manager being considered for a senior position in an international company must have spent a successful period as a manager abroad. Appraisal of individual performance will form a key part of the development exercise and an accelerated appraisal scheme may be introduced for the management stream, whereby appraisals are undertaken frequently, not just annually. Such appraisals may be incorporated in a Management by Objectives approach where applicable within an organisation.

(vi)   Recruitment of managers will be affected by the development programme. Shortage of time to fill a position, or disappointing appraisals, could lead an organisation to recruit to fill the gap. Some companies (eg Tesco, Marks and

Spencer) have a policy of strong internal management development; such companies are infrequent recruiters of established managers.

(vii) The success of a management development scheme can be measured by the simple test of 'did the organisation get the right person in the right job at the right time'. This is the fundamental test of success. However, the organisation will need to know that this has been achieved at a reasonable cost. It is therefore important to develop a set of objectives for Management Development section that link achievement with budget stages and that performance should be audited by a senior manager.

Note: that the question requires 'the steps than an organisation should take'. Therefore detailed discussions of individual management responses has only marginal relevance.

35   INFLUENCING BEHAVIOUR: LABOUR PRODUCTIVITY

Key answer tips

(a) Remember only 'major' factors required – Consider using the Hawthorne studies to exemplify your answer.

(b) A more technical question – but only 6 marks so be brief.

(a) **The major factors which affect labour productivity**

Increased productivity does not necessarily mean more production, but rather more efficient, cost-effective production. The same output with lower costs is just as much increased productivity as greater output without increasing the previous costs.

Many variables affect individual performance in any activity, particularly at work. Physical working conditions and the task itself are important, as are individually-oriented elements such as safety or monetary rewards. Many of the factors that motivate individuals to perform are social in nature eg, prestige or recognition, but motivation is not wholly, nor even primarily, an individual variable. Its force and direction are certainly functions of the social situation in which it arises and is exercised.

Another influence on performance is competition between one individual and another, or many others. Allport cites studies that compare an individual's normal solitary performance with his or her performance when other people are present. The results indicate that group situations produce a greater output of energy and achievement.

Productivity is also an important measure of managerial performance, which depends, in turn, on leadership effectiveness. In terms of human resources, there should be enough technical help for staff and supervision to enable coaching. Individuals should be properly trained and not switched from inappropriate areas of work to respond to peaks in production.

Although labour productivity is based mainly on human factors, as the task becomes standardised, the human influence becomes less important than the non-human factors. Hence, in rather ill-defined, white-collar jobs, much emphasis is placed on human factors, whereas in blue-collar jobs, working is paced by the environment, not the operator, so productivity is based on delays between component operations. Looking at both the human and non-human factors, the way that they affect productivity is outlined below.

Human factors

- The ability and intelligence of the person is critical where productivity is concerned. It may depend on whether the individual is capable of learning the job or on whether training has been able to capitalise on the current skill/ability level.

- The complexity involved in motivating people and tapping latent talent arises because of the many factors that are involved. Managers may consider Maslow's higher order needs such as esteem and self actualisation, but they cannot ignore physiological, security and social needs.

- Managers can emphasise motivators such as the work itself, accomplishment and recognition but cannot ignore Herzberg's hygiene factors such as pay, supervision and working conditions.

- Both intrinsic and extrinsic rewards are important, but they have differential impact. Some individuals will perform better with increased responsibility while others would rather have more pay.

- Expectancy theory argues that productivity has to be seen as a path to valued goals. Behaviour depends on the outcomes that an individual values, and the expectation that a particular type of behaviour will lead to those outcomes. The theory states that if a person needs more money, and expects to be given more for working hard, then the individual will decide to work hard.

Other factors

- Job design can influence the outcomes that an individual values. The task should be possible and the job's sub-tasks well-designed.

- The system must be able to provide appropriate work on time with raw material input of sufficient quality to enable the job holder to get on with his/her job.

- The financial resources should be available for proper equipment, training and reward systems.

- Tasks which are urgent tend to attract more status and supervisory effort, and frequently produce a resultant pride and feeling of importance for operators.

(b)　The relationship between labour productivity and the difficulty of achieving budget

Individuals and sections in an organisation can be given financial targets to guide their performance. These targets may concern the level of expenditure that the section has, the level of costs incurred or the level of sales volume to be achieved in a month. Production budgets may involve non-financial standards such as labour hours used, machine downtime, materials used and waste materials.

Expense items may be easier to target and monitor, but the elimination of waste and the control of quality demand significant contributions from all levels of staff. The achievement of budget targets for expense on the one hand, and sales on the other, is closely related, not only to the closeness of management control, but also to the efforts of the people involved in the process. The theories of Herzberg and Maslow give useful pointers towards what might motivate. Herzberg's motivators include achievement and challenge, while Maslow cites status/acceptance by peers as a strong influence. At lower levels both include the notion of basic economic forces as requiring to be satisfied.

Budgets need to be set which are public, and to which clear status rewards are attached as well as economic ones. Also, they will need to be challenging while not set so high as to be seen as unrealistic.

Setting expectations is the job of management, while monitoring performance and coaching employees towards achieving those expectations is partly the role of the control systems and partly the role of supervisory management. Edward Lawler has argued that management control strategies can lead to rigid bureaucratic behaviour. The standards in the control process tell people what they have to do to perform well and maybe to get promoted. People then behave in this way and this may not be in the interests of the organisation as a whole. Lawler cites research in a shop which set sales targets and a pay incentive to reward staff according to the volume of sales they achieved. Staff were so busy grabbing sales that other essential tasks such as display work and stock checking were ignored. The control system did not set any standards for stock and display work, only for sales volume.

36   INFLUENCING BEHAVIOUR: REWARD SYSTEMS

Key answer tips

Simple question, best split into several 'main' features rather than a list.

On the assumption that people are at the lower levels of Maslow's hierarchy of needs (basic/physiological) and need money to buy food, the employment relationship is usually characterised by an economic exchange. This means pay for work done, although it is must be emphasised that vast numbers of people work as volunteers, by definition they must be in higher levels of **Maslow's hierarchy**. Clearly in a modern society they or their family must have income - part of an economic exchange somewhere in the background.

To attract people to do work, therefore, employers must provide an attractive reward package. This is a complex amalgam of affordability, perceived internal statuses and the needs of a variety of applicants. Unskilled applicants living with their parents near to the place of work have fewer needs that those with children living some distance away. The cost of working for some is greater than those afforded by state benefits - the 'poverty trap'.

Local labour markets vary with age as well as skills, as older workers often will have paid off debts in raising a family such as mortgages and their dependants may well also have left home. Nevertheless, psychological factors make it unlikely that older applicants will accept lower wages - nor can internal structures and relativities cope with volunteers or age-related pay in most organisations.

What occurs therefore is a hierarchy of jobs, rated in a job-evaluation scheme or by collective bargaining, or by a management 'remuneration committee'. These jobs are often grouped into a number of levels requiring similar levels of skills - for the sake of simplicity if nothing else.

Pay is then attached based on market rates (especially local union rates for skilled workers or minimum wage legislation). Internal relativities are then set - in some firms, supervisors are automatically paid 10% more than those they supervise. For clerical and managerial jobs, skills develop in the job and are paid in a **progression of increments, rate-for-age scales** or **merit (performance-related) pay**. This usually involves a formal annual Appraisal of Performance.

Non-managerial jobs are very often hourly paid whereas managers receive an annual salary. In these cases, additional hours worked are voluntarily given and compensation at a higher rate is usually offered. This may be the hourly rate (time) and 25% - time and a quarter, or T + 50% - time and a half - with 2T double time - on days of rest, public holidays etc.

Further, some jobs attract bonuses or commission usually based on increased profitable sales, or production output. It is difficult to calculate the normal rates of performance above which bonuses are paid: **F W Taylor's scientific management** gave birth to a plethora of 'time and motion study' experts who measured effort and job difficulty to come to standard times. Sales managers are not fortunate and have to look into the future to estimate budgets and structure commission payments in excess of these. In Japan, profit-related-pay can account for up to one-third of earnings but in the UK it tends to be somewhat trivial, except in partnerships and professional firms (like solicitors).

Added to pay is a wide range of **non-incentive benefits from pensions**; through sick pay to expense allowances, even company cars, subsidised canteens and so on. The job of the 'compensation and benefits' manager becomes more complex daily.

37   TRAINING AND DEVELOPMENT STRATEGY

Key answer tips

(a)   Begin by discussing strategy, perhaps using Porter – low cost leadership and differentiation. These require different training and development policies.

(b)   Give a brief explanation of the psychological contract.

(a)   While there is a scientific and objective component **in training**, there are cultural and motivational aspects also. Traditionally training was geared to providing the technical skills needed for employees to perform their current and then subsequent jobs, often by way of apprenticeships or other traineeships. This was extended to personal 'process skills' such as time management or supervisory skills and added to by techniques such as quality control, health and safety issues and so on.

Development is usually a more general, long term activity combined with training but usually on-the-job in real time assignments. These may be sideways ('developmental assignments') gaining experience of other functions, or upwards (promotions) to gain supervisory or management experience. These are evaluated by Appraisals of Performance whereas training events may be evaluated by the participants rather than by trainers or the ultimate line manager of the participant. This is why training is often seen as an act of faith rather than a scientific way of increasing performance of individuals.

Increasingly, both activities serve higher goals. One is the visibility of training or development plans, the rise of 'development centres' akin to assessment centres, and the use of external qualifications. These serve to cement the relationship of individuals to corporate goals and to create a 'future reward' atmosphere of continued development of the individual. In-house MBAs are a good example.

More prosaically, a strategic, formal plan assists senior management in assessing the ability of the organisation to realise its strategic objectives. An expansion into Eastern Europe may look good on paper until the HR plan reveals a lack of expertise in the local culture and language of the target economies. Thus it can be adapted to provide a **strategic framework** for expansion and the essential need for succession planning.

Internally this process has a role in emphasising performance standards and changing the aspirations of employees. The need for professional qualifications such as CIMA can be formally programmed into the system; newsletters listing the exam successes of colleagues can emphasise the need for continual personal development - not necessarily funded by the organisation.

Externally, having 'kitemark' standards such as Investors In People status in the UK suggests the recruitment might be made easier, as reassurance of good treatment once employed. Similarly, internal schemes send out positive messages both to suppliers and customers and therefore may increase quality of supply and sales revenue. Figures show that 93% of top UK companies invest in training but 81% of the poor performers did nothing. This suggests a strong link between strategic success and HRD, though, as discussed above, there may not be a simple relationship.

(b) Induction training is very often seen as a one-day-event. It often covers essential form-filling, safety policies and procedures, and a tour of the organisation facilities and introduction to its personnel.

However, induction most importantly should set the level of expectation for the new recruit, emphasise managerial standards, inculcate the idea of excellence and loyalty rewarded by promotions and benefits. Actually, some of these elements are internalised from the organisation's PR, especially its recruitment advertising. They are deepened by the professionalism (or otherwise) of the selection process especially the interaction with the interviewers.

This process is important if new staff are not going to be subject to the underlying organisational culture which **Schein** uncovered - the local rituals of ways of working - which is independent of the corporate culture to which the management applies. Sociological studies of the world of work attest to the strength of conformity to norms of the work group - such as 'gold-bricking' or the restriction of output, absenteeism rates, attitudes to overtime and authority, and safety practices. All of these can be counter to organisational effectiveness - and even national competitiveness - so, induction of the most appropriate norms and values is a vital opportunity for management to claim the moral high ground and ultimate gains in effectiveness.

38   EXPLAIN THE PLANNING AND DELIVERY OF TRAINING COURSES

Key answer tips

This is a detailed question about formal off-the-job 'courses' so omit other types of training. Remember 'main' methods and remember it is only communication methods that are asked for, not evaluation or monitoring of training courses.

Most training courses still use the 'classroom' method which gives scale economies and is useful for imparting knowledge - if not skills.

Trainers traditionally used blackboard and chalk and then whiteboard and pen to put up the main points of their verbal presentation. Details however would need to be covered separately, usually by numbered handouts corresponding to each part of a presentation. These may well be attached within a specific folder produced in A4 with a logo and course name. Occasionally a course booklet, which might be a more professional, glossy affair, would be supplied.

In order to programme the training, many professionals began to use numbered overhead transparencies (OHTs) for use on an overhead projector (OHP). These could be hand-written onto acetate sheets, often with a stiff cardboard border, or printed so that they were permanent. By coding and numbering and ordering them in the trainer's own specific folder, these could be used time and again - for different courses if applicable and save preparation time and in-class writing time.

Where a standard format across an organisation was required - such as a Pension Plan or car launch presentation, slide/tape shows became popular. Here specially produced 35mm slides were taken of the OHTs and linked to a commentary produced centrally. In some instances, a script was produced instead for the local trainer or manager to read, giving the impression these were his/her own words. The advent of better computer hardware and software led to the electronic presentation of slides via a laptop and projector. These did not need to be printed off beforehand and could be sent electronically to delegates by email.

Where the classroom situation needed to be broken up into 'syndicate' or group work, the flip-chart was developed. These were essentially easels to which a wad of large paper sheets could be clipped - and plastic strips, like picture-rails, developed for management centres enabled the individual sheets to be inserted for display. The syndicates worked separately on a problem then returned to a 'plenary' session with their notes written in large letters on flip-chart sheets to discuss with the other syndicates. The flip-chart paper could easily be rolled-up and carried and so many itinerant trainers, this was used instead of a cumbersome white board for making presentations - such as in the franchises of car manufacturers where space and equipment was limited or absent.

To apply the ideas and genius of the presenter, a range of dry-wipe, semi-permanent and permanent marker pens (felt-tipped) was developed: and even light-pens. Lasers were used to point, by a spot of light, the emphatic words of the presenter and demonstrate a commitment to hi-tech training.

39   EVALUATE A TYPICAL APPRAISAL

Key answer tips

(a)   A simple question needing discussion on the process (and pros and cons) of appraising performance.

(b)   A more tricky question linking appraisal to reward, but only 8 marks so some general points should score marks.

(a)   The informal process of appraisal is constant: we are evaluating ourselves and others while at work, often unconsciously. The formal process however aims to orientate this appraisal to goals and objectives set by the organisation and to make it free of bias and subjectivity.

Traditionally, performance has been appraised by output-piecework and other **payment-by-results systems** (PBR systems) merely counted the number of items produced by the employee, often irrespective of merit. This same process is with us today in the ratings (viewing figures) of TV and radio audiences, newspaper circulation etc. With work organisations however, attempts have been made to move away from output-maximisation to norms of output consistent with quality. This led to standard times for jobs which replaced PBR in the UK car industry by measured day work - MDW. More recently **Management by Objectives** (MBO) attempted to measure intangible outputs as well as tangible ones by combining ratings for loyalty, innovativeness, management expertise etc with sales results. The pursuit of performance-related-pay (PRP) stems from the widespread application of measurement of individuals from easily-quantifiable sales jobs to less-easily categorised positions in nursing or the Inland Revenue.

Who does the measuring can be as important as objective measures. Traditionally the immediate supervisor or manager would appraise a subordinate's performance annually. With 180o feedback this meant the process was two-way - a mutual investigation of the way results were achieved rather than the results themselves. Further refinement as in Tesco required $360°$ feedback which brought in the views of colleagues and/or customer departments. At the same time, measures moved from external verifiable data to internal 'competences' or skills, and the attempt to link all jobs - even manual ones - to PRP followed a trend identified as 'financial flexibility' by **Atkinson.**

This movement - heavily bureaucratic - is intended to produce more effective organisational performance by introducing the idea of individual accountability. It does however seem to run counter to the introduction to teamworking and group technology initiatives which stress the interaction of individual skills in group settings. This can be rationalised through an internal competency - based appraisal of an individual's contribution to the group, as opposed to the traditional output measures, which are now applied to the group or cell.

(b)   The relationship to pay follows the scheme of **Fombrun et al's 'performance cycle'** where reward is simply a product of performance or achievement. In the simple PBR case, each item of output has a price - £0.1 per nail; £4 per square metre painted etc. Even here of course a shortage of supplies can lead to low wages rather than any fault of the operator. MDW and other schemes pay rates for bands of performance above the 'norm' and in salary progression for staff these may represent 'increments' along a spine. A more flexible system is merit pay expressed as a percentage of basic pay. These appraisals therefore put an additional strain on the process because they have financial impacts. They may also have positive or negative impacts on future prospects, training plans and promotions all of which carry an economic reward or penalty in the longer term. For this reason many organisations perceive appraisal more as a developmental process, an end-point in time of a continuous coaching activity, geared to individual goals but not specifically to rewards and punishments as such.

That many PRP schemes have proved not only ineffective but counter-productive to effectiveness has questioned the link from vaguely determined performance to a very precise pay packet figure. Especially as Director remuneration linked to overall organisational performance seems to be out of control, HR functions are having to re-appraise appraisal.

40   APPRAISAL AND REWARD

Key answer tips

A detailed question about the link between personal appraisal and reward requires discussion on:

- formal systems of evaluation, i.e. appraisals

- formal systems of reward, e.g. scales/career development plans.

Appraisal of performance sits in the centre of Devanna et al's 'HR cycle' which begins with recruitment. For these HRM theorists, the performance of individuals is a crucial need in order to 'cascade upwards' to the ultimate performance and competitive advantage of the organisation. The appraisal then leads to training and/or reward systems - though sometimes a poor appraisal will lead in the opposite direction - to discipline and possibly dismissal on the grounds of capability.

The 'positive' **Devanna cycle** is an optimistic forward-looking model based on motivation. Though motivation exists primarily in the job, theorists recognise that, for most people, an economic element is essential - if only for survival. Maslow saw this at the bottom of his needs hierarchy and Hertzberg described the meeting of these basic needs as 'hygiene'. As the HR department has little influence on job design, and so job satisfaction and motivation within the job, its role is concentrated into organisation-wide systems.

Formal appraisals of performance usually take place annually between the supervisor (or their boss) and the worker. These are changing to include team appraisal, $180°$ (by worker on boss) and $360°$ (involving colleagues) but the mainstay of the HR planning system is still the practical annual appraisal. Possibly generated by objectives, occasionally by a formal system such as MBO **(Management By Objectives)**, performance of the worker is reviewed by the manager under a number of headings. From this two systems usually come into play from the Devanna model: training and reward. **Training needs** are usually identified from deficiencies in performance, occasionally there are forward-training opportunities e.g, for new legislation about to come in, or for assisting the worker in obtaining a promotion. **Reward systems** are usually based in the first instance on job-evaluation, and occasionally an appraisal results in an upgrading, or the identification of the need to re-evaluate the current position. More often, appraisals are coded numerically or alphabetically into grades to which percentage pay rises are attached. The appraisee who meets requirements but no more should receive a modest increase, which the majority of staff also receive. High performers, if not promoted as well, should receive exceptional increases – in comparison with poor performers. This set of information goes forward under the salary budget into a salary plan. The levels are reviewed by the board and amended or approved. Amendments might occur where a pattern of over-or under-appraisals is perceived within a department or section. Individuals who performed exceptionally last year but not this are also scrutinised by aware HR staff to see if a change of manager could be de-motivating these key staff.

Finally, the plan is set in motion to produce salary increases at certain times for the individuals concerned. To spread the load, some organisations use quarter-days in the year and assign individuals to the one nearest their recruitment date. This also smoothes cashflow.

41 DISMISSAL, RETIREMENT, REDUNDANCY

Key answer tips

An open question about leaving both planned (fixed-term contracts, retirement) and unplanned (turnover, dismissals). Consider the issue of redundancy which can be either planned or unplanned.

Planned leaving normally refers in the HR plan to retirements at the state retirement age. An age profile of current employees is easily built up and scheduled retirements each year can be filled in quite automatically so that future demand can be anticipated and recruitment planned for. Typical examples might be in manufacturing, where many employees joined 'en masse' when a factory opened, and were in their 20s. Thus, 40-45 years on they will be retiring 'en masse' over a period of five or so years. Mass recruitment may be needed at that time.

Unplanned leaving is of course more complex and disruptive, often called 'turnover' or 'labour turnover' and is **voluntary** – i.e. employees leaving by resignation for better jobs elsewhere. Monitoring turnover can give indications of poor management or working conditions, stress, or low wages compared with the market-place. A reasonable level - 5% - 10% is healthy however as it enables the introduction of 'new blood' and the possibility of promotions. **Involuntary leaving** is not usually measured - this involves dismissal for various reasons under the contract of employment.

Capability often is given as a reason and may include long-term or frequent sickness absence. Early retirement on grounds of ill-health is an option for those in the pension plan and with sufficient service, while others must rely on state-provided benefits. Frequent absences however are difficult to handle as it is not easy to appear fair and reasonable: employees are usually counselled, then given targets to achieve well before dismissal, and this type of treatment spills over into an issue of 'conduct'. Poor job performance is similarly quite hard to prove definitively - there is always an element of judgement and comparison with other jobs/personnel. Issues of bad faith by employer's inept recruitment of people who prove unable to do the job can sometimes by circumvented by transfer to other work in a different department. Otherwise, dismissal is the only option.

Conduct, likewise, is a difficult area unless the firm has strict, written rules, which are made public to all employees (such as during induction training). Fighting, drunkenness, theft, refusal to follow a reasonable instruction, absenteeism and the like are more easy to handle than insubordination and rudeness to colleagues. The issue is whether dismissal is really necessary.

Redundancy is an acceptable reason and quite clear - but so long as criteria for selection are open and fair. Redundancy exists where the business ceases to be, where the job the employee is performing becomes outmoded or disappears, or when work is transferred to another location. This last category can be quite confusing especially in major cities where employees live near to main roads or railway lines which they habitually use to get to work. If the Head Office moves across town it might become extremely difficult for those employees to reach the new location in good time and so they may claim to have been made redundant. Employers also must consult staff, minimise the effect of the scale of the redundancy and its timing, giving advance notice, calling for volunteers, reducing overtime and part-time/temporary or contract work and so on. Following the redundancy the employer then has the problem of maintaining the morale of those left: not an easy proposition.

42   REDUNDANCY

Key answer tips

(a)   A simple definition is required for 6 marks indicating at least three types of redundancy (2 marks each).

(b)   An extensive question – discuss the management and the process, with explanations and examples.

(a)   **Redundancy** occurs where the work of an employee 'ceases or diminishes' or is 'expected to cease or diminish' under UK law. This can occur with business failure where a firm is liquidated. It may be bought later, but initially anyway the employees are redundant. There are of course degrees of failure and a general down turn might result in across-the-board reductions simply in order to save costs, often by voluntary redundancy schemes.

Secondly, the work can cease or diminish in the location due to a factory or office closure and a subsequent move of production or a administration to a larger unit or a more convenient location (e.g. nearer the market or near a port or airport).

Thirdly, specific work can cease or diminish, due to changes in consumer demand or changes in internal technology. For example, many accounts clerks are redundant when IT-based systems are installed; highly skilled car mechanics who can diagnose faults are redundant when car manufacturers introduce IT-based diagnostics or where parts become so cheap that a simple exchange/replacement is cheaper than a complex repair job.

(b)   The effects of redundancies can be managed best when employees affected are treated with care, and, if possible, found new jobs, and, for those who are left employed, some assurances of continued job security.

In the first case, were skills become redundant, re-training, job moves (e.g. to a semi-skilled or unskilled job), transfers to divisions where the skill is still required or to other firms all relieve the financial stress on the individual.

If **volunteers** can be called for, and given a good financial 'package' then this too can benefit both those leaving and give reassurance to those left. Typically, leavers will be those near retirement age who will soon be drawing a pension, and younger employees who will hopefully find it easier to get another job elsewhere.

Banning recruitment, limiting overtime, cancelling contractors to bring work inside the firm, are other measures to obviate a general turn-down in business revenues. Linked to redundancy there might be a scheme to enhance the pensions of those near retirement age and encourage early retirement. These measures show the management as attempting to limit the effects and retain jobs where feasible, and this assists in preventing morale from plummeting.

Where **compulsory redundancies** are inevitable, a full system of consultation and possibly a scheme of 'out placement' should assist. Consultation with employee representatives is compulsory in the UK where more than 20 redundancies will occur in a period or 3 months, but this must be 'genuine' and not a paperwork exercise. In some industries, like coal, local Enterprise Schemes have been set up to encourage self-employment and development of local services. Such schemes have direct (employment/financial) benefits as well as a P.R. value.

Finally, where redundant employees are not able to be found other employment or are not qualified by service to take early retirement, a **generous payment scheme** will enable those redundant to cope financially – by paying off debts such as mortgages for example, or by putting the money in a savings scheme in order to draw income from it gradually.

43   X

(a)   **Human resource planning** (HR planning) was previously described as manpower planning, and has been defined as 'a strategy for the acquisition, utilisation, improvement and retention of an enterprise's human resources'. Manpower planning still provides a good starting point for the development of a human resource plan, but in recent years it has been recognised that there is more to people planning than quantitative estimates of the demand and supply of personnel.

Four main phases are involved in manpower planning:

(i)   an analysis of existing staffing resources - its strengths and weaknesses, age spreads, experience and training levels etc;

(ii)   an estimation of likely changes in resources - flows into, within, and out of, the organisation - and the ability of relevant labour markets to supply existing or future demands;

(iii)   an estimation of the organisation's future manpower needs in terms of numbers, type, quality and skill composition; and

(iv)   the identification of gaps between supply and demand and the development of policies and plans to close these.

The HR planning process goes beyond this simple quantitative exercise by taking into account the broader environmental factors eg, patterns of employment and developments in automation and uses qualitative techniques, such as scenario planning, for estimating future manpower requirements. The process is also linked to the development of the organisation as a whole, and should be related to corporate objectives and to an organisation structure capable of achieving those objectives. It is also concerned with developing people so that they have the skills to meet the future needs of the business and with improving the performance of all employees in the organisation by the use of appropriate motivation techniques.

(b)   **Briefing paper: Development of a human resource plan for the finance department**

The key considerations for developing the human resource plan for the department will focus on three main areas:

(i)   making the required reductions, in line with the downsizing strategy;

(ii)   addressing the changes that are affecting the department; and

(iii)   identifying the future role, in playing a fuller part in the management of the business.

Reducing staff numbers from 24 to 17 over the next two years and to 12 by the target date (in five years time) will be by using natural wastage and early retirement wherever possible. Hopefully, this will avoid (or at least reduce) the need for compulsory redundancies, and will avoid or reduce the adverse effects on staff morale and motivation.

There is a good chance of achieving the reductions over the time period set, provided that the necessary steps are taken. Three of the older members are within five years of retiring; two more will move into this category within the five years set by senior management. If those employees nearest retirement could be encouraged to leave by offering them a generous retirement package and an enhancement of their pension, it would be the least painful option.

One or two of the younger qualified members of staff are already looking for posts elsewhere, so they may be encouraged to leave earlier when the news that the organisation is looking to slim down the department has been communicated to the department. One of the trainees has applied for maternity leave. She will have the right to return to work, provided that she comes back within the period set out in legislation, so we have no room for manoeuvre there. Some of the trainees will qualify within the time period under consideration, and the reduction in costs will not allow me to increase salaries substantially, so I think that they will look elsewhere for work.

The age/experience of the existing people, spread over financial accounting, management accounting and the treasury function, is a mix of older, experienced specialist staff, a young to middle-aged group of qualified accountants (many of whom also possess MBA degrees), and a group of trainees with limited experience who have yet to qualify. I would like to keep a similar spread and one of the problems will be retaining the most able of my staff. This will mean planning a package of financial inducements and a clear career structure.

Reducing staff will be possible, but coping with the current workload with the reduced resources will be more difficult. There are several solutions to help me to deal with this problem:

- The department's existing operations will be thoroughly reviewed to make sure that it matches the corporate objectives, and its structure is capable of achieving those objectives. It may be that, following the general downsizing, there may be a reduced need for some of its services.

- There are many changes in technology and the department can make more use of IT and the latest developments in computer software. This could allow an increase in productivity and result in better quality output from the department. It will mean developing some of the staff, so that they have the skills to meet the future needs of the business. Although staff training is expensive, it will provide some motivation and reassurance to staff that the organisation is still prepared to invest in them and is ready to equip them with the latest IT skills.

- The department has been under increasing pressure to outsource transactions, and some of its other routine work, to one of the new service centres. Although I am not keen to do this, it may be the only way of coping with the existing volume of work.

For the **future plans**, the department will have to monitor its expenditure to keep in line with the budget. Early retirement and additional staff training will add considerably to costs, but perhaps outsourcing some of the routine work will allow us to offset some of these costs.

It is inevitable that some of the department members will have to become more flexible and be ready to take on a wider range of responsibilities. The younger staff will welcome this, as their education and training has already prepared them for wider management responsibilities, and those with MBA degrees are in a good position to accept more responsibilities. However, additional training and development to handle future demands will need to be planned for some members of the department.

44   MOTIVATION

> *Examiner's note* - Candidates who describe the use of incentive schemes largely in theoretical terms can gain substantial marks, provided the application of the theory is appropriate.

(a)   **Motivation is a perennial organisational problem**. The context in which it is faced, however, changes from generation to generation as economic and social values change. Motivation can be either positive or negative. Positive motivation, sometimes called anxiety-reducing motivation or the carrot approach, offers something valuable to the individual such as pay, praise or permanent employment for acceptable performance. Negative motivation, often called the stick approach, uses or threatens punishment by dismissal, suspension or the imposition of a fine if performance is unacceptable.

Money can never be overlooked as a motivator. Whether in the form of a salary, piecework, bonus, stock option, company-paid insurance or any other financial incentive that may be given to people for performance, money is important. Most managers and economists place money high on the scale of motivators. This stems from the work of Taylor and the school of scientific management. Taylor believed that there was a right (meaning best) way to perform any task and that it was management's job to determine the right way. Workers gain from this approach because the right way is easier and pay is enhanced as a result of increased productivity.

On the other hand, behavioural scientists such as **Maslow** and **Herzberg** tend to place money low on the scale as a motivator. Their content theories offer ways to profile or analyse individuals to identify their needs and they stress the limitations of monetary reward as the main, or even as a major, means of motivating people at work. Their work emphasises the need for employees to feel valued, to attain a sense of achievement in their work and to have an opportunity to exercise responsibility. Another approach, and one that many believe goes far in explaining how people are motivated, is expectancy theory. Victor Vroom's theoretical perspective stresses the role played by subjective factors, such as the employees' estimation of the chance of promotion, for striving hard to fulfil organisational objectives. Pay is only one of many work rewards that may be valued by individuals at work. When instrumentality and expectancy are high, pay can be a source of motivation.

When discussing money as a motivator it is necessary to recognise its effects at two levels. Money in absolute terms, as an exact amount, is important because of its purchasing power. Because money can be exchanged for satisfaction of needs, money can symbolise almost any need an individual wants it to represent. The next increase in salary could mean affording a better car, or an extra holiday. Money is also important as an indication of status. Increasing differentials between jobs creates feelings of a senior status in the person enjoying the higher salary.

Financial incentive schemes have been used to motivate people to perform well for a long time. All such schemes are dependent upon the belief that people will work harder to obtain more money. The most direct use of money as a motivator, is a 'payment by results' scheme, whereby an employee's pay is directly linked to his or her results. The system can be applied to individuals, groups or the whole of a plant. Traditionally these systems are common in the factory of a manufacturing business and have been less commonly applied to non-manual work such as administrative, managerial or professional.

Performance related pay (PRP) is a method used to motivate non-manual workers. However, research has shown that money will only motivate if the prospective payment is significantly large in relation to the normal income of that person. Small increases can prevent feelings of dissatisfaction but to create motivation in a person, who will be motivated by money, it is necessary for the amounts to be large. PRP comes in a number of different forms. The NHS introduced the system, starting with senior managers, in which up to 20% of the salary was dependent upon achieving short-term and long-term objectives. Performance was evaluated according to results achieved against these objectives and classified in five grades. The amount of bonus, which could be nothing, was dependent upon the grade allocated and had to be re-earned each year. An alternative approach is to pay one-off bonuses to reward individual or team performance. Under this alternative system the bonuses are not consolidated into base rates.

Other methods of seeking to motivate employees by monetary means include various kinds of profit-sharing schemes and profit-related payment schemes. The most common profit-sharing scheme is simply to pay employees a cash bonus, calculated as a proportion of annual profits.

(b)

Examiner's note - Again, candidates who make good use of theoretical models of motivation to explain the viability of non-monetary methods of motivation can gain substantial marks, provided the theory is applied appropriately.

There are many other ways that managers can increase the motivation of their employees apart from pay and incentive schemes. Several non-financial motivators that have been suggested by various writers include participation in decision-making and quality of work life. The content theories of Maslow and Herzberg point to the job itself as a source of motivation. The job content can be interesting and challenging and can meet needs for advancement, social standing, professional recognition and self-esteem. The methods used include job enrichment, job enlargement and job rotation. The human relations' approach expressed the importance of the work group and leadership style in determining levels of job satisfaction.

The work of Maslow and Herzberg emphasises the **need for employees to feel valued,** to attain a sense of achievement in their work and to have an opportunity to exercise responsibility. There is no doubt that people are motivated by being involved in the actions and decisions that affect them This view leads to an approach towards employees that encourages contribution and self-direction, advocating full participation on matters of significance to improve the quality of decision-making and the nature of supervision. Participation also recognises the value of staff, since it provides a sense of accomplishment and 'being needed'. A manager seeking to raise performance by increasing motivation could involve staff in the planning and inspection aspects of the work encouraging staff to participate in the design of the work planning schedules. Staff would be motivated to achieve the targets that they had helped establish.

An interesting approach to motivation is the recent development of **'quality of work life programmes'**. Basically the approach is a very wide-ranging application of the principles of job enrichment. The intention is to improve all aspects of work life, especially job design, work environment, leadership attitudes, work planning and industrial relations. It is an all-embracing systems approach, which usually starts with a joint management and staff group looking at the dignity, interest and productivity of jobs.

The team approach shares a similar philosophy to the new approach to job design. It seeks to harness the influence of the group, which provides its members with the opportunity for social interaction, and has been shown to be a source of job satisfaction. Associated with working in groups, two major aspects of leadership have been identified as sources of job satisfaction. Firstly the leader who has a supportive relationship with their subordinates and takes a personal interest in them is seen to contribute positively to job satisfaction. Secondly the leader who encourages involvement and participation in the group similarly enhances job satisfaction. **Management/leadership style** is of particular relevance in this respect. A democratic style has been found to assist in the motivation process because it provides a degree of worker participation and involvement. The achievement of employee involvement in turn is considered to be a useful contributory factor in the motivation process.

Goals are also important motivators. They not only provide a basis for the measurement of performance necessary for administration of payment systems, but they can also serve to assist motivation in themselves. A goal provides a target to aim at, something to aspire to. This means the existence of a goal generates motivation in a person to work towards the achievement of the goal. Goals provide a standard of performance; a person is doing well if they have achieved a goal or are on the way to achieving it. Feedback on an excellent level of performance can be rewarding in itself and can spur individuals to greater efforts. On the other hand failure to achieve a goal or at least to make some progress toward it is evidence of unsatisfactory performance.

Research has investigated the importance of goals in motivation and concludes that for goals to be significant motivators they must be specific, sufficiently difficult to be challenging and they must be accepted by the person as their own particular goals and not as something imposed from outside.

45   B PLC

(a)   The idea that people react directly to money has been used by many theorists – F W **Taylor, Maslow** (on the bottom rung of his hierarchy), even expectancy theorists like **Vroom.**

Money, of course, is not only symbolic and status-related but it also buys more intangible things like holidays, fishing or golfing and other leisure pursuits. The accumulation of money per se is unlikely to motivate many, but its effects are virtually unlimited.

The assumption is that people operate at a low level of need in many jobs as they are inherently uninteresting and unsatisfying. If, as **Hertzberg** suggests, the organisation can change the job design (enrichment, enlargement, rotation) then additional money will not be needed to generate higher levels of performance.

The ability to pay for additional performance depend ultimately on the contribution to profit – either by saving costs or increasing sales. In many instances, measures of these are lacking or incomplete, or depend on extended team-working and so are de-motivating for other members of the team (e.g. reception staff) when commission is paid to others (e.g. sales people).

The **motivation theory** which encompasses all these merits and limitations is that of **Expectancy theory**. In this theory, it is possible to add – in expected rewards in terms of money and /or job satisfaction. These become the aims of the employees' actions. Some kind of calculation is then made as to how much effort is required to achieve them, and how they may be achieved. This 'motivational calculus' is not wholly rational and known but theorists argue that people behave **as if** it is.

(b)   **Share incentives schemes** work to link the employee to the organisation and engender a general commitment to its goals, which may reduce labour turnover, absenteeism, wastage etc. In B's case, this behaviour is ultimately rewarded not only by a feeling of involvement as shareholders but also by share price increases and returns via dividends.

However, the link from actual performance of a business unit to overall share price can be extremely tenuous in a big firm, one products poor performance can affect the whole group adversely. Interest rate movement and trading cycles have nothing to do with employee commitment but affect share price.

Also, if conditions deteriorate generally, share price and dividend are depressed (as at B) and employees become worried about their shares resulting in lower morale.

The rewards can be tied more closely to performance by operating profit related pay (PRP) where profit is the local operating profit of a plant or location (e.g. a Strategic Business Unit or a Division). Here, the overhead and input costs can be easily seen and a baseline established. Thence forward any reduction in costs or increase in sales can be reflected in a formula to result in monthly (or quarterly) payments. It may even be possible to motivate all members of the sales team by agreeing different 'pools' of money across functions so as to reflect their general contribution. Then, direct actions like answering a phone for an absent colleague, can result in an additional sale and an additional benefit.

46   SMOG

(a)   Smog is fairly typical of small businesses but increasingly these are becoming aware of changes to management accounting required by environmental pressures.

IT has vastly affected the day-to-day handling of information, with paper-based systems being replaced, and a huge effect on the jobs and tasks of the management accounting practice itself. Where the function itself has changed little, the ability and speed for analysis has increased, as has the breadth and volume of transactions, enabling management accounting to become a more strategic practice.

In some cases the standardisation and routinisation of functions has led not only to job losses but to **'outsourcing'** of entire sections of the management accounting practice to contractors. Where electronic communication is possible, these contractors can be located anywhere-far away from the remaining management accounting functions-but requiring more close monitoring of security of data.

Organisational restructuring has been referred to above, but when widespread the nature of decisions must be linked to the MA data and subsequent to 'outsourcing' the management accounting practice must monitor and control contractor costs and quality of the service delivery. These features are becoming important in globalisation and internationalisation.

Quality and continuous improvement concerns have impacted on data-collection and decision-making and so also on the more strategic nature of internal management accounting, data: Software allows 'what-if' scenario development, techniques include **'backflush accounting'** ABC, and the more generic **'balanced scorecard'** approach. BPR and TQM benchmarking both require extensive data sets internally and from external sources, and all have changed management accounting practice.

Environmental pressures created globalisation and concerns over the sovereignty of nations versus multi-national enterprises. Different schemes are needed to cost and evaluate the different international trading divisions (especially transfer pricing) a local government legislate for MNE's to provide data, which management accounting most provide.

(b)   Smog needs a lot of training and development, and some of the following programmes would help:

IT training - both operational and systemic and for more senior staff in terms of consolidation of account spreadsheets and for professionals the scenario-building techniques. In many cases this can be linked to an external certificate and extended to homework and assignments (activity- based-training) perhaps assisted by loaning staff laptops to work at home.

Technical training needs to be more longer-term and linked to staff career development. For many staff in the UK the National Vocational Qualification (NVQ) Levels 1-3 would provide a framework, while for more experienced staff AAT or

CIMA qualification, linked to on-the-job training would provide a strategic basis for development.

This strategic basis, comprising a better understanding of the business and its environment might be added to by post-graduate Diplomas or Masters qualifications such as the MBA.

47   APPRAISAL

(a)   The **objectives of a formal appraisal** process are:

(i)   **To highlight areas of good/above average performance** in order to assist in reward systems and/or career development opportunities.

(ii)   To **highlight areas of poor performance** which can be rectified by a Training Needs Analysis.

(iii)   To **de-brief on targets set and achieved** thus creating a mutual understanding and opportunity for creative criticism. Some firms operate 180° Appraisal where the subordinate also appraises the supervisor.

(iv)   **As a control mechanism** e.g. as part of Management by Objectives ensuring the ongoing improvement in critical areas.

(b)   Appraisal systems are fraught by their very nature of formality.

Having a certain time for feedback may ensure it is done, formally correct, logged and actioned but may result in managers 'saving-up' issues for the predetermined time rather than addressing them as they occur.

Many managers see the process as one enabling them to set additional 'projects' for staff rather than an attempt to measure them against what they are supposed to do. This is easier than trying to create objective measures, for example in a finance department where adherence to standards is far more important than individual creativity and where many employees are doing very similar, repetitive tasks.

Frequently, managers see the Appraisal as an opportunity for criticism and to bring out all the faults of the employee in circumstances where this would otherwise not be possible. Employees whose everyday work is exemplary and who have no cause to be worried can face a very personal judgement about their personal characteristics within a formal, confidential, 1-to-1 appraisal.

They suffer from the 'halo and horns' effect in that human judgement is poor, often based on impressions, so it is easier for a manager to look for faults or success in an otherwise patchy performance and bias his/her judgement one way or the other – particularly when the appraisee is generally seen as having 'potential' and it is politically expedient to emphasise success (e.g. in graduates).

Finally, most managers are not trained in, nor are they comfortable with, the process. They may tend to do it passively, aim for a 'middle level' to avoid conflicts, and spend little time in preparation or execution of what can be an extremely resource-hungry activity.

Some of these problems can be alleviated by:

•   Education and training of managers and subordinates

•   Central direction of target-setting, scale and indices of performance

•   360° appraisal involving peers and a judgement of the managers

•   Increasing the frequency

All this can be greatly assisted by slick software, eliminating the 'paper chase'.

48   N PLC

Key answer tips

This is quite an interesting question in which you should look at the benefits of career planning from the perspective of an individual who thought she had a career ladder, but who has since experienced restructuring so that her career path is now far from certain. Your answer should also incorporate elements of succession planning, as this becomes an issue for a company which is in danger of losing good managers precisely because the career ladder has been removed.

(a)   **Benefits of a vertical career ladder for Josie** included the following:

- She had a goal – career advancement - towards which her efforts could be directed

- She knew her work had the chance of being tangibly recognised in terms of career progression

- She knew that a job that maybe was currently not very interesting had the chance of being superseded by a more interesting job which still had the security of being with the same firm

- Promotion within the company would have meant more pay and benefits, more responsibility, and possibly more interesting and varied work

Benefits of a vertical career ladder for N plc included the following:

- The chance to reward good employees with promotion

- A more motivated workforce who would seek to fulfil the company's long-term aims

- An enhanced ability to attract excellent recruits who would become engaged with the company's fortunes and so would stay, minimising staff turnover

- The opportunity to benefit from the hard work and commitment of a dedicated and well-trained workforce over a prolonged period of their working, productive lives

- The ability to retain good staff and prevent them from defecting to competitors

- An excellent corporate image of a company who behaved ethically and sensibly towards the ambitions of its staff.

(b)   Following the programme of restructuring there are fewer middle and senior management jobs, and fewer levels of management so that there is less of a career ladder – the gaps between the rungs have widened, as it were. It is obvious therefore that N plc will not be able to use the idea of a vertical career ladder, or even job security, to motivate its middle ranking staff.

The fear and disillusionment that Josie and presumably some of her colleagues are feeling will possibly prevent them from being fully motivated and committed. This may mean that they may make decisions which are sub-optimal in terms of N plc. They may also feel driven into the arms of N plc's competitors.

These effects of N plc's restructuring programme may or may not have been anticipated by the company. It may be that N plc has already accepted that Josie's level of management is unlikely to respond well, and will therefore move on in time to another employer. However, if the company is keen to retain these staff it should make sure that they are both happy in their current positions, and encouraged to apply for the few senior jobs that are available.

One way of fulfilling this objective is to enrich the job that Josie currently does, say by involving her in more decision making or by treating her as an 'internal consultant', whose opinions and ideas are sought on a range of topics. Alternatively, or perhaps in addition to this policy, the incumbents of the jobs at Josie's level could be circulated, so they all get some variety in their working lives. This gives an added benefit to N plc in that it will have a pool of experienced staff to call on each time a senior position does become available. It also means that the employees enhance their skills and experience so that they are more 'marketable' to other companies. Again, this may be something that N plc will just have to accept.

49   S SOFTWARE COMPANY

Key answer tips

(a)   This is quite a challenging question but only 8 marks are at risk. The attitude of line managers to training is not usually covered in textbooks and as there is no model, answers would tend to be descriptive rather than analytical, often relying on 'common sense.'

(b)   This is a fairly straightforward and is covered in most texts. The Examiner's answer using the Devanna et al (1984) performance model is an odd choice, but could be used to emphasise the contribution of development to company performance.

(a)   These views are typical of those expressed in many organisations, and at one level are due to the competing goals, objectives and consequent perceptions and attitudes of the employees who are conditioned by them.

Andy is a pragmatic, hands-on, production manager – with a strict schedule to complete. His down-to-earth style is suited to the solving of considerable numbers of relatively trivial production problems on a daily basis, but the thought of his people living a life of total luxury runs against his core values. To add injury to that insult, production may have to be rescheduled; some may be lost forever; some may be recouped naturally or overtime may have to be worked, pushing up his costs.

Colin has an external orientation as a marketer and is constantly worried about the activities of competitors. He may also have had considerable experience of the negative effect of training – where suitable opportunities are not available afterwards, trained staff often leave, not only will they take their labour and skills to competitors but in S's case, technical and proprietary sensitive information may be actually drained from S into T, U or V.

Maurice is only a 'bean counter' and without any objective way of evaluating training, the lack of faith school will serve no purpose in his area. Compared especially with other investments for which a rate of return of some kind is calculated, training runs counter to the norms and values inculcated in Maurice over the years.

(b)   Jean needs highly trained, loyal, flexible and yet focused people to create any competitive advantage. This area of the labour market is very difficult indeed to compete in and indeed she may need to bear in mind the possibility of using agency staff or sub-contracting some areas out.

Her basic strategy is to determine the needs of the line functions and using a TNA determine the match of existing skills to those needed. The subsequent 'gap analysis' provides her with two major options: upgrading the skills of current employees, or external recruitment. There are costs (very high) and benefits of internal development of staff. If the opportunities are there for subsequent promotion, and if the key skills are fairly specific to S, then labour turnover may not prove such a problem as in other firms in IT because loyalty will be built up and transferability limited. On the other hand such training will be very costly compared with the 'quick fix' of recruitment.

Her recruitment option is limited by the compensation and benefits policies of S versus its competitors – and also its reputation in the industry for creative innovation, which attracts 'techies'. Advertising may not be enough and costly head-hunters or agency staff may have to be used, or tasks sub-contracted.

This plan will have a great effect on performance. Unlike other sectors of the economy, IT has a strong reliance on individuals often approaching a 'star system' for constellation with a people culture (Harrison 1972). Without a 'LINUX' expert S cannot write LINUX code.

In capital intensive industries labour is not as important as commodity prices and technology; in the knowledge economy these roles are reversed. S needs not just an HR plan but an HR strategy which incorporates career development and training (via appraisals), appropriate rewards, and, unfortunately also a disciplinary policy whose standards weed out those 'creatives' who make continual mistakes in coding.

50   R COMPANY

Key answer tips

(a)   This is a straightforward re-iteration of the topic from texts and students should be able to score most of the 10 marks.

(b)   This is more challenging as it required specific reference to the organisations problems and then an analysis of these in terms of the content of an induction programme.

(a)   An induction programme is a programme for introducing a new employee into an organisation. Ideally, it should be planned and structured, rather than a variety of ad hoc arrangements. An induction programme should enable a new employee to:

- learn what they need to know about the organisation, how it operates, what its rules are, and its way of doing things and culture

- understand the work that they will be doing, and their responsibilities

- meet the individuals in the organisation that they need to or ought to know.

An induction programme should have a clear time frame. Typically, an induction programme might last three months, six months or as much as one year. At the end of the induction programme, the individual should be able to think of himself or herself as a fully-integrated member of the company's work force.

The key activities in a planned induction programme should be as follows.

Before the new employee's first day	The human resources department should write to the individual, with details of:

- the job title and job description

- conditions of employment, such as hours of work, holiday entitlement, sickness arrangements and so on

- rate of pay, including any entitlement to overtime, bonuses etc

There should also be a covering letter welcoming the new employee, and giving details of where to go on the first morning, who to meet and at what time.

On Day 1	The new employee should be met by a person in the HR department, who will welcome him/her, discuss 'personnel' matters such as the company's rule book and its pension scheme. The induction scheme should be explained, and then the new employee should be taken to meet his/her office manager.

The office manager will either act as a mentor for the new employee throughout the induction period, or (more likely) will assign someone else to carry out the tasks of mentoring. The role of a mentor is to explain the work environment to the new employee and deal with any questions or problems he or she might have.

The mentor will introduce the new employee to the work environment, for matters such as introducing work colleagues, touring the office building and facilities (canteen facilities, drinks machines and so on).

The mentor will also introduce the new employee to the work that he or she will be doing, and the computer software that will be used.

Early in the programme

The HR department should contact the individual again, to provide 'regulatory' information, such as information about fire drill, health and safety, discipline procedures and grievance procedures.

At planned intervals

In a planned induction programme, the new employee might go through a rotation of duties, assisting with different elements of finance work in order to familiarise himself/herself with the organisation's systems, and to meet a variety of colleagues.

The training needs of the individual might need to be reviewed. If there is a large enough number of new recruits each year, it might be possible to arrange an in-house course, where the employees are given a fuller introduction to the organisation and its operations, as well as a chance to meet each other.

At regular intervals

The new employee should have short, formal meetings with the mentor (in addition to any unofficial discussions they might have) to discuss how the employee is settling into the company and whether there are any problems. If problems arise, it might be possible to take action to deal with them, and remove the employee's concerns.

(b)   The problems that the finance department is experiencing are:

- the loss of several new employees within the first year

- under-performance by several of the staff.

It is by no means certain that the lack of a planned induction programme is to blame, nor that the introduction of such a programme will remove or even reduce the problem.

The process of recruitment might be inadequate. New employees might find that they are not entering the type of job that they had been led to expect. The HR department might also be failing to recruit people of the right calibre.

Alternatively, the problems could be due to poor management and/or low employee morale.

An induction programme might possibly help to reduce both problems.

Reducing staff turnover

An induction programme can help a new employee to become integrated more quickly into the organisation, by meeting work colleagues and learning how the organisation operates. If an individual feels 'at home' rather than an outsider, he or she will be less likely to resign.

Through introducing new employees to each other, it might be possible to create a 'self-help group' of individuals who are able to discuss their induction experiences and problems. Shared problems are generally more easily dealt with and resolved.

If an individual knows that there is a programme for induction, and can see a purpose to what he or she is doing, he or she might be prepared to be more patient in waiting for training, and to put up with mundane accountancy work in the short term.

Regular meetings with the mentor, if properly conducted, should provide an opportunity for the individual to discuss problems and concerns. To the extent that the mentor can help, the new employee will feel more valued and appreciated, and so might be less inclined to resign.

Improving performance

Lower-than-expected performance could be caused by a number of factors. These include:

- not understanding fully the tasks of the job and its responsibilities

- failing to appreciate the systems of the organisation and how they operate

- a lack of regular performance review after joining the organisation.

An induction programme could help to overcome these problems. The job responsibilities of the employee should be set out clearly in the job description, and the mentor should be able to give advice and guidance. An induction programme should also introduce the individual to the systems and the culture of the organisation, so that the individual appreciates more clearly how things operate and how his/her job fits into the 'general scheme of things'. By helping the individual to understand what is expected, he or she might perform better.

In addition, if the individual has regular meetings with the mentor, the mentor can give 'unofficial' guidance about the individual's performance, and discuss the difficulties the individual is experiencing.

MANAGEMENT OF RELATIONSHIPS

51   SOURCES OF POWER

Key answer tips

A simple question on sources of power (e.g. Handy) but discussion is required on each.

Tutorial note: students must be careful not to confuse power with authority.

Power can be defined as the ability to exert a positive influence over objects, persons or situations.

The major sources of power are:

(a)   **Reward power** – the power a person has over another because of his ability to mediate rewards for him such as promotions, pay, recommendations, etc.

Gerald has been appointed Chief Management Accountant and clearly is in a position to exercise 'reward power'. It will take some time for Gerald to familiarise himself with his subordinates, but he will be the major source from which they may receive promotions, pay increases, etc.

(b)   **Coercive power** – this enables a person to mediate punishments for others eg, to dismiss, suspend, reprimand or make them carry out unpleasant tasks.

Gerald may use his position to punish subordinates who do not show commitment to their tasks. This may take the form of withholding promotion or delegating boring work assignments.

(c)   **Referent power** – is based on the identification with the person who has the resources or the desire to be like that person.

Given the details within the case it cannot be stated exactly what resources Gerald would command other than 'information'. From this point of view Gerald can be said to possess a small amount of referent power.

(d)   **Expert power** – is based upon one person perceiving that another person has expert knowledge and is a recognised authority.

Gerald has been appointed on the basis of his expert knowledge and therefore 'expert power' can be said to be a major source of power for Gerald. In addition to being a qualified accountant, he has considerable experience and proven competence in developing and using information systems.

(e)   **Legitimate power** – is based on agreement and commonly held values which allow one person to have power over another eg, one who has been formally appointed or designated the group leader.

Gerald, being appointed to a position of authority and responsibility, has the right to command and enforce subordinates to undertake tasks to ensure the decisions made by him are implemented.

52   AUTHORITY AND POWER

Key answer tips

Split your answer into 2 sections; how power can be exercised and what form it can take as 'authority'.

Power may be exercised along with authority. Power without responsibility will lead to behaviour that is uncontrolled by the organisation and likely to lead to unintended and undesirable consequences.

McGivering recognises five distinct types of power:

(a)   **Reward power**

A person has power over another because he can mediate rewards for him eg, promotion.

(b)   **Coercive power**

In many ways similar to reward power, but more likely to work in a negative way i.e. the power to dismiss, suspend, reprimand, embarrass or order that unpleasant tasks be undertaken.

It will be seen that these two forms of power have limited application because they do not extend beyond the limits of the reward or punishment which can be mediated, and failure to exercise such power will cause rapid diminution.

(c)   **Referent power**

Psychologists believe that this is the most extensive power, since it can be exercised when the holder is neither present, nor intending to exercise his influence. It is based upon a desire to identify with someone who has resources, or the desire to be like that person. It is seen in the way children imitate their parents, independent of any coercive or reward influences.

(d)   **Expert power**

This is where there is recognition of specific knowledge. In the accounting practice the accountant who specialises in tax, executorships or insolvency will have expert power over his colleagues and clients in a given situation. Such knowledge is theoretical, but has far-reaching practical applications.

(e)   **Legitimate power**

This is based on agreement, and common recognition that permits one person to have power over the other. This power might stem from age, seniority or formal appointment and is classically illustrated in the Battle of Rourke's Drift where authority went on seniority to an officer of the engineers rather than to a line infantry officer, despite his connections and background.

Power can only be effective if it is held in balance. Loss of balance will cause forces to develop against it. A manager who is a tyrant, who abuses his power and is probably incompetent will find his staff may fear him, but not give of their best, nor will they support him. Rather, they will form a resistance cell to counteract his behaviour.

Authority can arise from any of three main sources:

Formal – where the organisation bestows the authority upon the individual by means of his job title and the reporting relationships specified. This is recognised in the organisation chart.

Technical – where the authority arises due to personal skills or special knowledge or training. Here the authority exists only within the scope of that special knowledge or skill;

Personal, informal – this authority is not recognised in any organisation chart. It exists because, without regard to the position he or she holds, the person is accepted as being particularly respected, or an elder citizen, or is simply popular and recognised by colleagues as being efficient.

53   RESPONSIBILITY AND ACCOUNTABILITY

Key answer tips

A simple question requiring a detailed answer – describe the three concepts separately – accountability, authority and responsibility, and then explain the relationship between them. Discuss the different types of authority and develop the close link between authority and responsibility and the consequences in the absence of either.

From the *CIMA offcial Terminology*, we have the 'accountability concept' which states, 'Management accounting presents information measuring the achievement of the objectives of an organisation and appraising the conduct of its internal affairs in that process. In order that further action can be taken based upon this information, it is necessary at all times to identify the responsibilities and key results of individuals within the organisation.'

We can add to this the definition of a responsibility centre: 'A department or organisational function whose performance is the direct responsibility of a specific manager'.

The concept of accountability relates to one person having to report to another for actions and results in the former's area of activity. From the diagram, it is evident that accountability goes upward. For example, a factory co-ordinator or charge hand is accountable to a foreman or supervisor who may, in turn, be accountable to a works manager.

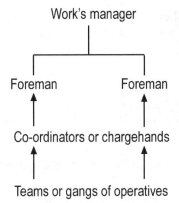

Authority refers to the scope or power of discretion that a person has to make decisions. This may arise from the person's position within the organisational hierarchy. This is regarded as line authority. In contrast, staff authority is where there is an advisory or service function within an organisation. Such authority could also be technical, a special expertise held by a person within the staff function. Treasury or taxation accountants on corporate staff will have technical authority.

From the organisational diagram above it is apparent that the foreman has both **authority** and **accountability**. He is accountable to the work's manager above him for the work that goes on below him. He thus needs the authority to tell the subordinates what is required. As part of his accountability, he must plan what has to be done, communicate instructions, assign work and follow up. He can delegate some of this to the lower level, the co-ordinator or chargehand to enable the communication to be more effective to smaller groups. He cannot delegate his accountability. He is still accountable to the work's manager.

Responsibility relates to the liability a person has when called to account. A person's responsibilities refer to the functions or duties that have to be performed within the organisation. A foreman may be responsible for fitting pipes to the deck of a ship under construction. He may have three gangs, each under a chargehand. He must give instructions to each chargehand, who must then assign the work and carry it out. However, the responsibility remains with the foreman to monitor the work and see that it is performed and report back to the daily production meeting. If the information is not available, then it is down to the foreman to make it available or to explain why. Non-compliance is a shirking of the responsibility of position. Thus there is a strong relationship with authority.

A problem would occur where a person has responsibility say for certain tasks, but no line authority. Such an unfortunate individual might be a course tutor in a technical college. She might have responsibility for all aspects of running a course, but no line control over the lecturers that teach on it. Thus if there is a recalcitrant lecturer who persistently refuses to comply with deadlines and misses classes, the tutor is powerless. The same applies where the management accountant has to rely on data from (say) foremen who regard him as merely a paper pusher, thwarting the prime progress of the business. The accountant has no direct authority to enforce her wishes. It is essential, therefore, that authority and responsibility move together.

As has already been implied above, authority can be divided into **expert and legal authority**. As its name implies, expert authority is derived from technical expertise. A taxation accountant would have technical authority arising from his special knowledge. The same might apply to an accountant with special knowledge and experience of insolvency or financial management and raising finance. Legal authority comes from any legal requirements. There is a legal obligation for management to provide for a safe system of work. Thus employees who persistently and blatantly flaunt the regulations, such as failing to wear harnesses and hard hats, riding illegally on fork-lift trucks or engaging in horseplay with hoses or other equipment, even if it is part of traditional 'initiation' rites, must be disciplined or even dismissed.

Finally, **authority may be implied** rather than specifically stated. A manager, by virtue of his position has authority even if he has no particular line control in an area. If he sees something that is wrong, he has the authority to take it up with the employee and take it further if necessary.

54   DELEGATION

Key answer tips

(a)   A fairly straight forward question. Consider the advantages (both practical and idealistic) and the disadvantages of delegation.

(b)   A fairly straight forward description of responsibility is required for 8 marks.

(a)   **Delegation** is the process whereby a manager or supervisor transfers part of his or her legitimate authority to a subordinate. Along with authority goes responsibility but whilst authority can be delegated, responsibility remains with the delegator; eg, while a Board of Directors may delegate authority to the managers, the directors are still responsible directly to the shareholders.

In all but the smallest of organisations some degree of delegation is necessary, as there are physical and mental limitations to the work that can be undertaken by any manager. This in turn allows subordinates to gain experience and demonstrate how they can perform. From these points the following practical advantages can be derived:

(i)   The workload of the manager is reduced leaving him more time to concentrate on strategic duties.

(ii)   Subordinates can gain good experience for future management.

(iii)   Delegation can lead to decentralisation, which can allow divisional or branch managers to react quicker to local changes than managers at Head Office.

(iv)   Allowing subordinates to perform work of a higher grade can aid their development.

(v)   Management can see how subordinates tackle work of a higher grade, and how they cope with extra authority.

(vi)   Effective deployment of resources fulfils value for money criteria.

Idealistic advantages could be seen as those that suggest delegation aids motivation in subordinates, and allows for an individual to grow in his work. Where an employee gains job satisfaction, the employer is able to have the benefit of much better work performance - which might thus also be regarded as a practical advantage.

Whilst there are many advantages to be gained from delegation, care must be taken to ensure that the process is carried out carefully, otherwise there may be potential disadvantages:

(i)   If there is not the right mix of duties passed down, a subordinate may only have the tedious tasks and quickly lose interest and motivation.

(ii)   The superior must recognise that he is still accountable for the performance of the subordinate - he must not abdicate his responsibility.

(iii)   With decentralisation, local managers may develop their own procedures, which may act against the objectives of the organisation.

On the whole, delegation of duties should be employed wherever possible and appropriate as the advantages will outweigh the disadvantages. With careful management control, the disadvantages can be minimised and optimum performance obtained.

(b) It is very easy to say, as a matter of theory that **authority** must be matched by **responsibility** in an organisation. Both are usually thought of as being determined 'from above', but in practise this matching process is hard to achieve.

In the first place, it is necessary, in determining authority and responsibility to know accurately what each member of the organisation should do (and what he in fact does). Thus an accurate formal organisation chart is of great assistance.

This may well need to be augmented by means of an informal organisation chart as well, since people very rarely operate in the way in which they are officially expected to. Once the organisation chart has been prepared, job descriptions can be established. These will first state the responsibilities and then organise the necessary authority to match those responsibilities. Of course, once again there is likely to be a difference between the formal and the informal pattern. Thus a forceful personality can very easily make up for a lack of formal delegated authority.

The process of delegating authority will vary very considerably from one organisation to another. It is essentially a question of power, and how power is exercised. It is of little use for a manager to have the authority to hire employees if he lacks the power to advertise for applicants, or to determine the rates of pay. But even if he has both of these, it will avail him little unless there are willing applicants. His authority cannot usually exceed that of his superiors, the significant exceptions being where he has specific technical knowledge, or unusual personal qualities.

For authority to be exercised responsibly, it is necessary for policies to be established for the exercise of the authority. These have to be set out clearly for the guidance of the subordinates involved, and control must be established by some suitable mechanism (based on a flow of appropriate information). A manager can only hold his subordinates responsible provided that he has made it clear what is expected, knows what has been achieved, and has some means of taking corrective action where necessary.

55   GROUPS AND EMPLOYEE COMMITMENT

Key answer tips

(a)   Explain the economic conditions underlying the need for short-term contracts in the early 90s and describe how the pendulum has swung 10 years later with increasing emphasis on gaining employee commitment.

(b)   A longer analysis is required, using HRM concepts. Try to avoid lists and to organise your answer under several major headings.

(a)   Recessionary times in the late 1980s and early 1990s encouraged employers to reduce their emphasis on employee commitment. The argument was that the costs of developing and retaining high quality permanent staff were hardly affordable at a time of economic difficulties. And in any event, it was argued, high levels of unemployment meant that replacements were easily available for staff who departed.

This was the background to an era in which many employers virtually ceased to offer full-time permanent contracts. Instead, there was an emphasis on using external labour, which could be shed without damaging consequences and at short notice if ever business conditions dictated. Where internal employees were taken on, it was often on the basis of short-term renewable contracts; again, employers were anticipating the need to lay off staff and seeking to minimise the adverse effects when that happened.

This situation has now begun to change quite noticeably in the UK. Reasons for this include the following:

(i)   Now that economic conditions are less harsh, the age-old realisation that committed staff are productive staff has reasserted itself.

(ii)   The costs of staff turnover are now understood to be high. It does not make economic sense to expend money and management time in a constant search for new recruits. A better policy is to retain the staff already in place.

(iii)   Increasing weight is given to the idea of improving staff productivity by securing commitment to organisational goals. Motivational theory demonstrates that staff respond well to involvement in achieving organisational objectives and productivity may well increase as a result.

(iv)   The quality of employees is increasingly seen as a key weapon in securing competitive advantage. Rapid response to customer needs, and the demands of world class production techniques, require that staff are 'empowered' as far down the organisational hierarchy as possible.

(b)   In the past, employers worked to secure employee loyalty and commitment by a mixture of job security and money (both basic salary and bonuses of various kinds). Nowadays, this is seen as too simple a model. In particular, employers are increasingly reluctant to accept an obligation on job security unrelated to the efficiency and effectiveness of the employees concerned.

The range of measures which may be taken by employers should be designed with organisational objectives in mind. In particular, the employer seeks to make tangible gains in productivity and profit in return for any incentives offered. This suggests that measures which simultaneously contribute to employee commitment and competitive advantage should be strongly favoured.

Money is still the most obvious starting point. However, in order to achieve organisational objectives, the focus nowadays is on incentives related to individual performance and/or organisational profitability.

Staff training and development similarly fulfil a dual role. Employees see this as providing personal and career advancement, while for the employer the reward in improved performance is tangible.

Increases in job satisfaction will promote employee commitment, and if this can be achieved by appropriate measures the organisation too can benefit. For example, careful job design carries two-way benefits, as does a system of management by objectives. The employee experiences the satisfaction of attaining targets that he has helped to establish.

Finally, the importance of participation and communication can hardly be over-estimated. Too often the employee feels little identification with the organisation simply because no information is available on how the individual contribution dovetails with overall goals. Modern ideas on team working and empowerment can make a large contribution in this area.

56   FAIR TREATMENT

Key answer tips

(a)   This is a very general question and no real theory exists to assist you in forming an answer. Discuss all types of discrimination: objectivity of the reward system and of discipline and dismissal.

(b)   Here you need to be familiar with equal opportunities legislation and policies.

(a)   **Fair treatment** does not mean treating everyone the same: issues like differential performance or conduct require organisations to discriminate in order to improve performance.

Fairness involves being treated justly – i.e. on merit. In the first instance, recruitment and selection policies and practices must ensure nepotism or favourism (or even bribery) is eliminated by segregating duties and roles of HR and line managers. At this stage, objective criteria should be established against the job requirements. In particular, discrimination on grounds other than merit should be eliminated: age, race, religion gender, marital status and so forth are not normally grounds for failing to employ someone, while level of educational attainment, experience, achievements and so forth are more objective measures.

Once employed, staff need to feel treatment is fair. Tasks should be allocated evenly based on experience, capability and workload; rewards should be based an objective criteria such as length of service, seniority, or measurable achievements rather than personality – based appraisals. Where there is doubt, organisations should have an open and objective Grievance Procedure which allows employees a voice; consultative forums and staff associations as well as trade unions can assist in legitimising complaints of unfair treatment.

Where employee conduct or performance gives cause for concern, there should be an objective and open **Disciplinary Procedure**. This needs to emphasise the aim of improving performance or behaviour rather than 'punishing' offenders'. To be seen to be fair, employees should be able to be represented (by a friend, relative or trade union official), have an opportunity to state their case, and have leave to appeal to a higher authority

Dismissal is an extreme measure and to be fair, it should give due regard to the circumstances of the case and the relative merits of the employee concerned.

(b)   Government can assist by setting a good example as an employer in the public sector, as most Governments employ very large numbers of people, and act as benchmarks for other organisations.

Secondly, its policies can result in organisations being formed and funded which can assist organisations or individuals seeking advice. In the UK charities such as the Industrial Society provide such a role, as do the Citizens Advice Bureaux. A particular body, ACAS (the Advisory, Conciliation and Arbitration Service), was set up precisely to assist in the tackling of perceived unfairness, and the resulting conflict. Other bodies set up by legislation form particular functions – the Equal Opportunities Commission, the Commission for Racial Equality, the Health and Safety Executive are examples.

Thirdly, and perhaps most importantly, the government can pass legislation to prevent or rather to alter particular unfairnesses from becoming the norm. Sex or gender (including marital status) is covered in the UK by the Sex Discrimination Act – which covers both direct and indirect forms and which applies to applicants for jobs as well as employees – and the Equal Pay Act. The Race Relations Act covers 'race, creed or colour' while the Employment Protection Act, and the ACAS guides, provide baselines for fair dismissals.

57   MANAGING CONFLICT

Key answer tips

(a)   Remember its the 'effects; not the causes or types of conflict which are required.

(b)   Management of conflict implies a theoretical framework of some sort.

(a)   The effect of conflict can become widespread if allowed to continue over a period.

Firstly, customers may detect a 'pass-the-buck' attitude when making enquiries, and employees may complain directly to customers about other departments. This lowers customer confidence and they may seek out other suppliers. Worse still, actual levels of service and delivery might suffer as co-operation between the different stages in the Value-Chain – as represented by different departments – weakens. This may well force customers to look elsewhere.

Secondly, rumours of problems may spread to other parts of the supply – chain, indeed if conflict is severe finance department may not pay the invoices of suppliers within the contractual period. Competitors' morale may be improved and their competitiveness increased, so that their sales staff actively seek more business than usual.

More generally, in a situation of continual conflict, targets are missed and an air of esperation may set in. Keen and lively employees with skills the market demands may be the first to leave, resulting in a further twist to the downward spiral of lost opportunities and missed targets. Individual managers who lose staff will be disheartened and distracted by the need to recruit replacements, while more generally managers become preoccupied with internal struggles to the detriment of strategies to overcome the external forces.

It is also possible that this horizontal conflict can result in vertical conflict if, say, shop floor earnings are affected by targets being missed and bonuses reduced. If the firm is unionised this may result in collective action.

(b)   Managers need to meet together to agree the current effects and identify simple solutions. Discussion may later result in finding some of these causes. Initial disciplinary action may be needed to 'unfreeze' the present situation by taking up one or two extreme examples of the conflict and making an example of the individuals concerned.

If they use **Lewin's Force-Field analysis**, they may identify those for whom the conflict provides benefits and those who, like the shop floor workers, are suffering. The management must then decrease the power of those benefiting, by decreasing the benefits, sideways moves, or even dismissals. The losers' camp should be treated carefully and consistently to prevent people leaving or engaging in other actions which might be detrimental. The aim would be to paint a picture of a new future without conflict, stressing its temporary nature.

The engagement of an OD Consultant as a **'change agent'** may be necessary to allow those benefiting to meet and air the issues which have led them to the situation, and for the OD consultant to check out causes and possible solutions through interviews, observation and perhaps a general staff attitude survey. This may pinpoint key individuals or situations which are important in maintaining the conflict.

Given that there will be some kind of plan to change the situation, management must then individually and collectively support it publicly and provide resources (time, money) for implementation. Such an implementation plan must specifically address the way resistance can be handled, as clearly conflict seems to benefit many people or it would not be so widespread or persistent.

58   TR

REPORT

To: Chief Executive

From: Manager

Date: 18 June 20X0

Subject: Conflict between the R&D and Operations departments

(a)   Within TR, there are many examples of how conflict is manifested. They include the following:

- constant complaints about 'the other department';

- a general sense of ill feeling and lack of co-operation between the staff of the two departments.

- communication between personnel in the R&D and Operations departments, except for some routine interchanges, has almost ceased;

- verbal disagreement between the departments, resulting in abuse that is considered usual;

- expressions of frustration about the behaviour of managers and members of the other department;

- unfair criticism of the achievements of the R&D department by Operations staff;

- the Operations department are perceived to be uncooperative and resistant to adopting some innovations developed by R&D.

The **conflict** between the Operations and R&D departments stems from a misunderstanding by each about what the other is trying to do. Operations claim that research personnel take too long to carry out projects because, instead of seeking practical, cost-effective solutions to problems, they go in for 'the perfect solution' - which is often very costly and often late. They do not appreciate that innovation depends partly on a mix of science and chance and is not something that can be scheduled and produced, like a train timetable. The misunderstanding on the part of the people in the R&D department is that they are unaware of the pressures that Operations managers and staff are under to implement an efficient service.

The heads of both departments are earnestly committed to achieving the aims of their respective departments and to achieving the goals of the organisation. They both want to produce a more efficient service for customers and ultimately to earn higher profits for the organisation. Traditionally, both departments have developed their own specialisation, which has produced barriers with other departments. Operations and R&D have become preoccupied with trying to achieve their own goals, even though it has sometimes been at the expense of the goals of the other department and of the overall goals of the organisation. Where, as in this case, the achievement of the goals of the two departments are interdependent, then the situation is aggravated by the frustration caused when the goal of one department is blocked by that of the other. Unfortunately, there is a structural problem within the organisation, because of the separation of the task of the development of new methods and techniques from the task of implementing the resulting innovations. This arises wherever a division of labour occurs in an organisation.

Another **cause of the conflict** is the clashing of personality types at the head of each of the respective departments. They are both strong characters with authoritarian personalities and a deep commitment to their own departmental goals, which is likely to exacerbate the conflict. Authoritarian people tend to be rigid in their beliefs and conform to rules and regulations, and are not inclined to change unless compelled to do so. Their commitment to their own departmental goals is a good thing in itself, but blind commitment without regard to the super-ordinate organisational goal of increased efficiency and effectiveness is not acceptable to the organisation.

(b) Resolving the conflict between these two departments will depend on each department head having an increased understanding of what the other is trying to achieve and of the pressures and difficulties that each faces in trying to meet its objectives.

This can be achieved using a programme of re-education for the staff of both departments. Members of each department need to understand each other's problems and perspectives. This process needs to start with the heads of the respective departments, who will require a degree of retraining and a reminder that co-operation between their departments is essential to the well-being of the whole organisation. Authoritarian people prefer to work in organisational situations that are highly structured and unambiguous, each needs to know what is expected of them. They are likely to respond to relatively autocratic and directive leadership styles.

There are a number of methods that are available to carry out this programme, ranging from briefing meetings, through to workshops in which members from the two departments come together to work on simulated, or even real, problems. However, real understanding will not come about unless there is an exchange of staff between departments. If members of the R&D department are actually confronted with the problems of meeting timetable schedules on a daily basis, they will come to appreciate the pressures facing operations staff. Similarly, if and when members of the Operations department experience the frustrations of trying to devise new methods and techniques for increasing efficiency, they will really come to appreciate the difficulties experienced by staff in R&D.

Alternatively, to encourage co-ordination and communication, TR management could change the structural arrangements and form temporary project teams to work on small projects, with members of both departments working together to solve the problems. A project leader with the relevant skills and a non-authoritarian personality could be chosen to lead the group.

59   SOFT CORPORATION

(a) Management style is the general way a manager behaves in a variety of situations and so can be distinguished from contingency theories. A 'style' is often not defined except for its perceived outcomes in the terms of behaviour – such as 'country club' management or 'task–centred'. One of the most enduring, and simplest, is the idea of power-sharing: managers can be authoritarian (fail to delegate, 'tell' etc), or democratic (open and involving, 'sell' ideas). Some avoid the issue of the complications of democracy by a 'hands-off' or *laissez-faire* style, an abrogation of management.

Joan Timmins has an 'authoritarian' style - giving 'orders' or 'telling'. This would have been acceptable in a military situation but SOFT company is more democratic, based on a rational-legal order (Weber's clarification). This is particularly problematic in a technical function like finance which is almost self-correcting based on strict rules and regulations, professional competence and ethics. Joan could therefore adopt a 'laissez-faire' style, leaving decisions to professionals and operate as a 'boundary manager' making life easier for her staff by introducing various improvements (furniture, lighting, easier forms or software etc).

In this way, her role would be seen by staff to be beneficial as well as confining her to larger-scale 'management-type' decisions rather than interference. There is limited scope for democratic style as professionals are often uncomfortable with a collective decision-making system, as individual experts, and the scope for change in a Finance department is severely limited by statutory and other rules and regulations.

(b)   Joan will have an extreme problem in adapting to *laissez-faire* because of her own personality - which is authoritarian and judgemental-and her years of military training and experience. She has to 'un-learn' these techniques, and really reverse the way she has operated so far – possibly losing face.

She probably cannot change her personality, but she can use it to enhance the status of the Department externally within SOFT by appearing well-briefed and having clear objectives at committees, indulging in research and surveys on new methodologies in Finance, even representing SOFT on industry committees. Internal to the department she needs to hold a general meeting to tell staff of her plan to make life easier for them-but expecting them to go through a period of stress as the new responsibilities are placed on them. They will like this 'selling' of an idea.

60   T AEROSPACE COMPANY

Key answer tips

The benefits and potential problems of team working are the main points to be covered in this fairly straightforward question. Make sure you consider the plan from the perspective of the company's existing managers, as well as from that of the company and the potential team members. Managing teams can be very tricky!

(a)   The essential feature of a team is that it is a group of people who share the same goals and together use the skills at their disposal to achieve those goals. Each team member is held accountable to the others for their performance, so to some degree the team's performance is self-regulating. A successful team is therefore much more than the sum of its parts: working in unison the team can produce much more than could the same people working together as a loose and uncohesive group.

(b)   T Aerospace Company can expect the following benefits from the adoption of team working:

- Increased innovation and creativity as the team members pool their creative energies in brainstorming and 'bluesky' activities

- Enhanced motivation and commitment from employees as they find that the fulfilment of the team's objectives also fulfils their own personal objectives

- Discipline and loyalty as the team is self-regulating

- Improved overall performance because of the positive synergy outlined in (a)

- Improved decision making as the motivated team makes greater effort to ensure that all decisions taken have been thoroughly and objectively evaluated

- Empowerment of employees as they take authority, responsibility and credit for their decisions and outputs

(c)   Despite the undoubted advantages that can accrue to individuals and companies with team working, the move to this approach is not without difficulties. This is mainly because, in group theory terms, not all teams are 'successful'.

- As the team is evaluated on its collective output it is possible for some individual team members to get away with not pulling their weight. Their poor performance may have a levelling effect on that of the other team members – in other words, there may be a 'dumbing down' effect.

- Another common effect of teams is what psychologists call 'group think', whereby the team members begin to conform to a set of beliefs and ideals which stifles creativity and which may actually be harmful to the organisation. Group think can make teams inflexible.

- There is no guarantee that the objectives of the team will coincide with that of the organisation. A team may become a force of its own, with its own agenda, rules and goals. Their objectives, say about pay and conditions, can conflict with the company's, and they can even become subversive.

- There may be conflict within the team, so that time which could be spent more productively is actually spent on resolving internal conflicts.

- While very successful teams can be highly innovative and creative, it is by no means certain that they are more creative and innovative than a well-informed and talented individual. The qualities of group levelling and group think do not apply to individuals, so they may actually be more useful in this respect.

- The mechanics of team activity may mean that they take a long time to reach the same decision that an individual could have reached much more quickly. This is particularly the case if the team is highly democratic and requires that all individual team members have an equal say. It may become logistically very difficult to achieve this, because of holidays, sickness etc.

- T Aerospace Company should also be aware that its more traditional existing managers may object to the creation of team working, either because they are resistant to new ideas, they doubt that it is actually a better way of working, or they have had previously bad experience of teams. As managers of teams they will be required to adopt, new more flexible approaches, and they may find it difficult to relinquish their role as prime authority for that of chief adviser to a team.

How these difficulties can be overcome depends critically on evaluating exactly what is the source of the difficulty. The following management action may be required:

- Implementing a system of reward that does not reflect only the overall output of the team but also the individual contribution and circumstances of each team member. This should counteract the levelling effect.

- Maintaining good communication with individual team members, and supporting their unique interests, should allow for management vigilance against the effects of group think. Where it is identified as a negative factor, the composition of groups should be varied over time. This should also help to protect against the possibility of groups pursuing interests which are not those of the company as a whole.

- Where there is evidence of negative conflict in a team (a small degree of conflict is often thought to be healthy), managers will need to counsel the team members involved. There may also need to be disciplinary action, or the removal of certain team members.

- Training and ongoing encouragement should be offered to existing traditional managers who are having difficulty adjusting to the new style of teams.

61   NYO.COM

Key answer tips

(a)   This is a straightforward re-iteration of the well known principles of a disciplinary procedure. If these have been absorbed, a good portion of the 12 marks is available.

(b)   A more challenging question but only 8 marks are at risk. It calls for evaluation which is not generally well covered in texts, and so many answered would draw on students prior experience or 'common sense'.

(a)   The guidelines for drawing up such a procedure should, in the UK at least, follow the handbook issued by the Advisory, Conciliation and Arbitration Service (AGAS). These can be used to defend any action taken by NYO.COM if an employee submits a claim through UK legislation to the Employment Tribunal.

These guidelines state it should:

- be in writing

- specify who it applies to

- provide a progressive procedure with leave for appeal

- indicate who is responsible for its interpretation and implementation.

- indicate the types of offences which result in progressive action, or, in the case of gross misconduct for instant dismissal.

- specify that investigation must be thorough and that the individual must be able to reply to accusations and if defined must be allowed to be accompanied by a TU rep or a colleague.

(b)   NYO.com should have a formal disciplinary procedure for several reasons. Firstly, as mentioned in part (a), its existence and use protects NYO from accusations of unfairness in operating discipline.

Secondly, any such bureaucratic means standardises norms and relieves managers of the task of explaining standards over and over again – hopefully it leads to the establishment of self-discipline so that fewer cases come to management for official action.

Thirdly, if gone through at Induction it protects employees from falling foul of the often unwritten codes of conduct which may be encouraged by colleagues (e.g. clocking-in a friend).

Fourthly, it can act as a measure of NYO reputation in that NYO can be seen as a sophisticated employer rather that a 'hire-and-fire' outfit.

MANAGEMENT OF CHANGE

62   DETERMINANTS OF CHANGE

Key answer tips

Split your answer into 2 sections. first of all discuss the main features of change, and secondly relate these to effectiveness. Allow equal time for each.

Change, and change management have become a recent management issue, though of course change is the only constant-according to Eli **Goldratt** in 'The Goal'. The problem is entrenchment of ideas and systems, which have worked well in the past. Moss **Kanter**

describes the process of teaching senior management of large organisations some basic facts about the environment as 'teaching elephants to dance'. The steps are easy - the problem is the mass of the elephant, as they are intelligent enough.

Change in the past has been seen as a trend - perhaps as a graph generated by sales as a regression coefficient. This incremental change lulls organisations into a false sense of security: Handy describes the awful situation of the frog in a beaker of water which is gradually heated. There comes a time when it's vital for the frog to jump out but the change of temperature is so subtle it defeats its sensing mechanisms and it dies in the boiling water. Reading the environmental changes, visioning the future needs scenario development - but not many firms seem capable of doing this, as Shell was before the 1973 oil crisis. Step-change is easier to see - a crisis caused by tripling oil prices, or a new piece of Government legislation, or a new competitor. Organisations can develop defensive strategies in advance of such events but usually are caught 'on the hop' and only when profits decline, and investors get worried, does senior management feel confident enough to act.

Recently, authors have talked about **'transformational change'** whereby complete changes of direction have taken place. This might have been better used to describe the wave of nationalisations of oil companies by host nations in the 1960s but recently 'double-loop' learning has taught organisations to question their 'raison d'être'. Many are now finding conditions so turbulent that they are selling off even profitable parts of their business to 'stick to the knitting' of their own 'corporate competences'.

Much of this is driven by stakeholder effectiveness models - yet another 'crisis of capitalisation'. In the US especially, shareholder value has become a motto, and subsidiary roles are allotted to the **Goal Approach** to effectiveness - external targets, to the **Internal Process** approach of efficiency and cost-reduction and to the **Systems Resource** approach of supply-chain management. All of these are still vitally important but have to deliver increased shareholders returns. In decline, the major oil firms in the US have engaged in direct strategies to increase shareholder value: buying back their own shares from the market'. This activity increases prices and reduces the number of shareholders - so increasing the dividend payable to each. This by-passes the strategic management of activities and concentrates purely on cash. Perhaps a sign of the future?

63   ORGANISATIONAL DEVELOPMENT

Key answer tips

(a)   A simple explanation is needed, although plenty of detail is required to gain the full 10 marks.

(b)   Plan your answer and explain why OD can be successful but remember to mention that it is often not seen as being effective.

(a)   OD is an attempt to use an **'open systems'** approach which is holistic in looking at all of the constituent parts of an organisation. Part of the reason for this is that certain elements – root causes – may remain hidden while the superficial symptoms of a problem attract the attention of managers. While a consultant may solve the symptomatic problem, it may have a knock-on effect on other areas, or even reappear in the same form sometime later. Also, the root causes, following Elton **Mayo's** Hawthorne studies, may well lie deep with group culture or individual needs. These cannot be accessed directly so a wide-ranging set of techniques was desirable. OD set out to be a systematic diagnostic framework – a conscious systematic and planned intervention to change the underlying cultures and/or values and behaviours of individuals and groups. According to **Thompson & McHugh**, many organisations used T-groups as sensitivity training as part of collaborative effort by managements and the behavioural/scientist 'change agents'. Team development also increased diagnostic and interpersonal skills.

Typically, it involves a cycle of investigation and feedback to the sponsors (senior management) while simultaneously engaging the involvement and participation of a wide range of opinion – by interview programmes, focus groups, observation and questionnaires. This requires active participation in the process by top management, identifying key internal change agents ('carriers' of the message), training and development of participants (both active and passive) and monitoring and evaluation cycles at different levels.

Large companies in the 1950s and 1960s used OD programmes, often to complement job enrichment contained within or separate from productivity deals with manual workers' trade unions. Such studies – like Glacier Metal, Shell, ICI and IBM became famous for unlocking the rigidities of attitudes built into management via history. Pettigrew's ICI study made it clear that this had to be done through existing structures – or attitudes would not of themselves change. OD largely ignored structure and reorganisations, concentrating instead an unfreezing attitudes.

This broke the paradigm of the organisation and allowed a range of initiatives – transformational or step-changes – either within the firm (such as productivity deals) or with regard to customers and markets. Gains were made largely by the enthusiasm generated by novelty. In some ways it prepared the ground for the changes that become necessary in the decades that followed – the 1973 oil shock which tripled oil prices, and the 1980s competitive market created by a freer trade environment and 'Pacific Rim Tiger' economies. The demise of OD as a panacea has been replaced by a more narrow, but still similar OD intervention based squarely an culture change programmes (from Harrison's 'role' to 'task') which requires commitment of employees allied to structural changes – de-laying, downsizing, outsourcing – and to process changes – empowerment, teambuilding, involvement and participation.

OD therefore has no particular outcomes but can be regarded as an enabling framework under which change can be isolated as a variable and managed more effectively than the past.

64   IMPLEMENTATION

Key answer tips

A simple question, already structured: four strategies for managing change giving the advantages and disadvantages of each.

(a)   **Participation**

This approach seeks to involve employees in the decision making process. There are cases where this has been extended to the designing of own jobs, payment systems etc. The advantage of this method is that it enhances commitment to change, since the employees have developed their own change. In addition, the wider range of input into the change process will bring in an equally wide range of knowledge and experience.

However, there are a number of significant disadvantages. First of all, there must be the culture and climate to permit participation in change. RC Townsend boasted how change worked in Avis with the same people. However, the type of person who would work for a car-rental firm is likely to be different, and probably more adaptable, than someone who is in a very highly programmed job with little scope for creativity.

Secondly, the greater number of people in the decision making process can give rise to an extremely protracted decision making process. Also, as is evidenced from the Japanese approach, no one is responsible and hence accountable for the decision.

Thirdly, there is a need for a high degree of trust between the management and work people. Again, there may not be the culture and tradition of this, with the result that the invitation to participate will be treated with considerable suspicion.

Fourthly, participation must be honest. Pseudo-participation is always exposed for the sham that it is, and only serves to exacerbate the problem. This can easily happen, since with the wide variety of people being involved, there is a high risk that plans for change degenerate into a talking shop.

(b) **Education**

There is a mistaken view that if people are better educated and trained, then they will be receptive to change. While better education and training may make changes easier, and create an environment where people are prepared to participate in the change process, it will also raise the expectation of the individual. This could mean an increased turnover as people become more marketable, or an exacerbated hostility derived from frustration where enhanced expectations have not been met.

(c) **Communication**

This assumes that if the plans for change are effectively communicated, then people will understand the need for change and accept the changes. This would lay the foundations for change to be implemented fairly easily and painlessly.

Sadly, the communication of the plans for change is subject to misinterpretation and, if the wrong medium is selected, manipulation into disinformation by self-seeking interests. In addition, communication can be a two-edged sword. People may learn of the need for change and morale may drop, exacerbating the current situation. Similarly, the more marketable people may move, and this will also create a situation where change is needed, but the best people to implement it have left.

(d) **Power**

This is where management exerts what is perceived as its 'right to manage' and imposes change unilaterally. Management has the formal authority to do this within the parameters of appropriate legislation, and the de facto situation in relation to the labour market. In periods of high unemployment, management may elect to take this option, knowing that if employees do not like the situation, then they should look very carefully at the alternatives. It is argued that this draconian method is a viable option only in times of high unemployment, but it could be argued that in times of full employment those who are not prepared to go along with the changes can be eased out less painfully.

Such a strategy has the obvious advantage of being easy and quick to implement, especially if the workforce is in a weak and demoralised position. However, there are two significant potential disadvantages. First, in the short term, there is the obvious problem identified by Etzioni that such a coercive strategy will fail to gain the wholehearted support of the workforce, with the result that the desired levels of motivation, morale and output will not be achieved. Secondly, in the long term the company may be building up further problems for itself. Unions have long memories, and a coerced, demoralised workforce provides a fertile area in which confrontation and antagonism will develop. As a result, when the time becomes ripe for a more co-operative approach, the management is unlikely to find the unions and the employees very helpful, or predisposed to comply with managerial wishes.

(e) **Manipulation**

This can be very similar to the power strategy. It is ostensibly less coercive. A management team may use the media of pseudo-participation and pseudo-effective communication to persuade the workforce about the need for change. Ideally it will be done through a mass meeting, similar to union meetings outside the factory gate. Agreement comes from position power and an unwillingness to step out of line. The benefits are the same as from the power strategy, as are the considerable disadvantages.

(f) **Negotiation**

This moves along the spectrum from autocratic styles to a more consultative approach, usually through the media of the unions. The objective is an acceptable compromise solution. Two possibilities exist. First, that one side wins and one loses. Compromises are often unsuccessful, so this approach may be the best way. Secondly, is the possibility to work towards a compromise. This option may not exist or it may be very unpalatable. The obvious example is where rationalisation is required. The unions may resist the closures, but the future of the whole company or even the industry may be at stake. This may mean that the path towards a compromise is really not available. It also means that one party to the negotiations is fighting with a considerable handicap.

The obvious advantage of negotiation is that it recognises potential conflict and seeks a solution without running the risk of creating damaging industrial disputes. It has the further advantage that the resultant agreement will produce a commitment to the changes and it will maintain the morale of the workforce and the output that management requires. However, it can be a protracted process and if it goes on too long, patience may be lost on both sides. It also depends upon the level of confidence that exists in the union and the negotiating team. If there is a feeling that the unions have sold the employees out, if they could have got a better deal, and if they feel they have been the victims of cynical manipulation, then the whole process will fail.

65 CRITICAL CHANGE FACTORS

Key answer tips

A simple question requiring extensive detail. Perhaps use OD to structure the answer.

Beckhard gave various conditions for failure to secure effective organisation improvements through change. These are listed below together with actions that should be taken to successfully overcome these issues and thereby implement change effectively.

(1) **Lack of senior management's total commitment** - managements visible commitment must be obtained from the beginning. Which means they must understand the issues, and the proposed changes and agree with them. Involvement in the formulation of proposals through working parties etc, can help in this process.

(2) **Use of OD techniques that do not meet the need** - there must be a full review of the issues that are affecting the organisation and understanding that change is a process that consists of a variety of activities.

(3) **Impatience for quick results and lack of internal resources** - whilst strategies for change will depend in part on the speed required, organisations must be made to recognise that quick - fit solutions can result in long-term problems. Therefore it is recommended that any change programme is designed and planned taking into account the issues, the number and level of internal human resources and the timescales.

(4) **Over-dependence on inside or outside help** - what is needed is an effective blend of the two types of resources, which bring together the internal knowledge and experience of the organisation and external technical expertise.

(5) **Gap between the change effort of senior management and middle management caused by a communication breakdown**. The issues, and reasons for change together with the change strategy must be communicated to everyone who is affected by the change, in order that they may understand the reasons and what is required.

(6) **Trying to fit major change into an old structure** - consideration must be given as to how the planned changes will affect the current organisation structure, the functions performed, the numbers employed and sometimes the geographical location of activities.

(7) **Resistance to change** - all of the above issues if not adequately addressed can result in employees resisting the change. Therefore, consideration must be given to developing an effective communication strategy at all levels; including employees as far as possible in the process and listening to views and suggestions. Employees must understand the need for change. Greiner comments that successful solutions are reinforced and accepted throughout the organisation through participation and rewarding employees for identifying problems and developing solutions.

66   OPPORTUNITIES TO COMMUNICATE

Key answer tips

A simple question requiring good knowledge. Split into five competencies (each has 4 marks attached).

Tutorial note: it is not quite clear what is meant in this question by the 'competencies' involved in building a learning organisation. The examiner's own answer does not make this clear, and does not refer specifically to five of anything. In the solution below we assume that the kinds of technique required are similar or identical to those identified by Pedler, Burgoyne and Boydell.

A **learning organisation** is 'An organisation that facilitates the learning of all its members and continuously transforms itself'.

The aim is to design an organisation which is capable of adapting, changing, developing and transforming itself in response to the needs, wishes and aspirations of people, inside and outside. These organisations will be able to achieve their objectives without predatory takeovers, mergers or divestments. They will be able to avoid the large scale restructurings that are now commonplace in industry.

When an organisation is going through a development phase that integrates its activities, employees and ideas, this is when the organisation starts to take a 'learning approach' to change.

Self-development and **action-learning** is also one of the foundations of the learning organisation; as the organisation learns from the actions that it carries out so does the individual.

Diversity is one of the most vital aspects of the learning organisation. How an organisation manages to work with diversity is one of the keys to learning and productivity. Organisations usually try to ignore or suppress diversity, as acknowledging it can lead to a loss of control.

The learning organisation approach takes the stance that learning begins in differences. Different interest or pressure groups may have different interests, the organisation needs therefore to identify what the key differences are. Each organisation has to decide what level of diversity and difference it is ready to deal with, and what is the potential for learning and development. In this way pressure groups are valued for their diversity and the possible new ideas they may generate.

Pedler et al have identified 11 characteristics of the learning company.

For the learning organisation to become reality there must be constant energy flows and connections between the individual and collective levels.

The eleven characteristics are as follows. (Tutorial note: any five of these would be sufficient for the purpose of the question, assuming the interpretation spelled out at the beginning.)

(1) **Learning approach to strategy**. The process of strategy formulation is designed with learning in mind and incorporates experimentation and feedback.

(2) **Participative policy making**. All members of the organisation are encouraged and given the opportunity to contribute to policy making as part of the learning process.

(3) **Information**. Information is a resource to be exploited by all members of the organisation, not a 'power tool' reserved for a chosen few.

(4) **Formative accounting and control**. Accounting systems are designed in such a way that members of the organisation can learn how the cash resource is used.

(5) **Internal exchange**. Members of the organisation are encouraged to see internal users of their outputs as 'customers'.

(6) **Reward flexibility**. Members of the organisation are encouraged to see the diversity of rewards they enjoy (not just cash) and there is openness about why some people are paid more than others.

(7) **Enabling structures**. The structures of the organisation - everything from office layout to managerial hierarchy - are regarded as temporary arrangements which can be altered in response to changing conditions.

(8) **Boundary workers as environmental scanners**. In other words, members of the organisation who have contacts outside the organisation - salesmen, customer service staff, purchasing staff etc - should impart the knowledge they derive from such contacts to improve the organisation's knowledge base.

(9) **Inter-company learning**. A common example is benchmarking, where one company studies a particular system or process within another company with a view to improving its own performance.

(10) **Learning climate**. Management must foster a climate in which workers understand that part of their task is to improve their own knowledge and to share knowledge with other members of the organisation.

(11) **Self-development for all**. A priority for management should be the provision of opportunities for structured learning - courses, seminars, etc.

67 DECLINE

Key answer tips

(a) Identify the three categories of decline – vulnerability, atrophy and environmental and explain, with examples where possible, the entropy causes of each.

(b) Only 4 marks, so suggest general ways of reversing the decline identified in (a).

Decline is the third and final stage of the life-cycle.

(a) **Decline** is defined as a year-on-year fall in profitability. The three categories are vulnerability, atrophy, and environmental entropy.

Vulnerability describes a situation after the initial start-up of small firms. Here, cash is provided initially from the owner – managers who may sell assets and raise bank loans, in order to buy equipment; begin advertising and hire staff. Gradually business may build up but the cash generated is often required to pay for ongoing expenditure rather than to reduce overhead costs.

After initial enthusiasm from staff, and the novelty effect on customers, initial growth may slow abruptly and future inroads into capital cause the owner – managers to seek further assistance from the Bank, thus increasing their gearing and their risk. Efforts to support failing products and services may result in overtrading or simply be 'throwing good money after bad'. Eventually cash runs out and liquidation proceeds.

Atrophy describes an organisation used to cash from its 'cash cows' but not investing this into its 'stars' or 'problem children' (using the BCG matrix terms). Where its environment has been relatively stable in previous years, a fall in profits may be seen as a 'blip' and covered up by various forms of what **Griffiths** calls 'Creative Accounting'. Internal ratios may not have been seen as important and so the warning bells do not ring. **Slatter** (1984) describes eleven such causes in his analysis of decline including poor financial control of acquisitions and big capital projects. Symptoms are treated in the short-term which eventually makes matters worse: de-layering, downsizing and outsourcing to reduce costs removes key internal competences and lead to a loss of morale.

Slatter does not deal with external forces except to suggest a lack of (internal) marketing effort in a more competitive market. However, environmental entropy is a common cause of the decline of whole industries. This happens in the movement of commodity prices, or when developing nations undercut costs and/or provide additional services or benefits on a global scale. Traditional industries like steel-making become threatened by over-capacity. This may be related to changes in technology and/or customer demand which were not anticipated. Many large firms are moving from bulk wholesale commodity products to special niches – including steel and chemical firms. Chemicals has traditionally been subject to wide variations in demand over a five-year 'boom and bust' trade cycle. Periods of entropy expose basic flaws within industries and organisations which may be exploited by competition e.g. supermarkets' take-over of petrol retailing.

(b)   Management may find decline difficult to reverse as cash has been used to prop up failing products rather than to acquire strategic businesses. Often, management is in a 'blinded' stage before 'faulty action' is taken, such an the cost-cutting referred to earlier.

Some firms manage turnarounds however – these were called 'sharp benders' as the graph of profits diving suddenly turned upwards after intervention of new management. New cohorts of managers typically 'unfreeze' the present situation and bring in new business ideas (successful 'recipes') from other firms or even from other industries. The internal structuring of the firm and its strategic direction are thus switched over: such as Rank-Xerox reinventing itself as 'document company' to ward off Japanese competition.

It is important, however, for managers to address what Goldratt calls 'root causes' lay going through a current reality free' of cause – and effect relationships. These start with identifying the symptoms (UDEs or undesirable effects) and mapping the causes of each. This process, as in many 'change' situations can be accelerated by the use of a change agent.

68   INFORMAL ORGANISATION

Key answer tips

(a)   A tricky question requiring planning as it is difficult to define. Remember to detail both the advantages and disadvantages.

(b)   This is also tricky. Do not forget to identify costs and benefits too.

(a)   The nature of the **informal organisation** is difficult to define precisely because 'informal' means 'unstructured', unofficial, and so is changeable. It can most readily be defined by the 'organisational iceberg' where tangible factors are above the water-line (the formal organisational structures) whereas the vast majority of structure lies beneath.

The informal organisation can be contrasted with the formal one: for instance, it has no hierarchical levels, jobs, positions, rules. It has no functional divisions or departments. Indeed the very nature of informal relationships means that formal positions are ignored – such as in social events, sport, common interest groupings – and these are slowly uncovered by informal chats between members. One major company discovered to its surprise that all of its best managers (who got on well with each other and cooperated to achieve common goals) were actually all part-time rugby players.

Communication is via 'the grapevine' often at lunch or round the coffee vending – machine, in lifts and lavatories etc. Sub-cultures emerge from departmental groupings around local facilities, whereas more communal spaces (such as a sports and social club) encourage far wider networks to form.

Benefits include; research which showed the 'grapevine' as adding to, rather than competing with, official sources. Formal sources will anyway be incomplete and much shorter, so that informal networks can explain deeper causes e.g. for changes and fill in gaps in knowledge, and the informal channels are often far quicker, adopt ordinary language and so are more understandable, and as the sources often have no 'axe to grind' they are usually believed.

Disadvantages to a business include the human nature problem of crises being more 'news worthy' than steady states, and disasters more interesting than success stories. Attribution theory stresses the common 'conspiracy theory' of many people, who see blame and deliberate planning as more preferable explanations than accidents. Rumours are therefore generally negative and spread quickly and are believed. These can result in insecurity, low morale, resistance, even overt conflict.

Secondly, the system needs 'gatekeepers' who to maintain their informal role promote new stories regularly to appear 'in the know'. They have their own motives and embellish stories to satisfy their audience. They may already hold positions of influence such as trade union representative, staff association member etc.

(b)   Managers can identify the gatekeepers and either make use of them by feeding them information (informally of course), or by isolating them if their stories are always negative.

Simply by recognising the existence of the informal networks, managers can manipulate them, by recruiting newcomers with certain attitudes or attributes which may break-up a coherent informal grouping, or using the induction process as a way of instilling norms – **Mardlington & Wilkinson** refer to this an 'indoctrination'.

Setting up informal newsletters, printed by the organisation (e.g. the Quality Committee News) allows individual members to write but editing (and vetoing some remarks) would still lie with the relevant managers.

69   Y

(a)   Change in organisations has positive and negative attributes. On the positive side, it means experiment and the creation of something new. On the negative side, change means discontinuity and destruction of familiar social structures and relationships. Despite the positive aspects, change may be resisted because it involves both confrontations with the unknown and loss of the familiar. Change presents those caught up in it with new situations, new problems, ambiguity and uncertainty. Many individuals, groups and organisations find change, or the thought of change, painful and frustrating.

Individuals - seek to protect a status quo because they have a fear of the unknown. They develop a vested interest in the perpetuation of particular organisation structures and accompanying technologies. Changes may mean the loss of jobs, power, prestige, respect, approval, status and security. In the case of 'Y', it may also be personally inconvenient for a variety of reasons. It may disturb relationships and arrangements that have taken much time and effort to establish. It may force an unwanted location or geographical move or alter social opportunities. There could be problems with learning new skills. Some employees will fear that they will fail and will be reluctant to take on retraining. Perceived as well as actual threats to interests and values are thus likely to generate resistance to change.

Groups - there will be groups of people who see their position threatened and who will combine to resist any threats to their position. In particular, the middle management groups, fearing de-layering, will feel threatened and will be looking to their trade union to protect their interests. There may well be calls for industrial action or action to obtain the highest possible severance pay or redeployment terms. Even without the help of a trade union, groups may collude informally to resist change. They may do this by withholding information or by not being wholly co-operative with those seeking to implement change.

Organisational - at this level there will be a number of factors that will make the change process difficult. These include the existing investment in resources and past contracts and agreements with various organisational stakeholders. It is especially difficult to renegotiate the terms of the contracts with stakeholders, such as the trade unions. However, the main factor is the existing structure and culture of the organisation. Firms that change from a role culture, in a relatively stable and a large-sized organisation, to a different culture that requires a flatter, more organic, organisational structure to cope with competition in the open market, will have problems in surviving such a dramatic change

(b)   There are a number of ways that change can be facilitated. Kurt Lewin developed a general-purpose diagnostic and problem-solving technique to bring about change and improve performance. His force field model suggests that in any situation there are forces that push for change (driving) as well as forces that hinder change (restraining). If the forces offset each other completely, it results in equilibrium and status quo. Change can be brought about by increasing the driving forces or by reducing the restraining forces. Lewin's force-field theory of organisational change is illustrated below:

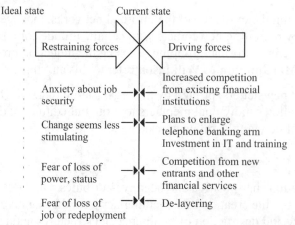

Using this model, we can show that the major driving force for change is the increasing competition brought about by changes in the industry environment. There are few options for 'Y' except to respond to it by becoming leaner and more effective. Reducing management levels and its consequent reduction in staffing levels should help to cut costs. The strengthening of the telephone banking division should help the bank's competitiveness, as should the investment in IT and training.

Despite clear evidence of the threat to the future of the bank, the plans that management have produced do not seem to have convinced the employees. The management should attempt to communicate the message to managers and other employees more effectively. It is not clear from the scenario what methods have been used to communicate to the workforce either the seriousness of the bank's situation, or the rationale behind senior management's plans to combat this situation, but this must be an early priority for the senior management team.

J Kotter and L Schlesinger suggest education and communication, along with other means, such as participation, manipulation and coercion as specific methods for overcoming resistance to change.

Resistance may be based on misunderstanding and inaccurate information. When this happens, it is important to get the facts straight and to discuss and reconcile opposing points of view. Managers should share their knowledge, perceptions and objectives with those who will be affected by the change. This may involve education eg, a training programme, face-to-face counselling, reports, memos and group meetings and discussions. However, the managers should tread carefully because bank employees generally have a high level of education and it would not help the case for change if management underestimated this.

A method associated with communication and education is that of facilitation and support. The management at 'Y' may be able to alleviate the fears of some individuals by the use of counselling and group discussion.

Participation is another way of reducing resistance to change, involving all employees from the start of the change process. Collaboration can have the effect of reducing opposition and encouraging commitment. It helps to reduce the fears that individuals may have about the impact of changes on them and makes use of their skills and knowledge. By putting the problem the bank is facing to employees in a series of face to face meetings, and offering the possibility of participation in the decision-making and planning process, it may be possible to get more employees to buy into the planned changes.

Given that the decisions have been made at 'Y' and that resistance has already been encountered it may well be that the best way forward is now through a process of negotiation and agreement with representatives of the workforce. Trade union officials will probably represent the employees' side. A process of negotiation and bargaining may result in concessions from management, in terms of built-in safeguards and appropriate compensation for the union members. The bank could then be allowed to continue without further interference.

Management could always try the manipulation or co-optation approach. They can put forward proposals that deliberately appeal to the specific interest, sensitivities and emotions of key groups involved in the change. Alternatively, they can use information that is selective and distorted to only emphasise the benefits of the change. Co-optation involves giving key people access to the decision-making process eg, 'buying people off' with the promise of some kind of reward for going along with the proposed changes. These techniques may work in the short run but create other problems. Manipulation will eventually be discovered and will discredit the reputations of those involved. Trouble-makers who are co-opted tend to stay co-opted and may continue to create difficulties from their new position of power.

The last approach - the use of explicit and implicit coercion - is where the management abandons any attempt at consensus and may involve mass redundancies without right of appeal. This would have to be the approach of last resort since the image of the bank would suffer and the morale of the remaining workforce would be badly affected.

70   DB COMPANY

(a)   OD is developed as a strategic form of Operational Research, often linked to technology (such as socio-technical systems) especially New Technology and IT. The approach is systematic-in that OD treats the whole organisation, and treats it as a system, an open system within a wider environment. This means that a 'rich picture' is often created where the actual linkages (as opposed to the formal organisation chart) are assessed, problems identified and strategic options and solutions developed.

The model developed by Pugh and others is a cyclical process, where initial data is tested against reality through education and communication with employees, and is constantly refined by re-engagement with employees after each iteration.

OD might be used with the DB company to good effect, as there are clear indications that problems of co-ordination are preventing expansion. OD specialists would identify the links between the expanding environment and DB and identify key 'boundary-spanning' activities to see if these were accurate in number and/or depth. The linkages would be followed internally via an audit trail of paper-often secretly labelling documents and timing their appearance later through internal stages. This would be accompanied by observations (e.g. a meeting) and confidential interviews to assess non-structure barriers (e.g. people like Joan Timmins!)

If DB is a manufacturing firm, an experienced OD consultant could concentrate on the linkages between sales (promising too much too early) and production (coping with unbalanced lines, demarcations, work-in-progress, and changes to specification).

These results would be fed-back to cross-functional teams who would be set up to investigate and report on solutions which would be acceptable to DB staff.

(b)   An OD practitioner requires firstly an attitude based on personality which seeks out problems, is curious, and persistent in examining the breadth of an issue, patiently and objectively. Many are specialists in a particular industry where generic problems exist. These can lead the OD consultant to specific areas of investigation- such as the conflict between car sales and servicing in dealerships. Knowledge of a range of techniques (such as diagnostic software) and socio-psychological methods like 'behavioural event interviewing' would also be useful.

Skill is required in practising the knowledge, and this comes partly with experience but also from basic attitude to people. Interviewing can be a lengthy process where concentration is needed to get reliable data; it involves patience, tact and diplomacy to feed back results to clients, and operating software like Power-point needs skill to design and deliver a good presentation meeting DB's needs.

71   K COMPANY

Key answer tips

Learning organisations and assessment centres are both fairly new concepts which have been found to be successful in certain companies. K Company, as it is involved in a rapidly changing world, is a prime candidate for using such up to date methods. You should not have had much difficulty with this optional question.

(a)   Learning organisations are those that encourage questions and explicitly recognise mistakes as part of the learning process. Edler, Burgoyne and Boydell define the learning organisation as 'an organisation that facilitates the learning of all its members and constantly transforms itself'.

Peter **Senge** identifies five core competencies for any company that wants to become a 'learning organisation':

- Building a shared vision or common sense of purpose, so that all members of the organisation are pulling together all the time, instead of only being brought together by an external crisis.

- Achieving personal mastery of the issues to be learnt through continuous self-development and learning, and passing this learning onto others through the organisation's cognitive systems and memories. In this way, the organisation maintains and develops it own norms, values, behaviours and mental maps over time, even though the individuals who first 'learnt' them are no longer there.

- Utilising mental models, so that individuals can both identify the assumptions that they bring to a situation, and develop alternative ways of doing things which will have a significant impact.

- Team learning, so that not only individual team members but the team collectively learns how to tackle difficult situations and decisions without losing the benefits of team working.

- Systems thinking, so that a situation is analysed for how it fits together as a whole, rather than just as a set of separate problems to be solved separately. In particular, this involves an understanding of how the organisation as a whole fits together and functions, so that the effect of an issue which impacts on one part of the organisation can be analysed in terms of its impact on the whole.

Building up a learning organisation should be undertaken in stages. Initially the emphasis will be on bringing all the organisation's workers round to an understanding of the importance of such matters as continual improvement, quality and benchmarking as ways to achieve improvements in 'how we do things round here'. Bureaucratic brakes on such improvements should also be removed at this point.

In the next stages the organisation's managers in particular can be encouraged to think of new ways in which the organisation could function – for instance, new technology, new markets, and new ways of delighting the customer.

The final stage is achieved when the processes undergone in the first two stages have become a way of life for everyone involved in the organisation. The important point about this stage is that it should be maintained in the long term so that the organisation can benefit fully from all the effort that has been put in. In other words, building a learning organisation is a continuous process rather than a project which can be implemented and then left. This is of particular importance for K Company as it operates in conditions of permanent, rapid change.

The implementation of the ideas implicit in the learning organisation is a significant effort which K Company probably feels it cannot afford to fail in. The company should also be aware that cultural changes will be required.

(b)   The idea of the assessment centre is part of a philosophy that grew out of the obvious shortcomings of the application, interview and references alone as selection techniques. Assessment centres allow assessment of individuals working in a group or alone by a team of assessors, who use a variety of assessment techniques depending on the requirements of the client.

The first step towards setting up an assessment centre is to make sure that the jobs on offer have been fully analysed into a set of competences, against which a set of criteria can be developed. The assessment centre activities can then be designed so as to test these competences against the criteria. The activities can include, as well as interviews and 'psychometric' tests, hands on simulations, in-tray exercises, role-play and presentations. There may even be outdoor, team-building exercises.

Since assessment centres became a more widely used technique it has been shown that they are much better at predicting a successful match between the selected candidate and the employer. The wider the range of techniques used, the more successful the result in terms of a good match.

Because there is such a wide range of assessment methods used at an assessment centre, it is thus argued that the approach is more thorough and therefore more successful than the more traditional approaches. If nothing else, the process takes longer and allows the potential employer to see the candidates over a longer period of time, and therefore 'get to know them' in a number of situations. This contrasts well with the very time-constrained, artificial interview situation. The methodology must be rigorous however, or else there is the temptation to select the person who just seems the most sociable etc.

The big disadvantage of assessment centres is the cost of setting them up, administering them, staffing them and producing the results. Many smaller companies simply cannot afford them , although recruitment consultants can stage them on behalf of a client if there is a one-off, very important appointment to be made. If this is the situation for K Company then selective use of assessment centres will probably be very beneficial.

72   F STEEL COMPANY

Key answer tips

There is a lot of material in the scenario and you should be careful in part (a) to include all of it, and analyse it carefully. The most obvious model to use here is Lewin's unfreeze-change-refreeze force field analysis, although you could have adopted a contingency approach and still gained marks.

(a)   The situation outlined for F Steel Company can be usefully analysed using Lewin's force field analysis, whereby the facts are identified as being either forces for change or forces for resisting change, and either internal or external.

Force	Internal force for change	External force for change
Newly-appointed CEO	*	
High costs and low productivity	*	
Rising exchange rate		*
Subsidised steel companies		*
Weak domestic demand		*
Strong overseas demand		*
Late deliveries	*	
Customers complaining about quality	*	*

	Internal force resisting change	External force resisting change
Trade union attitude	*	
Complacent managers	*	

(b)   Lewin's force field analysis, which identifies both forces for change and forces for resistance to change, is probably most appropriate for the CEO to use a change management model.

The main point of the model is that it highlights those forces for change in the right direction that should be encouraged, and those forces for resistance that should be diminished.

The model is not that straightforward, however. For instance, the fact that the force should be for change *in the right direction* is important; obviously the fact that costs are high and productivity is low is a force for change, but if it were encouraged the company would end up in liquidation! In addition, not all forces for change can be encouraged. External forces for change in particular are not always open to influence from the organisation. For example, it is unlikely that F can do anything at all about the exchange rate, as this is a macro-economic factor. Weak domestic demand for steel also probably cannot be affected by one producer, at least in the short term. The existence of subsidised steel companies overseas is difficult to affect, though in the long term pressure can be brought to bear on governments to level the playing field.

The main thrust of force field analysis therefore is to concentrate on those internal factors that can be influenced in the right direction. In turn these may affect external factors, such as customer complaints and the share of the strong overseas demand taken by F.

On the basis of this analysis the CEO should attempt the following steps for change:

- **Unfreeze**: develop understanding of the need for change, and reduce the factors that maintain and reinforce undesirable current behaviour. As the main forces for internal resistance are the attitudes of trade unions and managers, the CEO can unfreeze their behaviour by laying out clearly how far the company is threatened by the competition, and getting them to understand that without change the survival of the company, and therefore of jobs, is uncertain.

- **Change**: develop the desirable new attitudes and behaviour in all employees so that change is effected. This might be a lengthy and difficult process, as the facts can be difficult to communicate in a positive fashion that will encourage people to change their behaviours, Seminars, question and answer sessions, examples of other companies who have changed successfully, and committees of workers putting forward ideas, are all mechanisms by which change can be both encouraged and implemented. As well as employee involvement, the threat of redundancies and penalties, and the opportunity for rewards and new ways of working, should be made clear. These will need to be discussed and agreed by the trade unions. As the point at issue is effectively the survival of the company, it should be possible to achieve this. Negotiation is also required with the managers, and it may be that some of them will have to be made redundant if they continue to resist change.

- **Refreeze**: ensure that the new behaviours are firmly embedded by means of supporting mechanisms such as pay and conditions. The company should be sure to implement whatever promises regarding rewards and opportunities it made during the change process, but more importantly the pressure for constant improvement and continued change must be kept up.

73 BILL AND JOHN

Key answer tips

(a)   This is a fairly general question. The main parts of the answer refer to the problems of the entrepreneur. A diagram of the entrepreneurial organisation is not required however. The main problems cover the functional areas which have not yet developed – financial; control; marketing; HR; owners skills' in managing - a fairly easy 8 marks.

(b)   The mainstay of this specific question is the model of growth – most students are familiar with Grenier – and the answer is a fairly straightforward reiteration of this – difficult to gain the 12 marks unless you know the model perfectly.

(a)   Most commonly, entrepreneurs are skilled or technical people who want to be free of employment and use their skills in the market-place. Whiles this individualistic personality can be a strength, the tendency not to seek or follow advice often goes with it. Furthermore, technical specialists are frequently not skilled in general management and have difficulty delegating, motivating and controlling staff.

The start-up is often underestimated by the entrepreneur and the bank, commonly holding the personal assets of the borrower. Under-capitalised, charged high interest, and often naïve, the entrepreneur may be intimidated by late payment of bills and run out of cash. Frequent renegotiation of overdraft limits undermines the bank's confidence and adds to their charges and reluctance to be flexible over the terms of any loan repayment (e.g. capital 'holidays').

Frequently located where the entrepreneur lives or in cheap accommodation, start-ups do not attract staff with the skill and attitude required in an uncertain environment. In order to adhere to the business plan, pay is often targeted on the low side of local market rates, or jobs advertised as part-time. This leads to recruitment, retention and motivational problems.

Allied to personality and technical attributes, very many start-ups do not spend enough resources (time as well as money) understanding the market. The product or service usually comes first, and even where this is novel or high-quality its price may put off potential buyers, or its distribution via retailers may be difficult, inadequate, or incorrectly placed with the wrong type of dealer.

(b)   **Problems they are likely to face**

Greiner's (1973) model of growth encompasses stages of 'evolution' interspersed with crisis periods of 'revolution' and change.

Initially as entrepreneurs the organisation will grow through their own creativity but soon they will take on so much work they will need to delegate and face a crisis of leadership. If they can solve this the business will be on a firmer footing and grow by having a sense of direction. Later, those to whom power has been delegated face a problems of a lack of perceived autonomy, and may leave to seek responsibility elsewhere.

Further delegation – perhaps through divisionalisation – may solve this issue but the freedom given eventually reaches a point where the owners fear a lack of control. This control crisis is solved by better horizontal and vertical coordination – perhaps by a formal strategic planning function, or through a committee structure. The danger here is the issue of excessive bureaucracy of rules, regulations and stages of approval; a crisis of 'redtape'. This can be solved by a reversal of attitude to one near the founders' original ideas – senior management must re-invent themselves and create a shared vision which results in implicit collaboration.

Section 5

MOCK EXAMINATION QUESTIONS

SECTION A – 20 MARKS

ANSWER ALL TEN SUB-QUESTIONS – 2 MARKS EACH

1   MULTIPLE CHOICE QUESTIONS

1.1   An advantage of a centralised management structure for an organisation is that it is more effective than a decentralised organisation in relation to:

    A   flexibility of operation

    B   employees taking responsibility

    C   standardisation of procedures and methods

    D   the encouragement of initiative.

1.2   Mintzberg identified four broad types of organisational form. The most appropriate form for an organisation depends on the variety of the environment within which it exists.

What type of organisation structure is most appropriate for an organisation that has a simple relationship with its environment but where the environment is fast-changing and dynamic?

    A   Entrepreneur start-up

    B   Machine bureaucracy

    C   Professional organisation

    D   Adhocracy

1.3   Which of the following is inconsistent with the principles of scientific management?

    A   The empowerment of workers

    B   Tight control over the working environment

    C   The payment of incentives to workers

    D   Scientific selection and development of employees

1.4   An individual has influence within an organisation by virtue of one or more sources of power. Which source of power enables an individual to exercise influence through persuasiveness or negotiation?

    A   Resource power

    B   Legitimate power

    C   Position power

    D   Personal power

1.5   The so-called '4 Ps' of the marketing mix are product, place, price and promotion. For service organisations, the marketing mix is sometimes said to consist of the '7 Ps' rather than the '4 Ps'. Which of the following are in the '7 Ps'?

(i)   People

(ii)   Plan

(iii)   Process

A   (i) and (ii) only

B   (i) and (iii) only

C   (ii) and (iii) only

D   (i) (ii) and (iii)

1.6   Two of the objectives of human relations management (HRM) is to meet the social and legal responsibilities of the organisation towards its employees.

Which of the following HRM activities is relevant this objective?

(i)   Training

(ii)   Health and safety

(iii)   Welfare

A   (i) and (ii) only

B   (i) and (iii) only

C   (ii) only

D   (ii) and (iii) only

1.7   Which of the following items will appear in a job description?

(i)   Job title and responsibilities

(ii)   Who the job holder reports to

(iii)   The skills needed to do the job

(iv)   The rate of pay for the job

A   (i) only

B   (i) and (ii) only

C   (i) (ii) and (iii) only

D   (i) (ii) and (iv) only

1.8   According to Schein, what is the greatest cause of resistance to learning and change within an organisation?

A   Insecurity

B   Culture

C   Leadership

E   Human nature

1.9   Fiedler suggested that a relationship-oriented approach to leadership will be more effective than a task-oriented approach to leadership where the work situation is neither 'favourable' nor 'unfavourable'. The 'situation favourableness' depends on three variables: position power, task structure and leader-member relations.

In which combination of the following circumstances is a relationship-oriented leadership style be more effective?

	Position power	Task structure	Leader-member relations
	W = weak	S structured tasks	G = good
	S = strong	U = unstructured work	P = poor
A	S	S	G
B	W	S	G
C	S	U	G
D	W	U	G

1.10 **A company has established a team to advise the board of directors about corporate social responsibility. They include an environmentalist, a corporate lawyer, a finance specialist and the company secretary.**

The team has had several meetings to discuss a plan of action. Group members are still expressing strong but differing views about how to proceed, and arguments have become quite heated at times. The group has divided into two 'camps', one centred around the environmentalist and the other centred around the finance specialist. These two individuals have argued frequently and seem to dislike each other.

In Tuckman's analysis, what stage of development has the new advisory team reached?

A   Storming

B   Norming

C   Performing

D   Forming

SECTION B – 40 MARKS. ANSWER BOTH COMPULSORY QUESTION

2   THE B COMPANY

The B Company is in many respects a dinosaur, with a culture and structure from a time that has now passed. The company enjoyed much of its growth during the 1950s and 1960s under the leadership of its founder manager, Ben Tough. The company originally provided fittings for ships built in the local shipyards but, as the shipyards declined, the company moved into manufacturing a range of fixtures and fittings for the new homes being built for an ever-more prosperous population. As the company grew, it developed the characteristics typical of an organisation that enjoys a relatively secure market. In the interest of economies of scale it developed mass-production techniques and these, combined with good control systems, enabled the company to keep costs low.

Though Ben Tough retired long ago, B has maintained the hierarchical, centralised command and control structure that had been his hallmark from the early days. Over time, B also developed rules and procedures for almost every aspect of the business. In times of stable markets and steady growth, these set routines and procedures served the company well, but as the company moved into the latter end of the twentieth century, the market for B's products became saturated and senior management realised that, if they were to survive into the future, they would have to diversify into new products. Building on what they considered to be a core competence - B's manufacturing capability - the company moved into the growing and fast-moving world of consumer electronics.

At first, things went well. The company was able to transfer the skills it developed in the assembly of household fixtures and fittings to the production of a range of electronic consumer goods. However, as time went on, the market became increasingly competitive and less stable. This was partly to do with the increasing number of imports from developing countries, and partly to do with the increasing pace of change brought on by developments in microelectronic technology and by consumer demand for state-of-the-art gadgetry.

Despite its best efforts, senior management has found it difficult to cope. It is not that the management lacks an active approach to problems: the company has invested heavily in the latest production technology and recruited designers and electronic engineers to help it to respond rapidly to the developments in the market. Just why the company is not doing better is difficult to identify, but a chance remark by one of the designers leaving to work for a competitor provides a clue. Asked why he was leaving after such a short time, he replied, 'It's the way you do things around here. I just don't seem to be able to fit in. People at higher levels seem remote, and even those lower down don't appear to want to listen. Everybody seems cosy in continuing to do things in the same old way.'

Requirements:

As a consultant hired by the company, you have been asked to conduct an investigation into the degree of fit between the culture of the company and the demands it now faces in the market place, and to come up with a set of recommendations.

You are asked to structure your report into three main sections as follows:

(a)   describe the existing organisational culture of the company in terms of any well-known classification;   **(6 marks)**

(b)   explain the lack of fit between the existing culture and the demands of the market place;   **(6 marks)**

(c)   make recommendations for the type of organisational culture that you consider will best fit B's new situation, and justify your choice.   **(8 marks)**

                                                                                                        (Total: 20 marks)

3   GREG PYE

Greg Pye is the chief executive of a medium sized company that traditionally has been organised hierarchically according to function. After attending a management seminar, he decided to encourage inter-functional departmental co-operation by implementing a matrix structure in the organisation.

Greg agreed that a matrix organisation and cross-functional team working would provide flexibility and enhanced performance to the organisation. However, the company secretary drew Greg's attention to some potential drawbacks.

These include the possibility that 'people won't know who they are meant to be reporting to, supervision will be difficult for their line manager who thinks they are working in their teams and team leaders will have no real authority over the team members.'

After speaking to the company secretary, Greg began to have second thoughts about the matrix structure. Greg decides to ask for a more considered view of restructuring the company.

Required:

Greg Pye has asked you to explain:

(a)   the advantages of the existing hierarchical structure   **(7 marks)**

(b)   the advantages of introducing a matrix structure   **(7 marks)**

(c)   how Greg and his management team can address the concerns expressed by the company secretary   **(3 marks)**

(d)   how it might be possible to gain some of the benefits of a matrix structure without fully restructuring the organisation.   **(3 marks)**

                                                                                                        (Total: 20 marks)

SECTION C – 40 MARKS. ANSWER TWO QUESTIONS ONLY

4   STAKEHOLDER OBJECTIVES

Explain, with examples, the importance of both internal and external stakeholders in setting objectives for an organisation.   **(20 marks)**

5   ORGANISATIONAL STRUCTURE

You are required to discuss the research work of Lawrence and Lorsch into organisational structure, and comment on their conclusions.   **(20 marks)**

6   RECRUITMENT CHANNELS

Your organisation is a dynamic IT services firm seeking technical and creative staff to design websites for demanding blue-chip customers.

(a)   Discuss the traditional and modern channels of advertising these vacancies.**(15 marks)**

(b)   What would you include in the advertisement 'copy' to attract applicants.   **(5 marks)**

(Total: 20 marks)

7   MANAGEMENT STYLE

It has been observed that different styles of management are required at different stages of an organisation's development.

Requirements:

(a)   Define 'management style' and illustrate your answer with reference to any one well-known classification.   **(8 marks)**

(b)   Explain why the style of management may need to change as an organisation passes through the various stages of birth, growth, maturity and decline.   **(12 marks)**

(Total: 20 marks)

Section 6

ANSWERS TO MOCK EXAMINATION QUESTIONS

SECTION A

1   MULTIPLE CHOICE QUESTIONS

1.1   C

Flexibility, responsibility-taking and initiative-taking are generally associated with a decentralised management structure.

1.2   A

Environmental variety depends on the degree of complexity and the pace of change. The environment and the relationship of the organisation with its environment can range from simple to complex. The pace of change can vary from stability to dynamic change.

Mintzberg's four organisational forms are as follows.

Form	Complexity	Pace of change	Features
Entrepreneur start-up	Simple	Dynamic	Direct supervision
Machine bureaucracy	Simple	Stable	Standard processes and outputs
Professional organisation	Complex	Stable	Standardised skills
Adhocracy	Complex	Dynamic	The innovative organisation.

1.3   A

Scientific management is most commonly associated with the application of work study techniques (e.g. Taylor). The scientific school also favoured the close supervision of workers, which is inconsistent with empowerment.

1.4   D

Personal power describes the ability to persuade others, i.e. by reason of his or her personality, even if he or she does not have any other source of power or authority. An influential diplomat at the United Nations, for example, would owe his influence to personal power.

1.5   B

The additional three Ps are people (i.e. the people who deliver the service), process (i.e. the method by which the service is delivered) and the physical evidence of the service (e.g. a hotel might publish a brochure showing photographs of its facilities).

1.6   D

Health and safety is a legal obligation and welfare a social obligation. Training is neither of these.

1.7   B

A job description sets out the job title, the purpose of the job, and the main responsibilities of the job, who the job holder reports to, and which subordinates report to the job holder. It describes the job, but not the qualities required to do the job well, nor the rate of pay or salary for the job.

1.8   B

Schein suggested that organisations fail to 'learn' and change because of a lack of communication between different 'cultures' within the organisation. He identified three different cultures existing within an organisation that did not communicate well with each other.

(A)   The culture of operators. This evolves 'locally' in an organisation and is based on human interaction.

(B)   The engineering culture. Engineers are technology-oriented. They have a reference group outside the organisation that shares the same education and work experiences. They seek to 'design people out of the organisation'.

(C)   The executive culture. This is concerned with the financial health of the organisation. The reference group of executives is also outside the organisation. As executives reach a higher status within their organisation, they become more impersonal and see their employees more as a cost rather than as a capital investment.

As an organisation changes, these cultures collide. Engineers and executives are task-focused and see people as the barrier to change.

1.9   D

According to Fiedler, a relationship-style of leadership is more effective for combinations WUG, SSP and WSP. These are the combinations where the situation is neither very unfavourable nor very favourable. The other five possible combinations lend themselves to a task-oriented approach to leadership.

1.10 A

During the storming stage, conflict between group members can be strong and quite open. At the same time, there is much enthusiasm within the group and new ideas are being put forward. Leadership of the group can become an issue, particularly if there is no officially-appointed leader.

SECTION B

2   THE B COMPANY

REPORT

To: The Board of Directors, B Company

From: Consultant

Date: 15 May 20X0

Subject: Recommendations on the changing cultural environment for the B Company

The existing organisational culture could be described as a 'role culture', as identified by R. Harrison and others. In this type of organisational culture there is a formality of organisational structure, procedures and rules, which determine what is to be done. It is a role culture in that people act in terms of the roles specified by the job description. It is typical of large organisations, which operate in a relatively stable environment, such as that occupied by the B Company until recently. The Civil Service is probably the best example of a bureaucratic organisation, but large hospitals, large educational establishments and big corporations all exhibit aspects of this cultural type to some degree.

The increasing competition faced by B, together with the decreasing length of the product life cycle for consumer electronic products, has made for greater uncertainty and the need on the part of the organisation to be more flexible. The 'role culture' as outlined above is best suited to an environment, which is relatively stable and large sized organisations, as was the case with the B Company until relatively recently. Although it can adapt, this ability is restricted and the company will have problems in surviving a dramatic change, because the detailed rules and procedures, and the hierarchical centralised control structure will inhibit any kind of innovation. The chance remark by one of the designers leaving to work for a competitor seems to support this idea. His comments suggest that the only communication is downward in the organisation and that there is a reluctance to listen to employees. Individuals who work for this kind of company tend to learn an expertise without experiencing risk; many do their job adequately, but are not encouraged to be over-ambitious. This attitude is not conducive to changing market demands requiring flexibility.

The organisational type that would fit the B Company's new situation is the task culture, where management is seen as completing a succession of projects or solving problems. It is called a task culture because of its task, job or project orientation. This type of culture is reflected in a matrix organisation that is characterised by a lack of rules and a 'can-do' attitude to getting jobs done. Teams are established to achieve specific tasks, with team members having the requisite drive, skills and expertise to achieve the organisation's objectives. In such organisations, there is no dominant or clear leader. The principal concern in a task culture is to get the job done. Therefore, the individuals that are important are the experts with the ability to accomplish a particular aspect of the task. Individuals in the team have more influence than they would have if the work was organised on a formal 'role culture' basis. Information is likely to flow freely up, down and horizontally, so that the conditions of organisational learning are more easily met in this climate of co-operation. This type of culture is particularly suited to cope with rapidly changing product markets and production processes, such as the B Company is experiencing.

A change in the corporate culture of the B Company is a vital ingredient of the long-term success of its programme of change. The recommendation of this report is for the company to make a start on changing from its present role culture to a task culture. Because the culture of an organisation is very difficult to change, due to its deeply ingrained sets of values, beliefs and behaviour patterns of which participants may not even be conscious, the company may require some outside assistance to facilitate the change.

3 GREG PYE

Key answer tips

This question tests your knowledge of the fundamental issue of organisational structure, its importance as a communication system and your understanding of structural differences brought on by change. Don't waste time by drawing very detailed and involved structures - the majority of the marks in this question lies in listing/outlining the main ADVANTAGES of hierarchical and matrix organisational structures.

(a) The **organisational structure** defines the communications pattern, the control system and the command structure. The traditional hierarchical structure provides certainty, clarity and clearly. Such a structure defines:

- the communication pathways; the scalar principle provides an unbroken vertical communication line
- the linking mechanisms between management roles
- the allocation of formal responsibilities and authority
- the co-ordinating structure
- the relationships between departments, tasks and people and their duties
- the power structure; where power, control and decision making exists; strong leadership is possible
- management roles and official tasks
- the functional distinction between departments
- specialisation in departments, skills and management; procedures can be standardised
- unity of command; one superior and one source of influence
- the exception principle; decisions can be programmed and planning can form the basis of management
- decisions are made from the perspective of the whole organisation

(b) The **Matrix structure** allows cross functional activities to be undertaken whilst maintaining the function, skills and loyalties of departments. This type of structure is often associated with organisations which are product driven. The **advantages** of such a structure can be described as:

- Improvement in communication which will be lateral as well as hierarchical
- improved quality of decision making throughout the organisation
- direct contact between managers and employees replaces rules and bureaucracy
- management motivation is improved by greater involvement in decision making and control
- product driven rather than department driven and thus more aware of the market
- improved product knowledge by all the management
- improves quality of decision making, specially at times of change
- adaptive to local geographic conditions
- removes the problem of 'management islands' associated with the departmental specialisms inherent in the hierarchical structure
- managers are able to see and understand the whole picture
- reduction of stress on senior management
- provides flexibility across the organisation
- allows training and greater involvement for junior management
- improved control through de-centralised functions such as product budgets and profit centres

These ideas may well be more appropriate to a smaller firm such as Greg Pye's and are essential in an environment where there is constant adaptation to markets and technology.

(c)   The concern that individuals and managers may not adapt to a more flexible structure may be addressed by:

- team development and building
- balancing the demands of uniformity and diversity inherent in the matrix structure
- creating appropriate reporting systems
- creating product teams and customer groups
- addressing problems of trust and confidence that will arise from the removal of role certainty in the traditional organisation
- a system of performance evaluation
- ensuring clear communication paths and patterns

(d)   It should also be noted that many organisations display combinations of structure. A manufacturing division may be organised along traditional lines whilst the marketing department may be organised along the lines of a matrix organisation.

In reality, organisational structures are often a mix of formal, hierarchical structures and other forms. However, there is the danger that Grey Pye might end up with an inappropriate and clumsy construct. The benefits of both could be achieved through a hybrid structure.

The production department, with its need for uniformity and certainty could remain as a traditional hierarchical structure. The marketing department requires less formality and exists in a more uncertain environment, thus a matrix organisation, based in teams and products, might be more appropriate.

Overall however, a team based, product drive approach could be developed.

SECTION C

4   STAKEHOLDER OBJECTIVES

Key answer tips

Split the answer into 2 sections, internal and external.

Remember to include examples.

Explanation should focus on objectives.

There are three broad types of stakeholder in an organisation, such as a company, as follows:

(a)   internal stakeholders (employees, management);

(b)   external but connected stakeholders (shareholders, customers, suppliers, financiers);

(c)   fully external stakeholders (the community, government, pressure groups).

We shall consider each of them in turn.

Internal stakeholder - because employees and management (which includes the Chairman and the Board of Directors) are so intimately connected with the company, their objectives are likely to have a strong and immediate influence on how it is run. Within the organisation there are different stakeholder groups. All employees have objectives *as employees,* but also different departments compete for resources and influence in the organisation as a whole. For example, sales and marketing departments, for a variety of reasons will have objectives that the production department cannot meet. There might be a trade-off, for example, between market share and profitability.

External but connected stake holders - the objectives of **shareholders,** which are generally that of making a profit, are often taken as the prime objective that the company's management seeks to fulfil. But clearly **financiers** such as banks have similar objectives, which must be met (usually the payment of loan interest is a contractual obligation whilst the payment of dividends is not). The **customers'** objectives, in a market-led company, must also be fulfilled if the company is to be successful. Other stakeholders 'connected' with the company are **suppliers** and **distributors.**

Fully external stakeholders - these groups e.g, the government, local authorities, pressure groups, the community at large and professional bodies, are likely to have quite diverse objectives and have a varying ability to ensure that the company meets them.

How stakeholders relate to the management of the company depends very much on what type of stakeholder they are - internal, connected or external - and on the level in the management hierarchy at which they are able to apply pressure. Clearly a company's management will respond differently to the demands of, say, its shareholders and the community at large. This is because both the character of the relationship and the means by which the relationship is conducted depend on the relative bargaining power and philosophy of the stakeholder on the one hand and the company on the other.

The relationship may be characterised by a number of stances. Each party (stakeholder and company) may actively seek dominance or they may each adopt defensive roles. Ideally they should seek a **balance of objectives** but in turn this can mean that they may actively seek agreement or may merely react to circumstances as they arise. Hence the company and its employees/trade unions may have a relationship characterised by each party seeking dominance over the other, whilst with its customers the company may find itself reacting to the demands made of it by them. This shows that the ability to influence management does not necessarily arise from mere closeness to the company (employees are internal to the company but often the shareholders' and customers objectives are more important).

The way in which the relationship between company and stakeholders is conducted again is a function of the relationship's character, the parties' relative bargaining strength and the philosophy underlying each party's objectives. This can be shown by means of a spectrum as follows.

Weak			Stakeholder's bargaining strength			Strong
Command/ dictated by company	Consultation and consideration of stakeholder's views	Negotiation	Participation and acceptance of the views of stakeholders	Democratic voting by stakeholders	Command/ dictated by stakeholders

Stakeholders can influence the management of a company at a number of different levels:

- the strategic level (the main mission and objectives of the company)
- the planning level (how those objectives are going to be met) and
- the operations level (how plans are put into practice day-to-day).

When deciding on the company's mission and objectives, and the strategies to be adopted in meeting them, the company's board will almost certainly be constrained primarily by the interests of the shareholders (profit) but also by those of the customers (price, variety, reliability) and of other financiers (interest and capital repayments, value of security, value of shares). But the extent to which management has discretion to make profits for shareholders is itself constrained by the demands of customers for value and of financiers for reducing risk to their investment. A balance must clearly be reached.

The company must comply with identifiable constraints such as its statutory duty to exercise 'stewardship' over its shareholders' assets, its contractual duty to pay interest on loans and its legal duties regarding employment and environment protection. These may come into conflict with other stakeholders' interests and even with the company's preferred strategy such as to be 'market-led'.

Finally the company's strategy may be influenced by intangible constraints from the external stakeholders and the environment as a whole such as 'green culture and concern for Third World development and good employment practices.

Clearly many of the constraints affecting management at the strategic and planning levels will also filter down to the running of day-to-day operations. Certainly consumers will affect production aims (size, quality, colour) and procedures (planning, stockholding, computerisation) when demand is variable (as in the fashion and high-tech industries). Health and safety legislation for employees and consumer protection legislation also mean that day-to-day operations must be constantly reviewed for compliance. In some industries, customers can be very demanding and can exercise significant power. The big supermarket chains have a powerful influence over farms and food prices. In the industrial context, an important supplier can enforce major changes such as quality assurance and JIT.

In addition, management is constrained at every level by the legal environment in which it exists and the regulations with which it must comply. These can be said to arise from the objectives of the community at large and of the government, and can affect such things as employment rights, financial control and reporting, safety and environmental protection and the way in which competition is handled.

In practice, it is possible that objective setting will mean that there is a compromise between stakeholder demands. In a business, however, shareholder objectives, in theory at least, are the most important.

5   ORGANISATIONAL STRUCTURE

Key answer tips

An open question on differentiation and integration – but split into 2 sections.

Lawrence and Lorsch are known for their area of work called the 'contingency view' of organisational design. Their theory views organisations as open systems. These open systems in effect receive input and use resources from the environment and then export outputs as either services or products.

It becomes necessary at this point to consider how an organisation's internal characteristics are affected by external environmental influences.

Lawrence and Lorsch studied the environments from three different industries. These were food, containers and plastics. They approached this work by interviewing the managers and discovered it was possible to describe environments as being either uncertain and changing, or stable and certain. Following on from this they divided each firm into these areas, production, development, research and marketing, and viewed the sub-environments faced by them. The results were as follows:

(i)   Environmental uncertainty – varied for each area, lowest in production, highest in research and development. The research also suggested that the level of structuring in operation within the areas depended on the degree of environmental uncertainty.

(ii)   Research and development leaned towards a low degree of structure whilst production areas practised the highest.

(iii)   Marketing usually fell in between the two areas discussed in (ii).

The way in which units within the organisation are related was also researched. Results showed that varying levels of integration, i.e. units working together, occurred and also differentiation in the level of specialist work, particularly in manufacturing. It is helping with planning, resourcing and control throughout all stages of manufacture. Computers are used for controlling production, aiding design (CAD) and aiding manufacture (CAM). The result of using computers in this way has led to improved control of the production process, improved use of equipment and reduced stock held, thereby facilitating the use of JIT (just in time system). Other benefits are reduced labour costs and faster output by reducing the time between the stages of manufacture.

The use of CAD enables companies to cope with shortages of skilled workers. By using a small group of people working computers, a greater work output can be produced, therefore improving productivity. The use of the CAM system quickens the production of components and improves quality as well reducing the company's need for skilled workers. This results in financial savings as well as better productivity.

A computer offers vast storage enabling masses of information to be gathered and processed. Therefore the number of staff a company once used to handle processing etc. can be drastically reduced. This development has come to be called the 'de-layering' of organisations and has resulted in fewer levels within staffing structures.

As decision-making has undergone total re-organisation a faster overview of operations etc. is now possible. Also, the database is readily available to local managers and they can now take decisions when possible, without needing to refer to head office. Finally, as the decision-making process can be automated, it is possible for lower management to take on the responsibility freeing top level management to handle other matters.

In conclusion, all this new technology is constantly changing as it is updated. It has been necessary for staff to alter attitudes to such changes as well as accept the need for constant re-training etc.

6   RECRUITMENT CHANNELS

Key answer tips

(a)   The question wording is a bit of a giveaway – split into 2 sections, traditional and modern advertising channels.

(b)   Remember there are 2 types of staff – technical and creative but only 5 marks means a general answer is needed.

The traditional channels of recruitment rely on the press. For technical jobs, there may be specific days in the quality press at national level, or sections in the Sunday papers. Appropriate trade journals might also be used but these are often published monthly and so the time from writing the advertisement copy to applicants reading it can be several months. Daily papers have a weekly turnaround as do the Sunday papers. Additionally, there may be a paper which is nationally published but which is read by the target audience (in the UK the Express tends to advertise technical jobs), or in the larger cities an evening paper might be appropriate. Choosing the quality papers is not only expensive but gives the impression that these are very important jobs - with an expectation that salaries will be high. Choosing regional or 'tabloid' papers runs the risk of appearing less important. This is a question of judgement and using an Advertising Agency can help as they deal with many other firms similar to yours and should be able to show you success rates and costs. They are not cheap, but may be effective. Occasionally, for mass recruitment on a local level (such as a marketing survey or cultural 'event') local radio or even TV might be useful, though listener numbers may be low. Where there is an ongoing need, larger companies created the 'milk round' of universities in the UK so as to interview graduates 'en masse' directly. Government Agencies and schemes, though traditional, are often the wrong level for IT. Slightly less traditional, and sometimes seen as underhand, in the use of Agencies and Executive Search ('head-hunting'). Many firms have a database of categories of employee looking for alternative work - some of your own people may be on their books! They will approach people on your behalf, often not mentioning your name, and draw up lists for interviews.

More firms are now resorting to a wider range of ways of attracting good people. Nominations from existing staff is cheap if not very effective, for example, but the use of the Web, especially jobs websites is increasing. In the UK, universities have set up 'jobs.ac.uk' and some sites offer an email service which informs job-seekers of vacancies according to categories they have indicated they are interested in. This must surely be the future for job advertising.

The best way to attract applicants in number has to be balanced with discriminating selection. An over-emphasis on positives may result in an overwhelming response which takes weeks to sift and results in an unmanageable 'long list'. The career prospects, positive work atmosphere and technical details are important, but a salary package which is above the competition has to be a prime factor - despite many adverts keeping this confidential. At the same time, criteria must be inserted to keep out the unsuitable - essential qualifications, essential types of IT experience, length of experience. Perhaps some honesty too 'you will be expected to work late, travel frequently, be flexible and regard your weekends as essential IT-related self-development time rather than a leisure opportunity'.

7 MANAGEMENT STYLE

Key answer tips

(a) A simple question requiring a definition illustrated by just one theorist e.g. McGregor, Likert, Heckman etc.

(b) Your answer should be broken down into 4 sections: birth, growth, maturity and decline. A diagram may also help to embellish your answer.

(a) Management style can be defined as the approach used by a manager to exercise influence over other people, enabling them to achieve their objectives. There are a few well-known classifications of leadership style. The

Human Relations theories include contributions from Douglas McGregor - Theory X and Theory Y, and Likert's four systems:

- exploitive authoritative
- benevolent authoritative
- consultative authoritative
- participative group management.

Huneryager and Heckman identified four different styles of management:

- **Dictatorial style** – where the manager forces subordinates to work by threatening punishment and penalties.

- **Autocratic style** – where decision-making is centralised in the hands of the leader, who does not encourage participation by subordinates. Many of the most successful businesses have been led to success by autocrats who are paternalistic leaders, offering consideration and respect to the workforce, but retaining full rights in decision-making. Often they find it hard to delegate, to bring on successors, to stand down at the right moment, to switch off and go home, and to appreciate the views of others.

- **Democratic style** – where decision-making is decentralised, and shared by subordinates in participative group action. It is important not to allow a preference for democratic social systems to blind managers into favouring democratic management styles in all situations. Businesses can stand (and often need) firmer, more single-minded management than nation states would generally find healthy. Those who lead using the democratic approach suffer from being unable to move as quickly as competitor businesses led by autocrats and from people in the ranks not being clear as to exactly which direction they should be pulling in.

- **Laisser-faire style** – where subordinates are given little or no direction at all, and are allowed to establish their own objectives and make all their own decisions.

(b) As an organisation passes through the various stages of birth, growth, maturity and decline, the management style may need to change. One of the ways of explaining this process is to use Greiner's Life Cycle model.

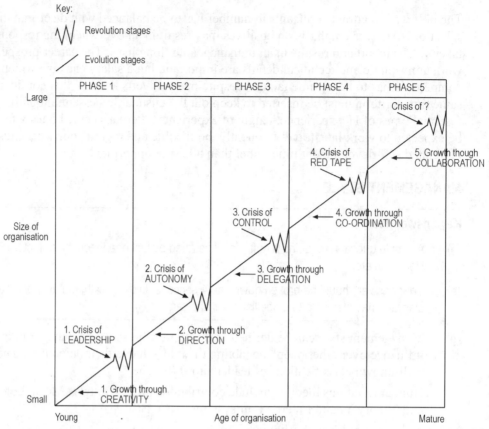

Greiner identifies five phases of growth. Each evolutionary period is characterised by the dominant management style used to achieve growth, while each revolutionary period is characterised by the problems that must be solved before growth can continue.

When the organisation is small, the leadership is personal and informal. The founders of the young business are generally actively involved at this stage. With their energetic and opportunistic leadership style, the creative potential can be channelled into growth. As the organisation grows, production becomes more efficient and there comes a need for skills relating less to products and marketing issues and more to the co-ordination of the organisation's activities. This is a crisis of leadership.

As the business expands, the organisation becomes 'structural' with a hierarchy of positions and jobs moving to greater specialism. This phase of growth exposes weakness in delegation. Management finds it more difficult to keep detailed control as there are too many activities and it is easy to lose a sense of the wider picture.

The response to the business problems of phase two is delegation. This has the advantage of decentralising decision-making. The person at the top of the management tree gets further away from the bottom and relies more and more on systems and bureaucracy. The managers needs to delegate, requiring less of a hands on approach and more of a people person and manipulator style of leadership.

During the fourth phase, the addition of internal systems and procedures helps to co-ordinate the activities and use the resources optimally. Management reward emphasises profit share and stock options that focus on both short and long term growth. However, the increased complexity can lead to a crisis of red tape as the procedures inhibit useful action.

The crisis of red tape is resolved by increased informal collaboration. Control is cultural rather than formal. Growth is encouraged through participation and mutual goal setting. Managers focus on problem-solving activities, which ensure the organisation's survival but also emphasises innovation for continued growth. The leadership style should encourage collaboration and co-operation, whilst managers focus on long-term high-level strategic development matters.

Section 7

NOVEMBER 2002 EXAMINATION QUESTIONS

SECTION A – 60 MARKS

ANSWER ALL THREE QUESTIONS

1   L COMPANY

L Company, a large multinational manufacturer of automobiles and delivery vehicles, has just announced that it is to close five of its automobile plants and to make a third of its 110,000 employees redundant. This represents a sharp decline from the exciting days of the mid 1990s when it released a range of best-selling models and generated record profits. Like many other successful companies, however, L Company became complacent and has lost market share to aggressive competitors. There is, however, some positive news for L Company in that its delivery vehicle division has just reported a slight increase in its annual sales. In publishing this news, the Chief Executive Officer (CEO) has promised that any jobs arising in its delivery vehicle division will be offered first to those made redundant in its automobile plants.

Required:

(a)   Using the scenario for L Company, explain the relationship between human resource planning and planning at the corporate and business levels.   **(12 marks)**

(b)   Assume that the Human Resource Managers in L Company are committed to a 'soft' RM perspective where employees are regarded as the organisation's most important asset. Explain how this might affect their human resource plans in the restructuring process.   **(8 marks)**

(Total: 20 marks)

2   S COMPANY LIMITED

S Company Limited assembles mountain bikes and related products, and retails them by mail order. The company was started by Sunil (a cycling enthusiast) and grew rapidly in the 1990s as mountain biking became popular as a leisure activity and competitive sport. Like many entrepreneurs, Sunil employed relatives and friends in the early days of the business and, even today, still prefers to employ people recommended by his own employees rather than go through any formal recruitment process. In fact, this is typical of the way the business is run. There is an absence of formal rules, systems and procedures. The organisation structure is flat, with Sunil making most of the decisions. Sunil's style of management means that relationships with employees are generally friendly and informal.

But not everything is going well. The company is experiencing a number of problems that are minor in themselves, but taken together are proving damaging to the company's performance. The most serious of these is the increasing number of returns from customers who are dissatisfied with bike assembly, missing parts or product quality. But there are other problems such as late deliveries, lost invoices, slow response to customer requests and complaints that, taken together, are having a negative impact on the company's profitability.

In the face of all these problems, Sunil has reluctantly hired a management consultant to conduct an investigation into the running of the business. The consultant's report has now been completed and the main recommendation involves the implementation of bureaucratic procedures. Sunil read the report with disbelief. He had always been led to believe that bureaucracy was something that produced inefficiency!

Required:

(a) Explain why the adoption of the features of bureaucracy (such as those advocated by Max Weber) would assist S Company Limited to overcome its problems and improve its efficiency. **(12 marks)**

(b) Explain why Sunil may be right to be suspicious of bureaucratic procedures as a solution to his company's problems. **(8 marks)**

(Total: 20 marks)

3   H COMPANY

H Company, a high-street clothing retailer, designs and sells clothing. Until recently, the company name was well-known for quality clothing at an affordable price, but the situation has changed dramatically as new entrants to the market have rapidly taken market share away from H Company.

One marketing analyst has commented that the problem for H Company is that it has never moved from being sales orientated to being marketing orientated and that this is why it has lost touch with its customers.

Required:

(a) Describe the difference between a company that concentrates on 'selling' its products and one that has adopted a marketing approach. Advise H Company on how to develop itself into an organisation that is driven by customer needs. **(10 marks)**

(b) Explain how the management in H Company could make use of the marketing mix to help regain its competitive position in the clothing market. **(10 marks)**

(Total: 20 marks)

SECTION B – 40 MARKS

ANSWER TWO QUESTIONS ONLY

4   D SOFT DRINKS COMPANY

The D Soft Drinks Company has become so convinced of the benefits of empowerment that it has decided to introduce empowerment throughout the company. As Director of the finance department, Mary has been instructed to empower her staff to bring the department in line with company policy. Mary is not enthusiastic. She has managed her department very successfully for 15 years and cannot imagine how empowerment would improve things. She already delegates some of her responsibilities to trusted members of her staff and regards any further delegation as likely to have a negative impact on the smooth running of the department rather than to improve its efficiency and effectiveness.

Required:

(a) Explain to Mary how empowerment can help improve the efficiency and the effectiveness of the organisation. **(6 marks)**

(b) Advise Mary on the steps she needs to take to ensure that empowerment is successfully introduced within the finance department of the D Soft Drinks Company. **(8 marks)**

(c) Discuss the main difficulties that Mary might anticipate when introducing empowerment. **(6 marks)**

Total: 20 marks)

5 X COMPANY

Until October 2002, Sheila was the Chief Executive Officer (CEO) of X Company, a manufacturer of washing machines and similar products. As Marketing Manager in the late 1990s, Sheila had been responsible for adding new products to the company range that boosted company profits, a success that had been largely responsible for Sheila's promotion to CEO.

In 2000, however, the company suffered a number of setbacks, and Sheila, in order to boost sales by bringing products to the market sooner, ordered that all testing of new products should stop. The consequences were disastrous; X Company was overwhelmed with returned merchandise.

In an effort to keep the share price high, Sheila ordered the Finance Director, Bob, to omit the recording of returned products. Bob initially protested that this would be unethical accounting, but eventually complied with Sheila's order. Under further pressure, Bob was also persuaded by Sheila to show an increase in sales and respectable earnings per share figures. Bob managed to do this by adjusting the way the company reported sales, by understating expenses and by generating several hundred false invoices.

A year-end audit exposed the misconduct of the two executives. Sheila was sent to prison for two years. Bob was imprisoned for one year and was struck off from membership of his professional body.

Required:

(a) Describe the sources of power and authority that would enable someone in Sheila's position to persuade Bob to behave as he did in the above scenario. **(12 marks)**

(b) Discuss the measures the Board of Directors of X Company might take to ensure that the abuse of power and authority that occurred in X Company does not occur again.

(8 marks)

(Total: 20 marks)

6 T INC

Sam is the Chief Executive Officer (CEO) of T Inc, a tobacco company. He has traditional views about the purpose of business in general and his own organisation in particular. Though he is frequently pressured by a variety of groups and organisations that think he should run his organisation differently, he sticks firmly to the view that the overriding purpose of business is to make money for the shareholders. His son, Frank, who is being coached to take over the CEO role, takes a very different perspective. In his view, T Inc has a responsibility to a wide range of stakeholders.

Required:

(a)　Explain how

    (i)　Sam would justify his view that the overriding purpose of the business is to make money for the shareholders;

    (ii)　Frank would justify his view that T Inc has a responsibility to a wide range of stakeholders. **(12 marks)**

(b)　Recommend the stages Frank should go through in determining the priority of the goals of T Inc when he becomes CEO. **(8 marks)**

(Total: 20 marks)

7　Z BANK

In order to meet the threat from new competitors, Z Bank has decided to implement a new strategy. The first part of the strategy involves supplementing its current services to customers by providing them with on-line Internet and telephone banking services. The second part of the strategy is to reduce costs by closing many of its rural and small-town branches (outlets).

In an attempt to pacify the employee representatives (the Banking Trade Union) and to reduce expected protests by the communities affected by branch closure, a senior Bank spokeswoman has announced that the changes will be 'incremental' in nature.

In particular, she has stressed that:

- the change will be implemented over a lengthy time period;

- there will be no compulsory redundancies;

- banking staff ready to take on new roles and opportunities in the on-line operations will be retrained and offered generous relocation expenses.

For customers, the Bank has promised that automatic cash dispensing machines will be available in all the localities where branches (outlets) close. Customers will also be provided with the software needed for Internet banking and other assistance necessary to give them quick and easy access to banking services.

The leader of the Banking Trade Union is appalled at the intended action of the Bank. He has argued that the so-called 'incremental' change is in fact the start of a "transformational" change that will have serious repercussions, not only for the Union's members but also for many of the Bank's customers.

Required:

(a)　Using planned change theory, recommend how the Bank's new strategy can be successfully implemented. **(12 marks)**

(b)　Describe the difference between incremental change and transformational change. Explain why the Bank spokeswoman insists on calling the Bank's plan for change 'incremental' while the trade union leader calls it 'transformational'. **(8 marks)**

(Total: 20 marks)

Section 8

NOVEMBER 2002 EXAMINATION ANSWERS

SECTION A

1   L COMPANY

Key answer tips

This is a fairly theoretical question which relies on particular knowledge of the HR plan as a functional level plan, as opposed to the higher level business and corporate plans.

It requires a general discussion of levels and their relationship to 'L'.

(a)   The general relationship between HRP and other levels of planning is that it is at the functional level. In other words, L has a corporate level strategy which affects all of its strategic business units. At this level it is said to be complacent and has lost market share to competitors. This has had a knock-on effect at the SBU level where five plants are closing and 110,000 people losing their jobs.

At the SBU level however, Delivery Vehicle (DV) Division, operating in its own market-place and formulating its own strategy on price, delivery, service etc has announced a slight increase in sales.

These business–level results then impact on the HR plan. It seems DV Division will need rather more staff in the coming period to match its increased demand. Clearly 110,000 staff from the other Divisions will, however, be losing their jobs. These ebbs-and-flows can be incorporated to some extent within the overall HRP; indeed the CEO has promised internal transfers to DV Division and will have priority over any external recruitment.

While this is still in progress, the HR planners should have data on planned out-flows such as maternity leave, terminal sickness cases and those due for normal retirement. This is a normal activity – conducting a static audit. In this case, however, those within a year or so of retirement can be identified and offered the same terms as if they were to retire later so as to absorb some more of the 110,000 redundancies. Thus the 'gap' analysis at functional level can react to the changes at SBU and corporate level.

Next, the future demands for labour need to be amended. While five plants have closed, new model launches may require ratter more staff in the coming years, and, rather than external recruitment, L can keep the redundant employees details on file and plan to offer a certain number future jobs. In the DV Division, this is clearer due to increased sales, and its managers will know approximate numbers required and so be able to begin internal recruitment.

Thus, the plans interlink naturally because of forecasting but currently the crisis means more internal than external recruitment.

Key answer tips

- Define 'soft' HRM (= commitment) and contrast it to 'Hard' HRM (= efficiency)

- Look for areas where 'L' has a decision to make based on its valuing people as its core assets.

- Discuss these (but briefly as only 8 marks)

(b)   'Soft' HRM is often quoted as if it were HRM. The core idea is that people are a firm's greatest assets – that they can make a contribution to profits, innovation, cost-reduction etc if assured of mutual commitment on the part of the employer. This may apply more to 'core' employees and involve various HR strategies such as functional flexibility (arising from additional Training and Development) career planning, performance-related-pay, and some measure of involvement and participation.

This contrasts with the 'hard' version which treats labour as a commodity – a cost which can be variable rather than fixed. This applies to 'flexible firms' and the move to outsource activities to lower-cost, seasonally adjusted contractors, so reducing overhead. Temporary, part-time and fixed-term contracts are also used.

For L to leave 'soft' HRM in its present circumstances will add significantly to its costs (by retaining skilled workers until they can be re-employed). It must therefore make some kind of Cost Benefit Analysis to convince its shareholders. Clearly all 110,000 cannot be re-absorbed but L could create, as Chrysler did, positive policies to enable their re-employment elsewhere. Its soft HRM approach may have to be re-evaluated if present market conditions are forecast to remain over the next 3-5 years.

2   S COMPANY LIMITED

Key answer tips

Requires a knowledge of the main factors (of the 8 available) within Weber's 'ideal type'.

Using these as a check list, identify areas 'S' would benefit from and discuss why these would improve performance.

(a)   Weber described the changes in society as moving from Traditional and Charismatic sources of authority to a more Rational/Legal basis.

Increased rationality led to the arrival of 'rule by the office' or bureaucracy, technically the most efficient method of distributing power. It relied on eight key premises which represented for Weber an *ideal type* – not all organisations would posses all eight.

'S' seems to have a lack of systems generally and could benefit from the following aspects of bureaucratic organisations.

(i)   Sunil is being nepotistic – traditional – in recruiting not on merit but on his own knowledge of people. This is a clear breach of the Rational/Legal basis and he should assess each employee against a job description / personnel specification and if necessary replace then from the wider labour market. Otherwise, if he keeps all or some, a proper system of performance management and accountabilities must be put in place.

(ii)   He has a kind of authority structure, with only one boss, which accords with Weber, but no system of delegated accountability which should precede the job description exercise in (i) above.

(iii)   Quality would improve by setting up standards (objectives, rational) which must be adhered to by all or disciplinary action would be taken (the legal aspect).

(iv)   Procedures for recording activities would be a priority so that control could be exercised by scrutiny of what was achieved versus what was planned. This would make employees realise their work was more important than they perhaps thought – especially admin where carelessness (alienation?) leads to loss of invoices and complaints in the system.

Key answer tips

A general and quite difficult question, luckily attracting only 8 marks.

It seems to require a 'common sense' view of bureaucracy which nowadays has become confused with the idea of 'red tape' and excessive formalisation and standardisation in a 'mechanical type of organisation.

(b)   Sunil is aware of the problems of bureaucracy in its generation of 'red tape': it has become synonymous not with Weber's idea of 'technical superiority' but with the opposite. Following set procedures is essential in some instances – such as safety or financial transactions – but adherence to sets of rules can of itself become a goal. The original reason for the rule is lost yet it is too easy to generate rules on the basis of a single crisis event, which then become part of the system (and its 'role' culture) and so very difficult to dismantle. *Burns and Stalkers* (1961) study showed that a 'mechanistic' system was unsuited to changeable environments which requires a more 'organic style'. While Sunil has reaped the benefits of this in the past, the formalisation stage (Grenier, 1973) has surely arrived, given the current problems.

He is rightly conscious of the need to engage staff in the goals of the firm, while problematically beginning to show them some control is necessary. He seems to have a wise head on his shoulders.

3   H COMPANY

Key answer tips

(i)   This is mainly theoretical in contrasting the 'marketing concept' of meeting needs with the selling of unwanted/unneeded products to unwitting consumers.

(ii)   This requires some advice and so a thoughtful approach.

(a) (i)   A 'selling' company probably aims a generic product at a wide market segment and so as almost a 'commodity' i.e. cannot differentiate the product. This means that a high-volume/low price strategy may be evolved and so the emphasis of the business is less on the innovation and creativity to create margin but on selling techniques to ensure its products are chosen over those of a competitor – such as clever merchandising, offers, competitors, goods distribution etc.

A marketing company however uses the 'marketing concept' which aims to establish customer needs first and then design a strategy to meet them. This may well include 'commodity' products and competition on price, but this should be a deliberate trade-off with other products which can be differentiated in Porter's sense and so create margin which can be used not to reduce prices by internal efficiency but by market research to influence patterns of demand e.g. women's perfumes at Christmas are sold to male customers buying them as presents so the ads must be attractive not to women, paradoxically, but to men.

(ii)   H can adopt this by a change in culture (role to task) and philosophy – 'customer first'. This needs to be the subject of a wide change – management programme, perhaps using TQM as a vehicle. In this way the various parts of it's value chain can be linked, backwards, from the customer through sales and marketing through to purchasing. Clearly marketing must lead the way (in terms of research etc) but other functions must be part of **Task Force** teams to reduce their resistance to change.

Key answer tips

Requires a knowledge of the 4P's and then these must each in turn be related to 'H'.

(b)   The marketing mix is often referred to as the 4Ps – Produce, Price, Promotion and Place, but nowadays authors have extended the number of factors – some up to seven items.

Product – though it depends ultimately on customers, H must be able to retail products at a reasonable price or, however chic, it may not sell in volume and so overhead costs would increase as a % - if for example its customers want 'designer labels'.

As it is a retailer, it is less constrained than a manufacturer with production facilities and design departments. It can alter its products to appeal to different segments and merchandise them accordingly – with differing point of sale advertising (e.g. larger and smaller sizes for ladies).

Price – It may decide not to put the price on items in the windows in order to tempt buyers in who like the basic product. However, this is a dangerous strategy as customers often do not have time to enquire about prices. H has high-street competition and so must match the prices of similar items, while also conforming to traditional sales times, offers, etc.

Promotion – If H has a marketing concept it must differentiate its above-the-line and if possible below-the-line advertising to meet the expectations and values of each of its segments. So, it may re-brand itself generally as The Youth Shop but target older people, the middle-aged, the young executives and children all separately.

Place – The high street is increasingly not the place to be – malls, franchises in-store, catalogues and increasingly the internet are becoming the prime channels of distribution. H must spend money on these.

SECTION B

4   D SOFT DRINKS COMPANY

Key answer tips

Simple asks for the advantages of empowerment from theory.

(a)   Empowerment is a new term for Herzberg's job enrichment/job enlargement categories often called 'vertical loading'. Partially it has been driven by firms cost-cutting by 'de-layering' management jobs such as line supervision and creating teams with team-leaders (who used to be called 'charge-hands'). This increases efficiency in terms of labour unit costs. Partially also it is reaction to create more 'organic' organisations in today's more turbulent times, so that able, competent and committed shop floor workers deal directly with suppliers poor quality, handle customer complaints, improve internal systems etc. This adds to effectiveness because, if properly trained and diplomatic, those on the shop floor know far more intimately the problems and potential solutions than do managers. This is apparently the basis of much of Japanese firms' success.

Key answer tips

This is a 'managing change' question which can be approached using any of the major models – OB, force field analysis, Kotter and Schlesinger etc.

(b)   That Mary herself is not enthusiastic rings danger bells as most change management research shows support from senior management to be vital for successful implementation – especially where problems arise.

Many may need to be persuaded therefore to adopt a soft, OD approach and appoint a change agent (probably an external consultant) who has a track record of success elsewhere in this area. She can then advise, and act on the final 'big gun' resort when policies act. Between them they need to determine:

-    what needs to change

-    what to change to

(in the words of Eli Goldraft). This may be problematic in a finance section where rules need to be followed to avoid fraud.

Then the drivers and resistors need to be identified (under Lewin's Force Field Analysis) and their fears/motives acted upon. This could be done via an Assessment/Development centre and subsequent Training and Development programme.

This will help to re-freeze the new behaviour, which can be supplemented by appraisal of performance and possibly performance–related pay if this is not expensive. This cost might be out-weighed by the reduction on level of supervision and/or the increased volume of throughput.

Key answer tips

This requires some knowledge of resistance, plus an identification of those for whom empowerment would pose a threat.

Note: (b) has 8 marks – 1/3 more than (a) or (c) and its length should reflect this.

(c)   There are many obstacles to change: Mary seems to be the prime one. Others occur where people's interests are seen to be or actually wish be challenged by the change. With empowerment there are several difficulties in that mangers may not want to relinquish power, status and possibly money, while their subordinates may be unwilling or simply unable to 'stretch' themselves. Even when they are able, there are many instances of employee goals subverting those which were once superordinate, and creating a sub-system based on group conformity and charismatic power which undermines traditional authority. Contrasting this, some groups who are empowered adopt an almost religious zeal, prozelitising and creating an atmosphere of chaos, over-reaching themselves in their enthusiasm.

Clearly then empowerment should not go too far in the Finance Department of 'D'.

5   X COMPANY

Key answer tips

First identify Sheila's source of power (position) and authority (from the board) then describe them. Then contrast Bob's expert power base as inadequate when it is lower in legitimate authority and position than Sheila's.

Adjust the marks 8 for the first part and 4 for the second to estimate the comparative length of both parts.

(a)   Sheila's sources of power may come from several directions. We know she has the position power delegated to her role by the board. This may be weak, or as seems likely, strong. Such power is stronger when the current Board have appointed the manger and any failure reflects badly on them. At the beginning of any tenure, Sheila would have a 'clean slate' and not carry any previous 'baggage' with her. Later, however, after a few indiscretions or problems, her position could be less secure – even successes pale as they are less novel, as time elapses.

Thus, some aspect of charismatic and personal power may be attributed to her in her role. She impressed enough at the selection process and may well be a powerful, dominant personality able to persuade others of her correctness or simply of the need to follow her lead in order to avoid painful consequences. These may be purely personal (eg. disdain) or related to her position power.

Also, as a Finance role is part of the CEO brief, she carries some aspects of expert power in that she headed up the Marketing function and her promotion amplifies her expertise in performing at this level.

Her position creates other sources – she may punish Bob by re-location, demotion, even dismissal so this generates fear, or she may reward him in various ways then ensuring compliance.

In contrast, Bob only has the expert power associated with his position, unless he has enough charisma to call her bluff and go to the board. He would probably need some tangible written evidence however and so may well be coerced into silence as her power outweighs his own. Resignation is a possible way out – both are 'negative power' – and if Bob is young he may easily get another job. Frequently the stark choice is: change the system, change yourself, or leave.

Key answer tips

A theoretical question requiring a description of ethics in terms of how implementation can be carried through – only 8 marks.

(b)   Apart from operating the usual segregation of duties (SPAMSOAP), the Board needs to have a whistleblower policy to avoid the frequent frauds which occur – often in claiming for expenses – in a similar way to the Sheila/Bob case. Where there is UK legislation on sexual harassment, the whistleblower idea is only in its infancy and protects whistleblowers from being unfairly dismissed – but the sanctions only occur after dismissal in the form of a Tribunal Award.

X needs an open door policy internally where a specific committee can hear fraudulent practices – not necessarily those about money but perhaps on quality or safety short-cuts being taken.

6   T INC

Key answer tips

(i) and (ii) worth 12 marks in total.

(i)   Theoretical – aims of business (may be worth 6 marks so needs a full discussion).

(ii)   Theoretical, requiring a knowledge of stakeholder theory and strategic choice. Assume also worth 6 marks.

(a)   (i)   Sam is using the idea of ownership and returns to capital in the traditional view of economists that the goal of capitalist enterprises is profit–maximisation and, by that means, in wealth-creation. GEC founder Lord Weinstock is alleged to have asked an interviewee what GEC made: all of his replies were wrong: 'Money' was apparently the correct answer. With money, (and tax taken by government) other issues relevant to society can be taken care of by those responsible – which a limited company (T is incorporated) cannot be responsible for, whether it makes dangerous cars, guns, warships or tobacco.

        (ii)   Frank is using a more modern and wider definition of ownership than the strictly legal one. He could well point out the division of control from owner-managers under traditional capitalism to the managerial ethos observed by Berle and Means in the 1930s. Though shareholders 'own' T, they have, by virtue of their large numbers and lack of organisation, no effective control.

                Frank would therefore point to managerial sub-goals, not profit maximisation as the way the *raison d'etre* is created for T. As well, he would be right to use Mintzberg's 1972 diagram showing 'power in and around organisations' which clearly shows how neighbours, customers and pressure groups normally feel they have a stake in the customers but can extort power to T's detriment. In other words there is a business case as well as a moral one for including both disconnected and connected stakeholders in any analysis of T.

Key answer tips

This is difficult, general question not covered by texts, and luckily worth only 8 marks. It requires a 'common sense' evaluation. Possibly based on planning theory but requiring identification of the different stakeholders, their goals, and the congruence of these with the goals of T.

Be careful not to over-write this complex answer as it is only worth 8 marks.

(b)   Frank has a problem in that goals can be virtually contradictions e.g. price – quality/variety/service. He first needs to identify *all* of T's possible stakeholders and may need consultants to do this as he will have his own 'bounded rationality' and may omit, for example the Health Service.

        Secondly he needs a focus group to look at each parties' possible priorities *and* their effect (if any) on T. The pressure group ASH (Action on Smoking and Health) has been powerful thus far but nothing has been heard recently – has it got financial troubles? Some stakeholders (e.g. tobacco growers) will support and might be persuaded to assist in legal cases; others may be neutral and only want more of a monetary outcome (e.g. Government's taxes, distributor's profits, customer's budgets).

        Finally he needs to determine any actions taxed on this analysis.

7   Z BANKS

Key answer tips

Theoretical explanation required at some length for 12 marks.

(a)   The first stage is to identify, according to Goldratt, the UDES or unintended outcomes – the mistakes, problems, issues and signals which have brought the idea of change to the fore. Some of these can be linked together, and through a Thinking Process (TP) links can be emphasised or eliminated to create a 'current reality tree' of the business. This is the rational process of determining what needs to change, and what target to change to.

Once management has a clear vision, it is time to prepare the ground for change. Many advocate unsettling the present situation, such as by rotating all the senior staff to remove their links to political support from their 'yes-men' subordinates. The idea is to un-freeze the present; to allow for new solutions and ideas to gain ground, a new 'present' has to be created.

Next, the ground is ready for change. This can progress slowly by involvement and participation in deciding on what and how to change, or it can be gradually accelerated through education and communication to bargaining and eventually through coercion. Often, small easy tasks are tackled first to show success can be achieved, and gradually more difficult areas attempted. Creating a new, better vision many motivate some to accept or even champion the change, while the resistors' power needs to be identified and weakened. This can include co-opting leading resistors to chair task forces, or by isolating or even dismissing them.

Successes need to be communicated, and frequently task force bulletins or even company newspapers carry positive stories each week or month while managers hold briefing meetings with key groups (stakeholders such as customers or suppliers can be very helpful). Employee representatives – trade union, consultative committees – need to be kept on board but direct communication is more effective.

Given a reasonable amount of success, the change must be re-frozen and so key appointments need to be made, Trade Union requirements renegotiated, and policies and procedures revised. This is best done by a training and development programme which can incorporate employee views, their involvement and participation.

Finally, results must be monitored and problem areas revisited. This is continual, ongoing and vitally important.

Key answer tips

This is in two parts

- Incremental v transformational (say 4 marks)

- Difference in perception between employer and trade union (say 4 marks)

Be careful again not to spend too much time on part (b)

(b)   (i)   Incremental or 'step' change is one stage further on from constant change, which in turn is one step on from stability. Whereas stability means a straight-line graph with no slope, constant change implies a trend line – straight or curved – which can be statistically analysed and predicted. Step-change however is sporadic and unpredictable in its frequency and its potency – introduction of new products can result in many steps of small height or a few, very large ones. However it is possible to plan for these contingencies in a generic fashion.

Transformational change however is totally unpredictable as it happens at the core – the *raison d'etre* – of the organisation. Coal suddenly made windpower redundant and via steam-trains, reduced the canal system to a short, 40-year, life-span. The internet should challenge all personal mail services, and so on.

(ii) The Bank wishes to diminish the effect of change on the workforce and reduce the fear which creates resistance. It thus discounts its proposals as being within the current paradigm and so, only a large step.

The TU has the opposite goal and to protect its members interests exasperates the effects so as to establish a bargaining position with the Bank.